Local Economic and Employment Development (LEED)

Breaking Out of Policy Silos

DOING MORE WITH LESS

Francesca Froy and Sylvain Giguère

OECD

This work is published on the responsibility of the Secretary-General of the OECD. The opinions expressed and arguments employed herein do not necessarily reflect the official views of the OECD or of the governments of its member countries or those of the European Union.

Please cite this publication as:
OECD (2010), *Breaking Out of Policy Silos: Doing More with Less*, Local Economic and Employment Development (LEED), OECD Publishing.
http://dx.doi.org/10.1787/9789264094987-en

ISBN 978-92-64-05680-0 (print)
ISBN 978-92-64-09498-7 (PDF)

Series/Periodical: Local Economic and Employment Development
ISSN 1990-1100 (print)
ISSN 1990-1097 (online)

Photo credits: Cover © Slavoljub Pantelic/Shutterstock.com

Corrigenda to OECD publications may be found on line at: *www.oecd.org/publishing/corrigenda.*

Preface

In the context of the recent economic downturn, carefully balanced strategies are needed so that agencies use their increasingly limited resources to help meet shared economic priorities at the local level and set local economies back on the track to economic growth. National government policies can make a great deal of difference in building economically viable, sustainable communities, but not if policies are fragmented, services duplicated and agencies do not communicate with each other on what they are trying to achieve. As government spending is reduced to pay off deficits, a drive is needed to make public policy more effective through reducing duplication at the local level and better aligning activities. Many lessons exist from different OECD countries on how to make local governance more effective, now is the time to put these into practice.

This book emerges from a longstanding interest by the OECD LEED Committee in better integrating policies at the local level. The impetus to launch a new project on "Integrating Employment, Skills and Economic Development" came from previous work carried out on decentralisation and partnerships. The research made clear that the difficulty of co-ordinating labour market policy and economic development strategies at local and regional levels was a major impediment to the success of local development initiatives, and that area-based partnerships and other existing forms of governance had limited capacity to correct this failure. A proposal to initiate a study on this issue was put forth by Poland, which received an enthusiastic response from the LEED Directing Committee. 11 countries volunteered to be reviewed as part of the study which also received the support from the European Commission. We are pleased to be launching the results of this major LEED project at a time when the results are more relevant than ever.

This project would not have been possible without the contributions provided by the DG Employment, Social Affairs and Equal Opportunity of the European Commission; Human Resources and Skills Development Canada;the Labour Market Authority of Greater Copenhagen and Zeeland in Denmark;the University of Athens and the OAED in Greece; ISFOL in Italy; the Department of Labor, Ministry of Social Development and New Zealand Trade and Enterprise in New Zealand; the Ministry of Regional Development in Poland; the Ministry of Labour and Social Solidarity in Portugal, and the Department of Labor and National Centre on Education and the Economy in the United States. I would like to thank them all.

Sergio Arzeni
Director, OECD Centre for Entrepreneurship,
SMEs and Local Development

Table of contents

Acknowledgements

Francesca Froy, Senior Policy Analyst, and Sylvain Giguère, Head of the LEED Division, prepared and edited this publication with the support of Lucy Pyne, Consultant, who compiled the country synopses on the basis of country expert reports. Debbie Binks, Elisa Campestrin, Lucy Clarke, Sheelagh Delf, Damian Garnys and Helen Easton should be thanked for their administrative and technical support.

The editors would like to thank the country experts: Antonina Stoyanovska (Bulgaria), David Bruce (Canada), Sanja Crnkovic-Pozaic (Croatia), Peter Plougmann, Peter Lindstrøm and Allan Wessel Andersen (Denmark), Anna Manoudi (Greece), Sebastiano Fadda (Italy), Paul Dalziel (New Zealand), Grzegorz Gorzelak and Mikolaj Herbst (Poland), José Manuel Henriqués (Portugal) and Sorin Ionita (Romania) and Mark Troppe, Mary Clagett, Robert Holm, Tim Barnicle (United States) for their significant contributions to this project.

Executive summary

Government intervenes in a myriad of ways at the local level, and rarely are these interventions co-ordinated effectively. Most of us are familiar with the policy "silos" which exist at the local level – employment offices, economic development agencies and local training institutions working separately from each other, following different policy objectives and working to different time scales. Such divisions are often taken for granted, blamed on historical working relationships ("it has always been like that") and organisational cultures ("they don't work like we do"). However, these divisions come at a cost. The issues and challenges facing local communities are often complex and require a holistic approach to be resolved.

Localities with entrenched difficulties such as multi-generational unemployment, social exclusion and high crime rates, require significant investment in multiple areas – housing, training, local transport – to be turned around. At the same time, harnessing economic opportunities in a knowledge-based economy requires simultaneous investment in infrastructure, skills, research and innovation, to raise productivity and adapt to new markets. Following the economic downturn, investment in skills is being seen as an important way of rebuilding future prosperity through making local people more adaptable to change and less expendable to business. However raising skills levels requires a joined-up approach between employment agencies, economic development bodies and also local employers, with a focus on both the supply and demand of skills.

It is rare in OECD countries to find holistic policy interventions at the local level which tackle diverse aspects of a problem simultaneously, are well targeted and have sufficient resources to succeed. Synergies between different actions (training benefits from economic development interventions for example) go unexplored, and local resources go unexploited. At the local level actors often respond by trying to build networks and improve communication. In recent decades local partnerships have been spawned across OECD countries, frequently focusing on particular localities, and/or particular themes (see OECD, 2001). Government agencies use such platforms to meet with other agencies and local stakeholders, including local employers, private agencies, the not-for-profit sector and civic society. However, it is not always the case that participating agencies have the flexibility to influence the delivery of nationally set programmes and policies to meet targets agreed in partnership. Also increasingly prevalent in recent years are jointly developed local strategies. In Europe, in particular, the influence of the European structural funds is such that local development strategies are now very common. Such strategies often set out broad aims and objectives and appear to "say all the right things" about working together to achieve common goals, however more rarely do they contain a proper implementation framework for how they are to be achieved, containing detailed agreements on joint actions, budgets, timescales etc. Too often such strategies become wish lists with many different objectives but no consensus on the most important cross cutting issues which need to be worked on together to achieve real economic growth and inclusion.

Agreeing on such a reduced set of priorities requires negotiating trade-offs, synergies and necessary sacrifices, which is challenging at the local level, particularly when local agencies do not have the decision making power to agree to such actions. It can imply a degree of conflict between local agencies which many local actors would find uncomfortable. Even if the will to make sacrifices and work towards a limited set of local priorities is there, a lack of flexibility in determining organisational targets means that many institutions, especially public or quasi-public, are likely to give priority to their own targets instead of those set collectively. The problem is accentuated because local strategies, and the mechanisms set out for their delivery, are not always legally binding. In many cases, partners feel free to participate in collective strategic planning but not necessarily obliged to translate the agreements into concrete action.

So how can governments make the changes necessary to encourage real policy integration at the local level? Why have strong joined-up approaches developed in some areas, while they seem always beyond the reach of others? "Breaking out of policy silos: doing more with less" explores the implementation of employment, economic development and skills policy in 11 countries to identify common obstacles to policy integration, and approaches which have led to policy alignment. The 11 countries include Canada and the United States; New Zealand; and the European countries of Bulgaria, Croatia, Denmark, Greece, Italy, Poland, Portugal and Romania. Each participating country and region has a different institutional framework, different economic strengths and weaknesses, and a different culture regarding collaboration and partnership working. However, the study has found that common factors are at play for all 11 and the opportunity for learning through sharing experiences is great.

The study produced both qualitative and quantitative results. Countries were each scored in terms of the degree of policy integration present on the ground, and the strengths and weaknesses of the supporting policy framework (in particular, the degree of national and local co-operation, flexibility in policy delivery and the extent of local capacities). The influence of labour market conditions was also taken into account. What has emerged has been the importance of flexibility in national policy frameworks, to give local actors enough freedom to adapt their programmes and actions to strategic priorities decided on the ground. In the 11 countries studied, policy flexibility was identified as having the highest influence of all the factors on policy integration at the local level. Whatever the degree of co-operation and partnership working between stakeholders, it has limited ability to produce change if organisations do not have the flexibility to adapt their policies and programmes to meet the agreed priorities. This book, therefore, has important policy messages for both local and national policy makers.

This book begins with a synthesis of the findings and international policy recommendations followed by a series of country synopses which set out the policy context, findings and policy recommendations for each country in more detail.

Box 0.1. **The methodology behind this study**

The study has been carried out with the help of country based experts in the 11 participating countries. The analysis was carried out on the basis of a series of interviews with national and local policy makers in the fields of employment, economic development and skills using a common methodology provided by the OECD. The findings from these interviews were discussed and validated during discussion and debate in a series of national and local roundtables which again involved senior representatives in the three policy areas of employment, skills and economic development. The study has looked at both the success factors and the barriers and obstacles to policy integration, along with the extent to which joined up working has contributed to the delivery of effective local programmes and a consistent vision for localities and regions. See Annex A for a list of the countries and the case study areas reviewed.

Part I

Synthesis of country findings

Why integrate policies?

The promotional slogan of Maryland Workforce Development Board, "workforce development is economic development", highlights the increasing overlap between the aims and objectives of policies to promote employment, economic development and skills. It is widely acknowledged that efforts to co-ordinate employment policies with economic development strategies and social inclusion initiatives bring significant benefits, and now more so than ever. Traditionally, the main goal of labour market policy has been to ensure that labour markets function efficiently, facilitating labour market adjustment by matching job-seekers with vacancies and by developing the employability of workers. However, in a knowledge based economy the role of labour market policy is expanding (Giguère, 2008).

One of the key advantages that a locality or region can offer a business is the quality of its human capital. In recognition of this, local economic development officials can benefit significantly from working with employment offices and using workforce development as a key instrument to stimulate local economic development. At the same time, labour market policy makers are increasingly dependent on other local stakeholder and actors to achieve their own goals. Promoting regional quality of life as a means of attracting and maintaining a high-calibre workforce is becoming increasingly recognised as a key regional labour market development tool. Business organisations, trade unions and community-based organisations often provide services that supplement those of the public employment service, such as vocational training, placement and re-integration programmes, so joint steering is required to maximise complementarity while avoiding duplication. Training organisations benefit from networking with economic developers and local businesses to ensure that courses reflect rapidly evolving demands for skills and to prepare for forthcoming local investments.

The OECD LEED Programme has identified a number of factors which make integrated local development important, with the following being the most critical:

- **Complexity:** Many of the issues which local actors deal with are complex. As identified above, the issues that are rising up the agenda in OECD countries (skills, worklessness, immigration, innovation) are often intrinsically complex, "wicked" and interdependent problems that cannot be solved without a joint approach.

- **Efficiency, duplication and service gaps:** Governments tend to have a large number of different departments and ministries, many of which have arms or offices at the local level. When policy makers work independently from each other this has a tendency to produce duplication and service gaps. This study has identified that duplication is both frequent at the local level in OECD countries and wasteful, leading to a drain on public resources. At the same time many issues (such as the need to upgrade the skills of low paid workers, see OECD, 2006) are rarely dealt with by any public agency. While officials work towards increasing the efficiency of individual policy areas, they often neglect to check whether efficiency is gained across government as a whole. Whereas local governments may have an overview of policy interventions at the community level, they do not often have authority over the deconcentrated bodies that they are working with to produce change. Partnership working is therefore perhaps the only way to map services and jointly agree to mechanisms that will fill in gaps.

- **Achieving critical mass:** A further important driver for policy integration at the local level is the need for prioritisation. Local problems are not only complex but also often require a significant amount of resources to be tackled effectively. It is important therefore that everybody is pulling together at the same time to invest in tackling a particular problem, as opposed to undertaking many smaller actions simultaneously which never achieve the critical mass to have any real effect. In many localities, local agencies do not seem to "see the wood for the trees", *i.e.* they are so busy tackling the many symptoms of a problem that they fail to spot its root cause. In rural areas, for example, employment agencies often become preoccupied with helping local companies to fire-fight labour shortages which are in fact produced by the low level of employment conditions on offer in a low productivity "low skills equilibrium" local economy (see Froy, Giguère & Hofer, 2009). Seeing the bigger picture would mean spotting that real investment needs to be made in improving the productivity of local firms, raising incomes and thereby ensuring that local jobs are attractive to local young people, preventing them from emigrating. However, tackling the "bigger picture" often requires taking a longer-term, joined-up approach which is not always supported by the performance management framework of individual policy areas.

- **Building social capital:** Finally, while integration of policies is important to ensure that localities achieve their longer-term strategies, evidence shows that building links between local organisations and agencies is valuable in its own right as a way of building valuable social capital (see Putnam, 1993). Problems do not just get solved with grand strategies, but also on a day to day basis through knowing the right people to achieve what you want to get done. Local social networks support the spread of innovation and ideas, increasingly important in the context of the knowledge economy (Coyle, 2001). Those areas with the most dense social capital networks are increasingly the most successful in today's globalised economy. In this respect formal partnership between agency heads may not be as important as the many lower level contacts which they allow to build up between officials who are actually implementing day to day policy – as long as these officials have the flexibility to adapt their policies within the framework of a "local problem solving mentality".

The study found that in most cases, policy integration at the local level was ad-hoc and could not be judged to be "business as usual". Where policy integration was effective, however, it had the effect of capitalising on local opportunities and effectively diffusing local threats. In the Lower Rio Grande Valley in Texas, for example, a number of key local leaders, including the representative of the McAllen Economic Development Corporation and the Workforce Investment Board helped to galvanise local actors into recognising the bigger picture facing their community and working together to produce real change for the region. Identifying that local policy makers had in the past been working separately in a mainly reactive manner, they sought to turn economic development "from a response to a journey".

Twenty years ago, McAllen suffered from 20 per cent unemployment in an economy that depended primarily on the agricultural and retail sectors, and faced competition from the growing number of manufacturing plants operating in nearby Mexico. Local leaders saw the potential for the region to become a centre for rapid response manufacturing, taking advantage of the fact that it fell in a foreign trade zone.[1] A major barrier was the poorly educated workforce, which leaders tackled head on through developing a new community college offering a Bachelor Degree in Applied Technology and a technology centre, working with schools to reduce drop outs, and better customising training locally. At the same time the economic development staff actively encouraged inward investment on the other side of the border in Mexico, while working with new arrivals to locate the higher skilled aspects of their manufacturing plants which would customise products to US markets over the border in Texas. Overall, the regional strategy has been responsible for helping to attract more than 500 employers and nearly 100 000 jobs to the wider region, with important reductions in local unemployment rates (see Box 12.1 for more details).

Figure 1.1. **An integrated approach to turning around the Lower Rio Grande Valley in Texas**

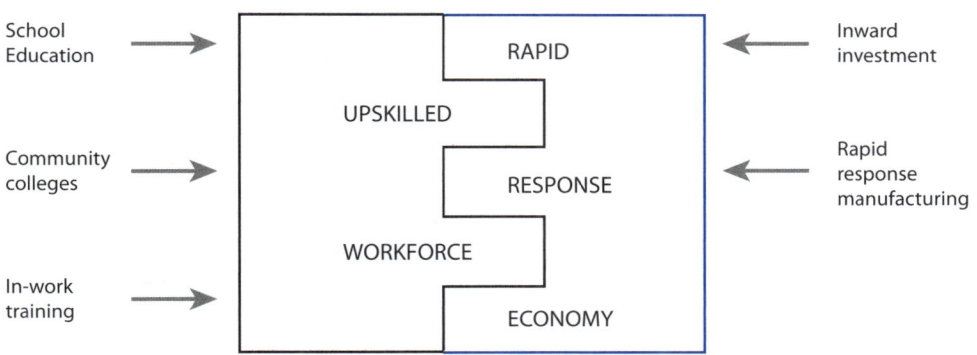

The success of the region in positioning itself as a "rapid response manufacturing centre" and turning around high unemployment levels and low skills levels may be a fairly unique case given the opportunities which the region had on its borders. However the principles of their success are transferable elsewhere. Achieving change in the Lower Rio Grande Valley has been highly dependent on strong but relatively informal collaboration across economic development, education, and workforce development leaders and organisations, based on agreement around a shared vision for the region's economic future. Flexibility has played a strong role, with local actors being particularly open in their definition of their local "region", with collaboration going across national borders to include a strong partnership with the city of Reynosa in Mexico. And in the process of implementing their strategy, local actors have also benefited from flexibility in the delivery of employment and skills programmes (for example through waivers which allow relaxation of employment legislation) to adapt programmes to local needs.

While this and approaches in other localities revealed the positive outcomes to be gained from policy integration, the study also revealed many cases of missed opportunities, with the principle assets of local communities going unexploited. For example, the rural case study regions explored in Bulgaria, Greece and Italy all had considerable natural assets which could have been much better exploited to produce tourism-related growth. Local strategies failed to combine resources and actions to build the critical mass of resources necessary to kick-start this part of the economy, through for example better environmental management and making more accessible these natural resources. In other regions, local actors were failing to tackle the overriding problem they faced in terms of their economies being based on a "low-skills equilibrium". In many of the case study areas an imbalance also existed in the focus of regional development, with investment in inward investment and infrastructure significantly exceeding necessary investment in the local skills base, impacting on the productivity of new and incoming firms.

The extent of local policy integration in the countries studied

For this study, policy makers in the fields of employment, economic development and skills were consulted at the national, local and state levels on the extent of policy integration between their respective policy areas. In the countries studied, in only two cases did policy makers perceive that there was a high level of local policy integration (Denmark and the United States). In Canada, Croatia, New Zealand and Poland, policy makers considered that there was a medium level of policy integration at the local level, while in Bulgaria, Greece, Italy, Portugal, Romania policy integration at the local level was considered to be low. Interestingly, countries ranked slightly differently when policy integration at the national level was assessed, with New Zealand being considered to have the highest level of policy integration between the three policy areas, and only Croatia and Bulgaria being considered to have low levels of policy integration.

Table 1.1. **Comparison of the level of policy integration in participating countries**

	National integration	Local integration
High (over 3.5)	New Zealand	Denmark, United States
Medium (2.6-3.5)	Canada, Denmark, Greece, Italy, Portugal, Romania, Poland, United States	Canada, Croatia, New Zealand, Poland
Low (0-2.5)	Bulgaria, Croatia	Bulgaria, Greece, Italy, Portugal, Romania

What factors influence policy integration at the local level?

Policy integration is not easy. Working together with other local actors takes time and resources. It can also lead to conflict – indeed it could be argued that the process of achieving trade-offs between different objectives at the local level inevitably creates conflict at one time or another. There is often strong inertia in the management of political and institutional systems, making the process of introducing greater co-operation and integration locally seem like a very steep challenge. In the United States, some localities do not integrate their policies because they have concluded that "integration – like most change is difficult to accomplish and not worth the political or emotional effort required" (Troppe *et al.*, submitted).

So what are the factors which ensure that localities overcome such challenges and achieve policy integration? The study explored the influence of five factors in particular in enabling or restricting policy integration locally:

- **National co-operation**: Does the degree of national co-operation between ministries and government agencies have an influence on the degree of policy integration locally? For example, if the national department of labour has consulted with the ministries for education and for regional development when developing a new training-based active labour market programme, will this make it more likely that local training courses are responsive to local economic development needs? Does the fact that different ministries sit in a cabinet together make it more likely that their local officers will collaborate with other local agencies on the ground?

- **Local governance**: What are the governance arrangements that make a difference locally? Does having a single local partnership on which all public sector actors are represented produce policy integration? Or is it better to have multiple theme-based partnerships which are set up quickly to deal with certain issues and dissolve as quickly when the issues are no longer pressing? Do business-led partnerships (such as the Workforce Investment Boards in the United States, and the regional Growth Forums in Denmark) support the delivery of policy that is more geared to local economic needs? Do demand-led partnerships inherently focus on more short-term problems, and lack the capacity to plan for the longer term?

- **Policy flexibility**: To what extent are the hands of local agencies tied due to the way that their own policy area is managed? Are performance management frameworks too strict, meaning that officials are constrained to meeting their own performance targets without the time or resources to work on broader community issues? Are they able to influence the nature and content of the policies and programmes that they deliver so that they are more responsive to local needs? Are local agencies constrained in the way they can use their budgets to develop common initiatives and solutions to complex problems? Does the legal framework in which they operate constrain them to certain activities and not others?

- **Capacities**: What is the influence of the skills and resources available at the local level? Does strong local leadership empower people with the ability to overcome administrative barriers and inflexible governance arrangements? Does a lack of resources mean that people are more likely to work together to maximise the value of what little they have, or do people become protective of limited budgets as they fear encroachment from other agencies? What sorts of skills are needed to work co-operatively with others and develop integrated strategies for the long-term? Can such skills be taught? Do local actors have sufficient analytical skills to really understand the information and data they collect, to plot trends and to identify how local assets will position the region within global markets?

- **Labour market conditions**: In any analysis to identify causal relationships at the local level, the influence of labour market conditions needs to be taken into account. For example, do certain situations of labour market stress encourage a more integrated approach? What constitutes a "burning platform" that will give rise to a joint approach? Do significant levels of unemployment spur people into action? Or are tight labour markets with high demand for skills more likely to encourage joint approaches by employment and economic development actors? Or perhaps it takes a more immediate industrial crisis to create a more integrated approach?

In the following sections we evaluate the impact of these five different factors on local policy integration in the participating countries, starting with co-operation at the national level.

Co-operation at national level

Employment, economic development and skills policies are implemented through a variety of different management frameworks in OECD countries (see Box 1.1 below). In most cases these policy areas are spread across different ministries, which co-operate to some degree on policy design and implementation. The frequency and level of formality of meetings between the ministries appeared to vary significantly between countries. While in North American and Australasian countries co-operation was much more informal, with meetings likely to occur monthly or in many cases weekly, in some European countries (such as Greece and Italy) ministries met mainly formally and less than once a quarter, at least outside of European structural fund implementation.

For the countries studied, the greatest degree of co-operation was found to exist between the ministries responsible for education and employment, with co-operation between the ministries responsible for vocational training and economic development being the weakest. For example in New Zealand, the Department of Labour, Ministry of Social Development and Tertiary Education Commission co-operated weekly through horizontal working groups, meetings, conferences, formal written communications, circulation of policy documents and newsletters. They consulted on policy priorities, strategies, programme design and delivery. However the Department of Labour met with the Ministry of Economic Development and New Zealand Trade and Enterprise less frequently (once a week and once a month respectively) and on-going co-operation was weaker.

Figure 1.2. **Policy co-operation between ministries at the national level**

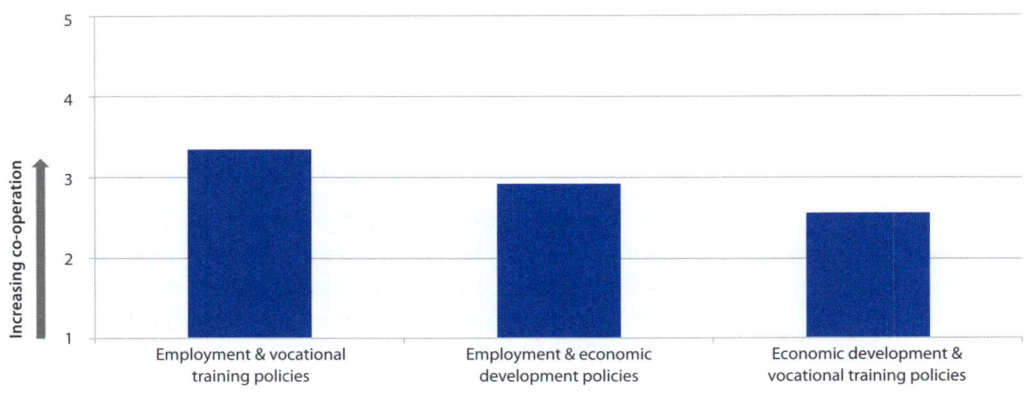

Notes: 1. Figures include both the federal and state/provincial level in Canada and the United States.

2: Where 5 is the highest ranking given and 1 is the lowest.

The higher frequency of meetings between ministries responsible for vocational training and employment was perhaps not surprising given the strong overlap in the management of training and employment policies at the national level in many OECD countries. Vocational training policy was at least partly implemented by the Ministry of Employment in many countries (*e.g.* Bulgaria, Canada, Croatia, Denmark, Greece, Portugal, United States). This overlap often led to problems of duplication: in Greece, for example, a lack of clarity regarding roles and responsibilities between institutions implementing training policies resulted in the development of two separate vocational training delivery structures – one under the Ministry of Education (providing formal vocational education) and one under the Ministry of Employment (providing non-formal, continuing vocational training). At the local level this translated into two different types of training institution offering similar services and causing confusion on the part of students and employers.

In several countries (Portugal, Greece and Bulgaria) national reforms have been put in place to bring vocational training and education policy closer together. For example, in Bulgaria, in 2005 a long term agreement was signed between the National Agency for Vocational Education and Training and the national employment service to build joint action at national, regional and local level and establish a unified information system on vocational education and training (VET) qualifications for the labour force. Similarly in Greece, a new law was passed in 2003 on the development of a National System for Combining Vocational Education and Training with Employment, a significant step in tackling the duplication between ministries at the national level, although initial implementation of the new system was relatively slow. In 2009, both initial and continuing VET have come under the supervision of the newly renamed Ministry of Education, Lifelong Learning and Religious Affairs.

Box 1.1. National governance frameworks

In order to understand the factors influencing policy integration in different countries it is important to understand their policy frameworks. The countries participating in the study all have very different governance structures. Canada, Italy, Poland and the United States are politically decentralised countries in that they have devolved a considerable amount of power to the regional level (that of the provinces and territories in Canada, the regions in Italy and the states in the United States) leading to considerable variation in the management of policies in different regions. Bulgaria, Croatia, Denmark, Greece, New Zealand, Portugal and Romania have all maintained a more centralised governance structure. In a number of these latter countries, however, the municipalities, and in particular local mayors, have an important degree of power. In Bulgaria, for example, there has been a gradual decentralisation in recent years to the municipalities which is expected to continue. In Portugal the municipalities have long been the central governance unit at sub-national level. In Denmark, municipalities have recently been given increased power in the context of a governance reform which also diminishes the power available at the regional level.

At the other end of the scale, international institutions are also implicated in efforts to create local policy integration. The European countries under study (including those which have recently acceded to or are acceding to the European Union – Bulgaria, Croatia, Poland, Romania) have all been heavily influenced by European programmes in terms of the governance of employment, skills and economic development policy, and also receive considerable funds to deliver policy in partnership at the regional level. A number of the countries studied, in particular Croatia, Denmark, New Zealand and Portugal, were undergoing or had recently undergone extensive reforms at the time of study which should be taken into account when evaluating recent practices.

The policy area of regional and economic development appeared to be relatively isolated at the national level, particularly from vocational training policy. The sheer number of ministries involved in the topic of economic development makes co-operation difficult in many countries. In Croatia, at the time of study there were at least ten national organisations responsible for the preparation and implementation of structural policy and economic development. With this number of institutions involved, each with its own diverse objectives, economic development policy was fragmented and unfocused. The Croatian Government Office for Strategy had taken over the process of national development planning and policy development but its capacity was still low and there was a need for more expertise, time and financial support. Likewise, in the United States economic development policy was split between ten different federal agencies with 27 sub-agency units and 73 programmes. Reviews of this policy area in the States found many activities were duplicated but efforts to consolidate the programmes have proved difficult, made worse by the fact that there was no single federal statute governing economic development. In Bulgaria, likewise, the fact that economic development policy was implemented by different agencies has resulted in duplicate programmes for entrepreneurship promotion implemented by both the Ministry for Labour and Social Policy and the Ministry of Economy and Energy, while two different municipal strategies have been launched by the Ministry for Labour and Social Policy and the Minister of Regional Development and Public Works.

In some countries, there has been an attempt to improve the link between economic development and other policy areas by assigning a single agency to economic development policy and encouraging it to play an umbrella role for other policy areas. For example in part of Canada, the Atlantic Canada Opportunities Agency was given the role of improving quality of life for all Canadians living in the four most eastern Canadian provinces (Nova Scotia, New Brunswick, Newfoundland and Labrador and Prince Edward Island) through an overarching policy oriented towards producing sustainable growth, building opportunities for people and focusing government. ACOA endeavours to steer the broad interests of the federal government in all of its work and co-ordinate horizontal initiatives. In Europe, the structural funds[2] often also give regional development ministries a guiding role in developing national strategic frameworks for implementation, although this does not necessarily give the ministries any greater powers outside of the European funding process.

The relationship between policy areas at the national level is often influenced by the political emphasis of different administrations. In the United States, traditionally employment and vocational training were found to be closest together, as both were driven through a supply side focus, however under the Bush administration, efforts were made to bring employment policy closer to economic development through a demand-led approach.

Whole-of-government approaches

Many OECD countries have experimented with "whole of government" approaches to certain cross-cutting issues, such as social exclusion or skills. In some OECD countries (for example New Zealand and Portugal) ministries come together at a very senior level in the form of cabinets, which sometimes form the basis for cross-cutting units. In the United Kingdom the Cabinet Office has been responsible for much cross-government work on social exclusion.

Involving wider stakeholders

Countries also vary according to the degree to which ministries co-operate with wider stakeholders at the national level. In Europe, social partners and trade unions are often key partners in the development of employment and training policies as part of the "tri-partite" system. From the late 1980s onwards, the drive to work in partnership also received a boost from the European structural funds which were to be managed on the basis of a "partnership principle".[3]

While in certain countries, such as Denmark, social partners play a strong role in the development and implementation of policy – leading to a form of "consensual" politics – in other countries their involvement can appear like a formality. In Bulgaria, for example, while the influence of the European Commission "partnership principle" has led to broad participation by social partners, it has also spawned a large number of different committees, each requiring substantial resources to be efficient and effective. The time and commitment of each stakeholder was found to be undermined through over-commitment to a large number of committees. In addition, a lack of clarity on the criteria for inclusion in some of the working groups had also raised serious concerns, creating mistrust and reducing the efficiency of these bodies. The lack of real co-operation between ministries was revealed when Bulgaria tried to tackle genuine cross-government issues through the horizontal Strategy for Poverty Reduction and Strategy for Roma Integration. Despite the myriad of committees and well-formulated objectives and measures, the strategy failed to succeed as it went against the grain of existing departmentalised policies and programmes.

The achievement of policy integration at the national level

Despite the difficulties in creating genuine cross-government co-operation, a number of governments have introduced overarching strategies which show some evidence of policy integration. In Portugal, the Portuguese National Sustainable Development Strategy (2005-2015) identifies four common issues which have now been incorporated within diverse sectoral strategies. These include a focus on "qualifications and skills", "competitiveness and innovation", "territorial approach to growth and innovation" and "modernising public administration". In Italy, similarly, the Plan for Innovation, Growth and Employment (PICO) launched in 2005 was intended to be an overarching strategy to unite different policy areas, while in this and other European countries the Lisbon Agenda[4] has provided the context for an overarching strategy for better adapting to the demands of the knowledge economy through technology transfer, research and innovation.

Many such strategies remain as policy documents, however, and have limited "teeth" in terms of implementation (see Box 1.2 below). The Globalisation Strategy launched in Denmark is one exception. In 2006, the Danish government presented a new strategy outlining an overall vision as well as 350 concrete initiatives to ensure that Denmark maintained a healthy economic position in a globalised economy. The Globalisation Strategy was broadly a call for further co-operation between relevant stakeholders, in particular the integration of business demands and education supply and was implemented through a series of regional partnership agreements that committed relevant parties in business development and the area of labour market policy. The fact that these policy areas had their own management structures and governance frameworks means that the ability to influence these other policy areas was somewhat limited. However, ensuring the implementation of the strategy through partnership agreements meant that it had a far greater galvanising effect in creating policy integration, at least at regional level.

It is rarer for national ministries to develop common targets for their policies in partnership. In the United Kingdom, Simmonds (in Giguère & Froy, 2009) points to the fact that a recent common target to increase the employment rate to 80 per cent under the Brown government was useful in bringing a variety of local actors together. Such targets, however, are rare in practice. In the United States the federal Department of Labor has tried to produce common measures across departments but has met with opposition from other agencies.

Box 1.2. **What constitutes real policy integration?**

The term 'integration' can be ambiguous and interpreted in at least three different ways. A first level definition of policy integration is when actions may be considered as integrated simply when they are listed together, without analysing the interactions or potential inconsistencies between them. Clearly, the positive results from this form of integration are in reality quite limited. A second level definition of integration requires that actions, where listed, actually converge towards the same objectives. This may be the case if actions are selected around common objectives, even if interaction and co-ordination do not take place in terms of their planning and/or implementation. A third level definition of integration is perhaps most essential to the requirements of good planning. According to this definition, actions and policies are considered integrated when they are complementary to and interact with each other as parts of a coherent and organic strategy designed to achieve a common set of objectives. For this kind of integration to exist, two elements are required: a plan consisting of common objectives and goals for which specific strategic actions and instruments are designed; an organic link between these actions and instruments, capable of producing positive interactions and synergies which lead to the better achievement of common objectives.

Source: Fadda (submitted).

Does national co-operation itself lead to higher co-operation and policy integration at the local level?

National level co-operation was judged to have a moderate influence on local policy integration within the study (see Figure 1.3 below). This study has highlighted that strong national co-operation between ministries in itself does not necessarily lead to strong co-operation at the local level. This is demonstrated by the case of Canada. At the federal level senior officials from Atlantic Canada had almost daily interaction with all federal departments on an informal basis and there were a variety of formal structures in place to facilitate planning and implementation. At the provincial level, likewise, a memorandum of understanding was developed between HRDSC (the government department responsible for employment and skills) and ACOA to align their policies in Nova Scotia,

Figure 1.3. **Relative importance of the different factors on local policy integration**

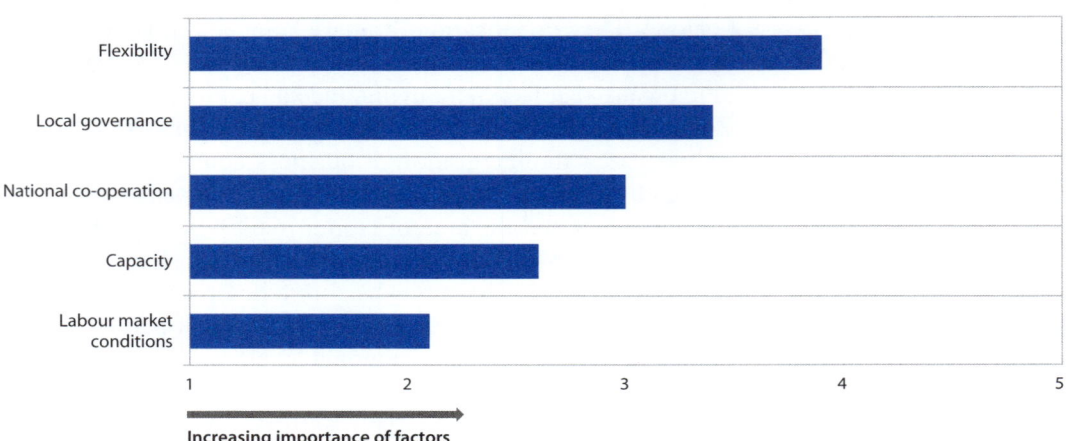

Note: This figure illustrates the average ranking allocated to each element by the 11 country experts on the basis of the country level research, where 5 is the highest ranking given and 1 is the lowest.

Box 1.3. **Summary of key issues regarding co-operation at the national level**

1. National co-operation is judged to have a moderate influence on policy integration at the local level.

2. Those ministries responsible for vocational training policy and employment policy are most likely to collaborate with each other at the national level, with economic development policy often seeming to act in isolation. This is largely because the responsibility for economic development is often fragmented across several different ministries.

3. In many countries the nature of co-operation remains at a relatively formal level, meaning that it does not translate into real policy integration in terms of joined up strategies with clear implementation criteria.

4. Still less frequent are common targets which would encourage joint working between different ministries towards common goals.

5. The simple fact of having co-operation at the national and state/provincial levels does not necessarily translate into increased co-operation at the local level.

leading to regular meetings at the senior level on these issues. At this level, the Office for Economic Development, Nova Scotia Business Inc, and Department of Education Skills and Learning Branch communicated at least on a weekly basis. However, at the local level in the case study region of Pictou, collaboration was much weaker, with no common work plan between the agencies and limited mechanisms for mutual accountability. While a regional development strategy was in place, it was missing an emphasis on skills and employment. The success of the federal-provincial working committees did not therefore necessarily trickle down and have a positive impact on local contexts and there appeared to be a gap between field officers of senior governments and local actors.

Local co-operation

Agencies co-operate at the local level to define local problems and challenges, identify solutions and realise joint objectives, and build trust and co-operative relations: all essential elements in local policy integration. Local co-operation was identified as more important to policy integration than national co-operation. Policy makers also assessed that co-operation was currently higher locally in participating countries than at national level (receiving a ranking of 3.4 out of 5.0 as compared with 2.9).

Of the case study regions, those in Denmark, the United States and New Zealand were felt to show a relatively high level of local co-operation while co-operation was perceived as lowest in the post-communist European countries of Romania and Bulgaria. In Denmark, for example, the Island of Bornholm established a regional growth forum under the Globalisation Strategy which has brought local people together to deliver a common strategy for improving the relevance of skills to the local economy and to work with industrial consortia to anticipate and meet business needs. The growth forum has "provided local stakeholders with a sense of common direction, togetherness and not least interdependency". In the United States, co-operation in the case study regions of Lower Rio Grande Valley and Coastal Maine was also high, in the latter case partly because of a federal programme to increase networking. In New Zealand skills shortages had led to strong co-operation at local level in the Bay of Plenty at the time of study, with the Regional Commission for Social Development playing a lead role in bringing local policy makers, colleges and companies together to tackle them.

Table 1.2. **Perception of degree of co-operation at the local level**

Degree of co-operation	Country
High (3.5 to 5.0)	Denmark, United States, New Zealand
Medium (2.5 to 3.5)	Canada, Croatia, Greece, Italy, Poland, Portugal
Low (1.0 to 2.5)	Romania and Bulgaria

At the other end of the scale, in Bulgaria partnership working was felt to be weak at the regional level because of limited devolved responsibilities. Institutions saw themselves as competitors for scarce resources rather than potential partners, and when partnership did happen it was the result of the goodwill of individuals rather than emanating from a coherent co-operation strategy. Where the incentive was there, things moved relatively quickly but incentives remained broadly lacking. At the same time, local municipalities had a limited budget or remit to act as a cross-sector organisation for co-ordination. In Romania arguably, the lack of incentives for organisations to co-operate was the main problem.

> ### Box 1.4. **Who is involved in employment, skills and economic development policy at the local level?**
>
> The actors involved in the three policy areas on the ground include municipalities, the local branches of government offices such as the public employment service, colleges, universities, trade unions, mutuals and cooperatives, and non-government and voluntary organisations. In European countries, municipalities often play a strong role in stimulating cooperation between other local actors, particularly in countries where they have been devolved significant powers, such as Bulgaria, Denmark and Portugal. In Canada and the United States, municipalities have a more reduced role, being small in size and mainly focused on infrastructure activities. The role of NGOs and trade unions also varies considerably between the countries. While in Canada and the United States, employment policy is extensively outsourced to NGOs, this is rarer, although increasing, in Europe. In Europe social partners and trade unions are much more likely to be involved in designing and implementing policy.

Which policy areas are the most co-operative at the local level?

Figure 1.4. **Extent of engagement in local co-operation**

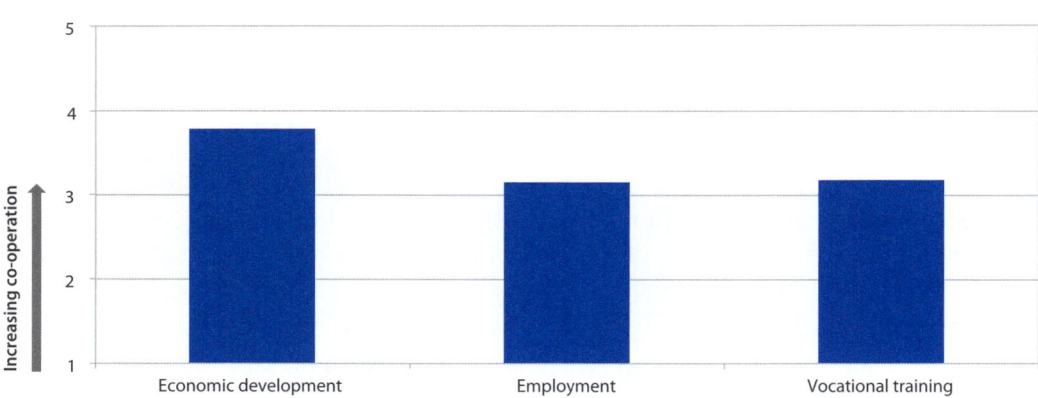

Note: This graph is based on a combined indicator taking into consideration the following: the number of partners with which the organisation has an ongoing active communication (where 1 is none and 5 is more than 5); the extent to which co-operation goes beyond formalities to involve substantive collaboration on policy development and programme delivery (where 1 is not at all and 5 is very strong); participation in multi-stakeholder partnerships (where 1 is very weak and 5 is very strong); and, the extent of information sharing (where 1 is very weak and 5 is very strong).

In terms of the three policy areas, economic development officials appear to be the most likely to co-operate locally in the participating countries, having the most partners, participating to a greater extent in multi-stakeholder partnerships and sharing the most information. The fact that economic development is the most co-operative area may to some extent be expected, given that economic development officials in local and regional governments and economic development agencies often have the clearest mandate to work with and involve different actors in developing regional strategies. Employment officials, who are more co-operative at the national level, appear to be less likely to work with others at this level, having fewer partners with whom they have ongoing communication and sharing less information and data. The degree to which their co-operation goes beyond formalities is also lower than for the other policy areas. For example, in Greece, the public employment service was seen by other stakeholders as "acting slowly and inflexibly in the context of local partnership and not helping enough in collecting and sharing local labour market data" (Manoudi, submitted). A key aim of Greece's new generation of employment offices (KPAII) has been to be more open to partnerships with other players.

It is not always the case that employment policy takes the back seat in terms of co-operation, however. In New Zealand, the policy makers responsible for employment and economic development were found to be equally co-operative with other institutions. The Commissioner for Social Development responsible for employment services in the Bay of Plenty region, has a broad responsibility to develop a strategic approach to development, and has been instrumental in developing partnership approaches to local issues (see Box 1.5). In the United States employment officials also showed a high degree of co-operation, as local Workforce Investment Boards are intended to perform the essential function of convening system stakeholders, resources, and service providers.

In the field of vocational training policy several countries, such as Denmark and New Zealand, have encouraged individual training institutions to take on more of a strategic role at the local and regional levels. In New Zealand, in particular, local polytechnics were expected to have a strategic presence at the regional level, while regional policy makers working in the Tertiary Education Commission had been re-located back to central government. As a result, local actors were more likely to collaborate directly with delivery agents, *i.e.* colleges or training institutions, as opposed to policy representatives.

Box 1.5. The role of the Commission for Social Development in stimulating co-operation in the New Zealand Bay of Plenty region

The Ministry of Social Development divided the country into 11 Work and Income regions: Northland, Auckland, Waikato, Bay of Plenty, East Coast, Taranaki/Wanganui/King Country, Central (North Island), Wellington, Nelson, Canterbury, and Southern (South Island). Each region was headed by a Regional Commissioner for Social Development who had considerable autonomy for participating in local labour market initiatives. Regional Commissioners are required to produce a strategic plan for social development in their region, which typically includes recognition of local labour market opportunities and threats. In the Bay of Plenty region, the Regional Commissioner for Social Development played a pivotal role in integrating economic development, labour market and skills/training initiatives, partly because they had considerable autonomy to contribute significant financial resources to find partnership based solutions to local employment problems. The framework for this autonomy is provided by an annual regional plan.

Instruments for co-operation

Generally, local actors were found to co-operate on an ongoing basis with at least four other institutions at the local level. The large majority of local actors also collaborate in multi-stakeholder partnerships, with participation being perceived as highest in North American countries and New Zealand and lowest in the Southern and Eastern European participating countries (see Figure 1.5).

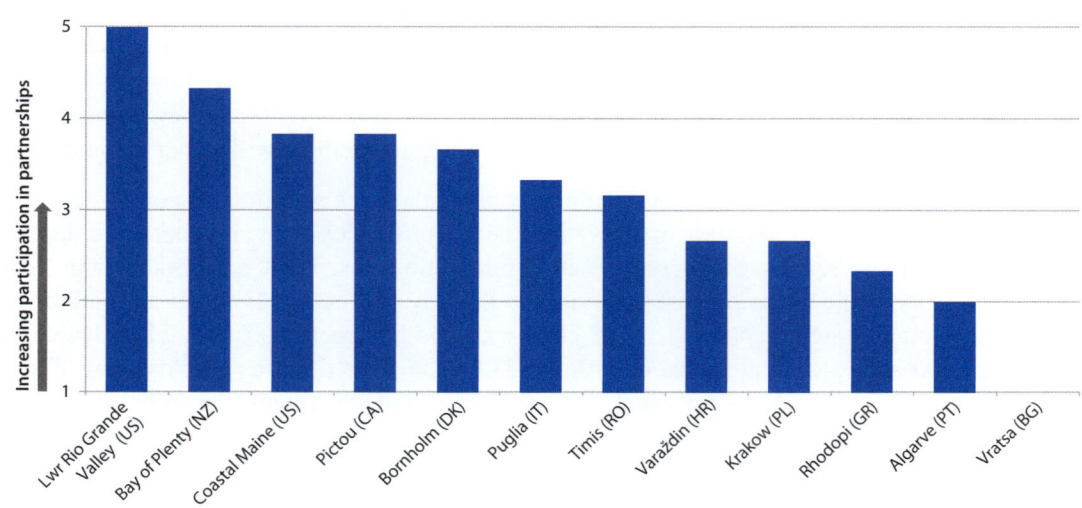

Figure 1.5. **Involvement of local actors in multi-stakeholder partnerships**

Note: This graph reflects the extent of participation in multi-stakeholder partnerships from very weak (1) to very strong (5).

Interestingly the correlation between the different factors associated with co-operation was relatively weak, suggesting that participation in multi-stakeholder partnerships does not necessarily improve information sharing or the establishment of ongoing relationships with other stakeholders. While information sharing was also highest in North American countries, Denmark and New Zealand, the distribution of the countries was somewhat different (see Figure 1.6 below).

Equally, despite high participation in multi-stakeholder partnerships in Pictou, Canada for example, institutions only maintained ongoing collaboration with between three and four partner institutions, compared with five and over in the majority of other countries, excluding Romania, Croatia and Greece.

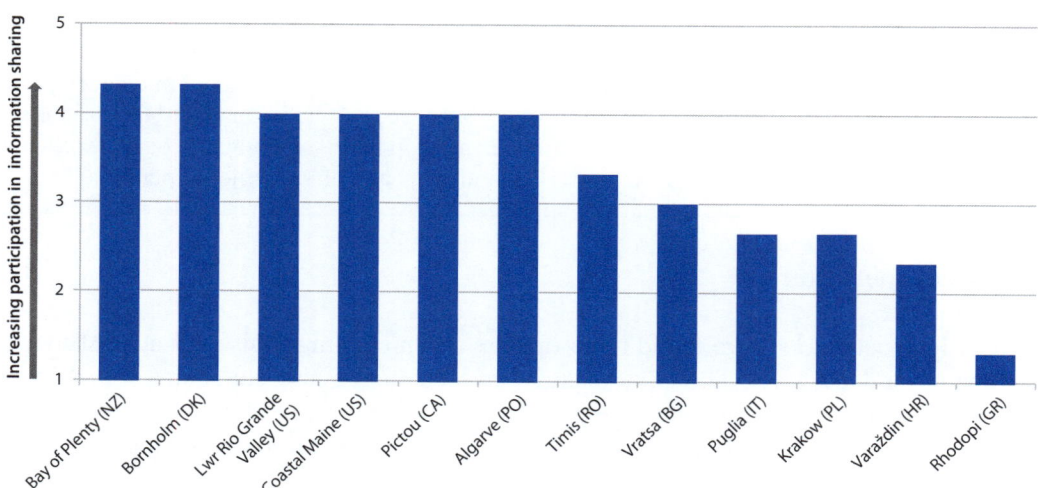

Figure 1.6. **Involvement of local actors in information and data sharing**

Note: This graph reflects the extent of information and data sharing from very weak (1) to very strong (5).

Formal committees and councils

There is variation in the degree to which co-operation between sectors at local levels is formalised (*i.e.* constituted in a formal partnership or committee). Multi-stakeholder partnerships have developed into permanent committee structures in many case study regions, mirroring those at the national level. Italy had the largest number of committees at local and regional levels, with at least 11 consultative committees operating in the Puglia region.

Formal commissions and councils are in many cases imposed "top down". In Bulgaria, Permanent Employment Commissions (PECs) met monthly at the local level to issue recommendations of projects to be funded in the field of employment and approve regional VET measures. In Vratsa the PEC had 27 members including mayors, the local educational inspectorate, labour office directorates and social partners. In Denmark, Employment Councils also exist at the local level and were given enhanced powers in recent government reform, bringing together trade unions, local municipalities, employers and employers associations to monitor and influence the implementation of policy locally. In Poland, Employment Councils at the *powiat* and *voivordship* levels brought together unions, associations, local governments, and non-governmental organisations. They met every three months and provided a useful point for co-ordination, but were seen to be overly formal and to function purely as "rubber stamping" bodies for decisions taken by local labour offices.

In the United States, the 650 Workforce Investment Boards at state and local level play a strong role in governing employment policy locally. They are elected by local officials from nominations by relevant organisations and are strongly business led, being both chaired by business and having to have a majority of business members, and also have designated seats for representatives from labour unions and local educational institutions etc. The extent to which they deliver local co-operation across policy areas varies considerably across the country, and in some cases they were seen purely as formal bodies which were bypassed by other efforts to create co-operative approaches at local level.

Parallel committees often exist in other policy areas. Within the countries participating in this study, it appears that educational committees are most likely to exist on the regional, rather than local, scale. In Denmark vocational colleges consult local education committees, comprising social partners and businesses, which are in some cases organised on a sector basis. Having several different formal structures operating in individual policy areas can risk accentuating the silo effect, however, if there is a lack of communication between them. In Denmark local employment councils and education committees were found to be operating alongside the new Global Forums which were implementing the Globalisation Strategy. The challenge was to bring together these different co-ordination mechanisms and this was being achieved by having co-representation across the different boards.

Another danger can be found in imposing too many co-operative local institutions "top down". In the post communist countries which have recently joined, or are in the process of joining the European Union, national learning from other countries has resulted in a series of co-operative structures being imposed at local level. However, if there is no simultaneous development from the "bottom-up" there can be limited ownership of these institutions. In Poland, for example, there is a lack of ownership and vision regarding the potential role of the *powiat* and *voivordship* employment councils bodies, stemming in part from the fact that they were implemented as part of a "top down" government initiative.

Joined up institutions

Outside of partnership and committee structures, certain institutions at the local level can act as interfaces which support integrated approaches and co-operative working with other local actors. In European countries municipalities often play a strong role in stimulating co-operation between other local actors, particularly in recent years where local authorities have been given a new mandate to look at local economic and social well being in several countries (such as the United Kingdom). Local and regional development agencies also play a role in bringing together different policy domains at the local level; regional development agencies in Romania, for example, had a broad cross-sectoral mandate, including human resource issues, which enabled a broad focus for local development policy in the regions during the pre-accession process. In the United States and Canada, community colleges also take on the role of integrating various policy objectives, through acting at the interface between employers, local students and local policy makers. The Nova Scotia Community College system, for example, saw itself as having a wide role to promote skills and labour force development to meet the needs of the provincial economy. Its mission is "Building Nova Scotia's economy and quality of life through education and innovation".

Box 1.6. **Policy trade-offs at the local level**

There are many policy trade-offs which exist at the local level, and which rarely get considered within fragmented governance systems. As an illustration, while some local agencies may be enthusiastic about encouraging immigration to meet local skills shortages, this will have an impact on other stakeholders (such as education providers) who will need to plan additional resources for training and schools. It might be that in the longer-term it would be better to spend such resources on better integrating the existing population into employment (including out of work newcomers) as opposed to attracting in new blood. As these issues are dealt with by different agencies, and indeed different governance levels, a necessary discussion on the best use of resources rarely takes place.

Co-operating with wider stakeholders

Co-operation with employers and the private sector varied considerably across the case study areas. Increasingly local employment agencies are being encouraged to collaborate with businesses to identify their employment and skills needs, although capacities meant that this is often an ad-hoc process. One such example was in Vratsa, Bulgaria, where the local district labour office visited 151 companies in autumn 2005 to assess labour market needs and inform of ongoing programmes and legislative changes. In many regions the private sector was unaware of what the public sector was doing, however, and whether it was relevant to them. In Pictou in Canada, for example, one stakeholder said that "Sometimes the private sector is reluctant to talk to us or seek our help as a government department, or they don't know we can help … once the private sector comes forward we find we can often position their concern and find a creative solution to meet their needs" (Bruce, submitted). In Maine, similarly, it was found that most companies, as well as individual job seekers, were unaware of the support and training services offered by the workforce system. In Greece, local employers tried to take an active role in a regional partnership to implement the structural funds in Eastern Macedonia & Thrace, but found themselves frustrated with a process that they saw as bureaucratic, self-serving and slow. Experts in the United

States found that employers were more likely to be proactive partners for the public sector in states which have consolidated programmes to reduce bureaucracy (such as Texas). Public actors often find it particularly difficult to co-operate with SMEs. One sub-region in New Zealand's Bay of Plenty was working to overcome this by developing a database of 9 000 to 10 000 local SMEs, which it regarded as an important resource to bringing in the employers' perspective and promoting local activities.

In some case study regions local public actors found it easier to work with private companies by uniting them in different sectors and clusters. Under the growth forums in Bornholm in Denmark, industry working groups based on local clusters emerged (in iron and metal, construction, victuals, agriculture, tourism, and the "experience" economy) which focused not just on economic co-operation but also on strategic thinking in relation to educational needs. In Denmark it was identified that "the clusters have led to an understanding of shared interests and goals amongst some businesses in Bornholm" (New Insight, submitted). Similarly in Murge, Puglia, local stakeholders focused partnership working with employers on developing a protocol for the reinforcement of the furniture manufacturing sector by measures such as developing agreements with banks to restructure debt, providing fiscal relief towards lowering labour costs and increasing the availability of targeted training for the sector.

Co-operation on strategy and on the delivery of services

While local actors in some of the case study areas were more likely to collaborate on developing local strategies (Puglia, Italy and Remth, Greece), in others they were more likely to collaborate on delivery. In many regions and localities, "one stop shops" became popular as a means of bringing together different agencies to provide a seamless service to local people. Under the Workforce Investment Act (WIA) in the United States each local area was required to establish at least one comprehensive one-stop center through which job seekers and employers could access all WIA services and each one-stop delivery system was required to offer a broad range of core services (information, preliminary assessment), intensive services (specialised assessments, in-depth counseling, individual employment plans, and short-term pre-vocational support), and training services. In other regions, day to day collaboration was encouraged through co-locating local branches of government agencies, even if they did not formally deliver joint services. In Pictou in Canada, the local agencies for regional development, business, education, were all in the same location thereby facilitating ongoing informal contact, important in a relatively rural region.

National and international schemes to encourage greater local co-operation

International and national governments have introduced schemes in several of the participating countries to encourage further co-operation at the local level (see Box 1.7).

In the best cases, national programmes to support increased co-operation at the local level can provide a healthy combination of tried and tested models, local creativity and leadership. They appear to have been particularly successful in rural areas: in Maine, for example, rural regions were the most enthusiastic about accessing the WIRED programme (see Box 1.7) to help build networks and join initiatives, whereas urban areas are more independent and self-sufficient in terms of these activities. Regions that are dynamic, growing and attractive to capital appear to be much less likely to collaborate vertically and to require help in developing

Box 1.7. **National and international schemes to encourage greater co-operation at the local level**

European Structural Fund programmes and community initiatives: In many European countries local and regional partnerships have developed to plan and deliver European structural funds programmes as the "partnership principle" is emphasised as much at the regional as at the national level. In addition to the mainstream structural funds, smaller scale community Initiatives introduced by the European Commission up until 2006 were also effective in stimulating co-operation; LEADER and EQUAL were found to have stimulated best practice projects in the Algarve region of Portugal, while the URBAN programme stimulated innovative co-operation in Puglia in Italy and Rhodope in Greece. In Romania the pre-accession programme PHARE was the catalyst for some strong and innovative co-operation, at least partly because it was insisted that investment in physical infrastructure should be limited to one third of total spend, leading to the introduction of softer issues such as human resources and training (for more information see the Romania country synopsis).

The United States WIRED programme: In the United States, the Department of Labor's WIRED (Workforce Innovations for Regional Economic Development) initiative supported an increase in the level of co-operation between stakeholders at state and local levels, providing USD 250 million to catalyse the creation of high-skill, high-wage opportunities for American workers within the context of their regional economies. A key component of the programme was galvanising regional networks consisting of civic, business, investor, academic, entrepreneur and philanthropic members with an action agenda and leadership commitment, as well as coaching from a select team of experts to provide guidance and technical assistance. In Maine the WIRED grant served as a catalyst for building co-operation by requiring potential grantees to collaboratively map the economic landscape of their region, and by obliging a regional network (the North Star Alliance) to form a consensus on, and leadership commitment to, a unified regional economic action agenda. The North Star Alliance focused on shop building and composite wood technologies, with 285 companies being involved in identifying common problems and shared agendas (for more information see the United States country synopsis).

Patti and PIT in Italy: the Patti – *patti territoriali* (territorial pacts) and PITs – *progetti integrati territoriali* (integrated territorial plans) have provided a useful framework for local partnership working in Italy, based on the model of the territorial employment pacts introduced in Europe in 1997. These pacts provided useful co-operation at the local level between many different stakeholders, but their impact on real policy integration appeared to be variable, with co-operation often remaining rather formal. In the locality of Nord Barese in Puglia, for example, participants felt that they had only been able to provide effective and concrete inputs into local strategy development and that when it came to the implementation of projects and programmes, co-operation was at a much lower level. The local PIT also appears to have had limited impact in terms of integrating employment policy into wider regional concerns. The national employment agency *Italia Lavoro* launched a national project called SPINN which provided assistance to PITs, while IFSOL (the national training agency) launched a similar scheme called FOCUS to encourage local governments to be more involved in co-ordinating VET and development at local level in conjunction with local education pacts. These schemes suggest that the national level needs to continue providing technical assistance when launching programmes to support co-operative working at ground level.

New Zealand regional partnerships programme: New Zealand launched a Regional Partnerships Programme (RPP) back in 2000, drawing in part on the research of the LEED Programme. It is a three stage programme which part funds regional economic partnerships for the development of regional economic development strategies, capability building and for a major regional initiative. Local organisations nominated partnerships in a bottom up process, however, as some of the regional development partnerships lacked the size, scale and capacity to create strong outcomes, the RPPs were being consolidated to a smaller set of regions.

horizontal relationships. In all regions getting adequate buy-in by local people may depend on building on the co-operation already developing locally. In New Zealand it was found that the best proposals for Major Regional Initiatives in the Regional Partnerships Programme "arose out of pre-existing local development processes in contrast to proposals initiated specifically to meet the new programme's funding criteria". Similarly, in Coastal Maine the WIRED grant was awarded to a network that had already collaborated around the Advanced Engineered Wood Composites Center.

Nevertheless, the ability of national and international programmes to produce sustainable change in the way in which local and regional institutions co-operate can be limited. This is particularly the case when programmes bring their own set of funding for joint initiatives, such as is the case for the European structural funds; such funding in many cases appears to result in a proliferation of short-term initiatives which do not alter the way traditional policies are delivered.

There is also the risk that national interventions remain short term and without clear exit strategies for when government funding runs out. This was the experience of local stakeholders in the Algarve region of Portugal who described their disillusionment with national government initiatives to promote partnership working in the area which were seen to end without either consultation or an explanation to local people.

Obstacles to local co-operation

Overall, the extent to which local co-operation went beyond formalities to involve substantive collaboration on policy development and programme delivery was ranked by local officials as "weak" in the case study areas. A series of factors appeared to limit co-operation:

Ambiguity of roles

A lack of clarity on the roles and responsibilities of different stakeholders was a key factor in limiting co-operation in many of the case study areas. Shifting and diminishing responsibilities for committee members and leadership issues undermined local action committees which had been set up to address skills issues in Pictou County, for example. Ambiguity created by a lack of awareness about the coverage of different organisations and fears that other agencies might take over particular "territories". Furthermore, when agencies have a limited awareness of what other agencies are doing it may be easier to maintain the status quo by not forcing collaboration or confrontation but such indifference can be a major cause of fragmentation and service gaps. Arguably, some degree of conflict may be necessary for policy integration to really succeed (see Figure 1.7 below), as it forces people to reduce duplication and consider the necessary trade-offs between different policy areas.

Tackling ambiguity can be even more problematic in localities which have a large number of institutions and networks operating at the local level. For example, the large suite of programmes on offer at local level in Pictou, Canada, was felt to create "a maze" not only for local people but also local policy makers. If such complexity is not managed effectively it can lead to anxiety and inaction. In the United States Texas has helped to create a more favourable environment for policy integration through, in part, consolidating existing programmes. In 1995 Texas merged ten agencies into one new agency, the Texas Workforce Commission, which meant that local WIBs had the capacity to manage a broader set of funding streams and programmes than in most states. The Lower Rio Grande Valley initiative began by mapping the services provided by different local

Figure 1.7. **From indifference to policy integration at the local level**

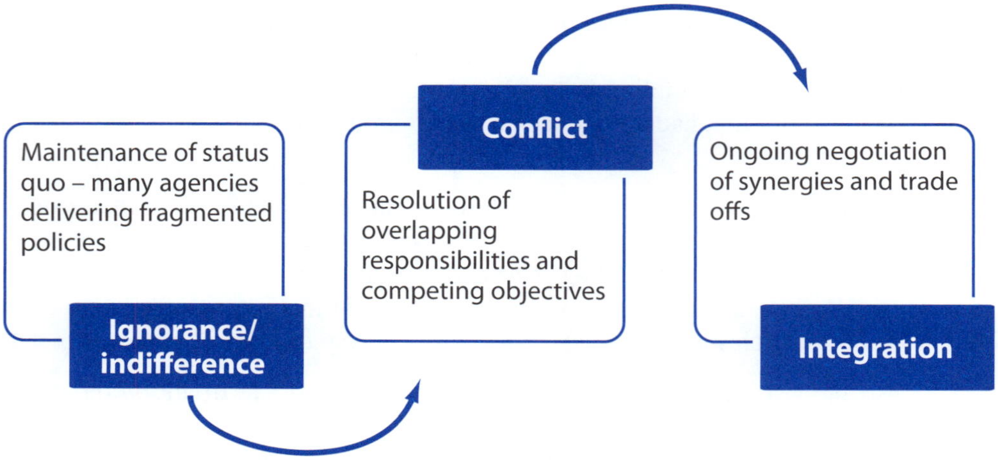

institutions. Similarly, in Maine the WIRED grant required a mapping of all employment, training and vocational education organisations funding sources, services and target populations, and uncovered 27 pre-existing and relevant government programmes.

Formal or informal co-operation?

A further issue is that formal co-operation at the local level does not always result in real collaboration on either strategy or delivery. In Italy, for example, the significant number of committees and councils at local level became bureaucratic steps to be overcome as opposed to constituting real mechanisms for collaboration, where partners pursued their own interests and raised visibility for actions. Such committees were felt to contribute little to policy integration, with concrete collaboration only occurring sporadically and mainly on the basis of situations of economic crisis.

In many cases, the study found that more informal collaboration was more likely to lead to real policy integration. This was certainly the key to successful joint working in the Lower Rio Grande Valley, where local actors only came together formally in partnership every year or so to review new data. The study expert in Croatia found that "informal relationships are usually the backbone of successful co-operation" (Crnkovic-Poziac, submitted) and pointed out that with good informal relations, local policy integration can in some cases be relatively easy: "All it requires is that a critical mass of people of a certain kind and with adequate mutual trust decide that they want to achieve something". However, in some regions, mutual trust is thin on the ground: in the case study regions in Southern Italy and Bulgaria, competition for resources and an uneven distribution of financing was found to cause widespread mistrust between institutions. This was made worse by an uneven distribution of information which meant that some participants did not have sufficient knowledge to participate in decision-making processes and, in many cases, were excluded from decisions made behind closed doors.

Relying on mainly informal relationships can also be dangerous when they depend upon the enthusiasm and leadership of particular individuals, both of which can be short-term and unsustainable as people move on and change jobs. In the United States integration in the State of Maine

---

Box 1.8. Management practices in industry – a model for the public sector?

Industry can provide a useful model for the public sector in terms of developing more flexible and integrated approaches. Companies are increasingly moving away from a "command and control" type of management structure, and towards a more network based method of management, steered in part by the power of the internet to link up people and provide a shared information and knowledge base which empowers decision making on the ground. Eberts (in Giguère & Froy, 2009) argues, for example, that in response to the forces of globalisation, large firms are allowing local productive units to be structured into horizontally co-ordinated networked structures which increase the capacity to innovate, react more quickly to external changes, improve product quality and cut down on operating costs. Such units co-operate flexibly on the basis of shared interests, coming together when necessary to achieve particular goals. A lead firm is important to continuously engage in attracting and selecting network members, sustaining network relationships by managing conflict and learning, positioning the network in the market and building the structure and the culture of the network.

Eberts makes the point that public policy makers may be slower to take up the same challenge. Unlike businesses that understand the imperative of changing their culture and capabilities to remain competitive in a global economy, governments struggle to grasp the essential elements necessary to make the full transformation; they are reluctant to shed their previously held ways of doing business and the culture embedded in their traditional government structures. Nonetheless, the evidence is clear that local communities that find new, flexible ways of co-ordinating workforce development and economic development activities can nurture the industrial competitiveness, worker development and social cohesion which are essential to compete successfully in the post-recession global economy.

---

was very much led from the top by the State Governor, who brought employment and economic development policy makers around him in a Workforce Cabinet; attempts to institutionalise collaboration further down the system, however, were weaker. Texas, in comparison, combined the necessary structure to promote sustainability and flexibility, leaving space to generate innovative solutions at the local level. In-depth systemic requirements for collaboration were introduced through the co-location and merging of agencies and the development of legal "Memorandums of Understanding" between institutions.

Geography and different governance levels

Geographical and administrative boundaries also form a strong challenge to co-operation locally. When agencies have different geographical jurisdictions and different levels of competence, it can make it very difficult to collaborate. In Portugal, branches of different ministries met in cross-sectoral co-ordination councils at the regional level, co-ordinated by the Commissions for Regional Co-ordination and Development, in what was a difficult process to oversee as the different ministries did not have equivalent competences and decision autonomy. The search for an appropriate scale to harmonise the deconcentrated bodies of the central government was a key feature of new governance mechanisms being implemented within the PRACE reform. In addition, a new law meant that municipalities were free to join forces at various government levels in order to tackle particular problems as they occur. In Poland, likewise, essential co-ordination between employment and social policies, particularly in the context of high rates of worklessness, did not occur as employment was managed at the sub-regional and regional levels, whereas social assistance was a local level competency.

Contested leadership

In many cases, local public agencies concentrate on collaborating with other stakeholders at the local level, but the focus is on social partners, employers and the voluntary sector, as opposed to other government departments. This can lead to confusion on the ground when each public agency sets up its own consultative partnerships without consulting other public departments. In the Bay of Plenty in New Zealand, for example, the Commissioner for Social Development, the regional council and the Tertiary Education Commission were all in the process of setting up committees and partnerships to develop a joined-up local approach, ending up in not only confusion but contested leadership.

Institutional mandates

Institutional mandates are important in determining whether or not local agencies feel that they need to co-operate with others locally. The three policy areas examined in this project are all very different in terms of their focus, aims and purpose. While economic development policy is area based in that it has broad aims to help promote endogenous growth, support business development, tackle deprivation, build infrastructure and support inward investment, education and employment policy are often more individually focused, helping individuals to find employment and build their skills. Employment policy is often seen to focus on disadvantage and equity issues while economic development officials concentrate on harnessing opportunity – as such, employment policymakers are not seen as an "equal partner in development". This was evident in Croatia where the policy areas were ostensibly working with similar target groups – local people, local businesses – yet the focus of employment policy was very much on those at risk of falling into long-term unemployment and on other marginal groups, meaning few meeting points occurred with a development orientated private sector looking for modern skills and high potential workers. Businesses and economic development professionals were seen to be less willing to turn to employment agencies as valid partners as they were not regarded as sharing the broader goal of creating a strong local labour market.

In some countries, employment agencies are now being encouraged to take on a broader role which may increase the possibilities for co-operation. In New Zealand, for example, the employment strategy included a priority for promoting sustainable regional economic development, a focus on high skilled jobs, and local industry partnerships to tailor skills development for emerging employment opportunities. In the United States Workforce Investment Boards could use their funds to devise and oversee strategies for lay off aversion, incumbent working training, local business retention and reduce failure rates amongst SMEs; more than 80 per cent of boards were engaged in sectoral strategies to meet the needs of employers. There is variation between countries in the extent to which economic development officials see their role to be broad or narrow. In recent years many economic development officials have been placing emphasis on human capital as a mechanism for economic development and growth, while in some regions the principal focus remains on promoting inward investment and developing infrastructure.

Training institutions also vary in the extent to which they work mainly to meet individual needs or take local employer and community needs into account. In Denmark a major refocusing of the VET system has shifted the emphasis from individually focused programmes to meeting competency gaps within the labour market as part of the Globalisation Strategy, forming a vocational training significantly more market led. In the United States the opposite has taken place: a drive towards better academic standards in the education sector is, to some extent, pulling in the opposite direction of employment policy which is moving towards more demand based vocational training.

The economic development plans of the Croatian and Canadian case study regions made hardly any reference to human resources issues, and focused primarily on capital and infrastructure issues, and in Canada the plethora of programmes and initiatives being taken forward made "effective, efficient and comprehensive strategies almost impossible to be developed and delivered" (Bruce, submitted). As a result of such difficulties, the degree to which local co-operation resulted in integrated strategies in the case study regions examined, was limited.

Box 1.9. Summary of key issues regarding local co-operation

1. Local co-operation is seen to have a relatively strong impact on the degree of local policy integration. Co-operation was perceived as highest in the case study regions in Denmark, New Zealand and the United States and lowest in Romania and Bulgaria.

2. Economic development actors seem to be the most likely to co-operate at the local level, particularly as they often have a mandate to develop local and regional development strategies. However, other policy areas can also take a leadership role, particularly employment policy makers in countries such as the United States and New Zealand.

3. Participating in multi-stakeholder partnerships does not necessarily strengthen ongoing relationships with other local agencies or increase information sharing.

4. Co-operation with the private sector proves a challenge in many localities, although targeting interventions on specific sectors and clusters can be particularly effective.

5. National and international schemes exist in some countries to encourage greater collaboration and co-operation at the local level. These can be effective – particularly in rural areas – as long as such schemes incorporate strong exit strategies and result in mainstream changes to the way institutions work, as opposed to the proliferation of parallel short-term initiatives.

6. Managed conflict is perhaps a necessary stage in the path from fragmentation to policy integration, at least in terms of promoting frank exchanges which will lead to a real consideration of trade-offs and synergies, and the effective prioritisation of resources.

7. Obstacles to co-operation include: ambiguity about roles, fear of conflict, differences in geographical boundaries, contested leadership, and narrow institutional mandates. A balance is needed between informal co-operation (which facilitates day to day delivery of objectives) and formal collaboration (which means sustainable forms of co-operation which are not just reliant on the personalities of individuals).

Flexibility

In the 11 countries studied the flexibility of national policies was identified as having the highest influence on policy integration at the local level. Whatever the degree of co-operation and partnership working between stakeholders, it has limited ability to produce change if organisations do not have the flexibility to adapt their policies and programmes to meet agreed priorities. It is not just the mandates held by individual institutions which are important, but the flexibility which exists in their management systems. In Romania the lack of power at regional and local levels to influence the content of policies, activities and programmes was seen as the principal reason why co-operation failed to produce integrated approaches. Resource constraints, although also important, came only second. According to one local stakeholder "those who know the problem best have relatively little power (and money) to act on them, and those with power and resources do not have direct responsibilities and a direct interest to take part in such efforts" (Ionita, submitted).

Policy flexibility can take a number of different forms. Mosley (2003) equates flexibility with "the density of generally binding rules and procedures", and at its simplest it can be understood as the ability of local and regional stakeholders to make relevant decisions and carry them through within the design and implementation of policies and programmes. Ultimately, governments limit the flexibility they hand down to their local offices for two main reasons; to achieve national objectives, and to achieve accountability. In the first case it is felt that too much freedom for local offices may limit their commitment to achieving national objectives, while in the second it is feared that funds may be misspent and audit trails not maintained.

Mosely classifies accountability into four different types: legal accountability (public agencies being expected to act on the basis of the rule of law and in conformity with applicable regulations), fiscal accountability (correctness and economy in the use of finances), performance

---

Box 1.10. What constitutes flexibility in the management of policy?

Programme design: Do sub-regional offices have any input into the design of policies and programmes? Are they consulted? Are they free to determine the programme mix and even adapt design features of programmes, including target groups, or are these largely centrally determined? May local public employment service offices implement innovative programmes outside the standard programme portfolio? Do they design local employment strategies?

Financing: Do sub-regional actors have flexible global budgets or line item budgets for active measures? Are they free to allocate resources flexibly between budget items for active measures?

Target groups: Are local offices free to decide on the target groups for their assistance locally or do programmes already specify particular target groups?

Goals and performance management: To what extent are organisational goals and targets centrally determined? Do they allow room for sub-regional goals and hence flexibility in adapting goals to local circumstances? Are targets and indicators hierarchically imposed or negotiated with regional and local actors? Is performance assessment based solely on quantitative criteria? Are sanctions imposed if targets are not met?

Collaboration: Are local offices free to participate in partnerships and do they collaborate with other actors? Can local offices decide who they collaborate with locally?

Outsourcing: Are local offices responsible for outsourcing services to external providers?

---

accountability (output-orientated effectiveness and efficiency) and public accountability (responsiveness to the needs of citizens and other stakeholders). Where strong accountability mechanisms are in place, even in a decentralised system, local officials often feel that they suffer from "micromanagement", having to ask permission to carry out any activity which is out of the ordinary. This can severely restrict the ability of agencies to plan strategically in partnership.

Flexibility in employment policy

In 2009 the OECD looked at the degree of flexibility in the delivery of labour market policy in OECD countries and found strong variation in the degree to which local employment officers were able to input into policies and programmes, decide how to spend their budgets locally, choose who was eligible for policies and programmes, negotiate performance targets, and outsource services (Giguère & Froy, 2009). As a result of this comparison, the OECD developed a flexibility indicator through which it benchmarked member countries (see Figure 1.8 below).[5]

Figure 1.8. OECD countries with the most local flexibility in labour market policy[6]

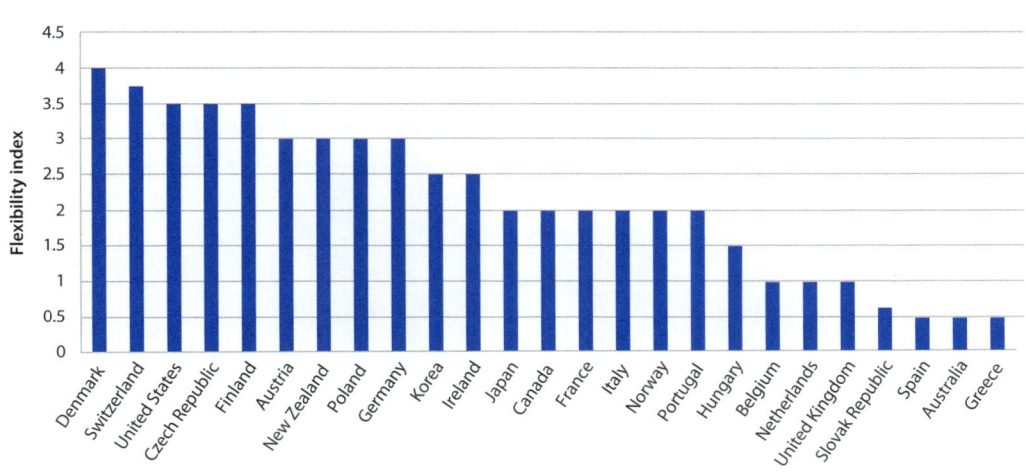

Note: This analysis was carried out using a flexibility index which ranked flexibility according to a number of different factors including (1) input into the design of policy, (2) budget management, (3) eligibility criteria, (4) performance management, (5) outsourcing, and (6) collaboration with other actors. The research drew on the results of the Questionnaire to the Employment, Labour and Social Affairs Committee (ELSAC) on Activation of Labour Market Policy in 2007. The findings were supplemented by further research in March and April 2008.

Source: Giguère & Froy, 2009.

The analysis included eight of the countries participating in the current study, namely, Denmark, Canada, Greece, Italy, New Zealand, Poland, Portugal and the United States. Of these countries, Denmark, the United States and New Zealand showed the highest level of flexibility in the implementation of labour market policy, with local offices having substantial powers to adapt their programmes and policies to priorities agreed in partnership at the local level.

In Denmark while three principle target areas for labour market policy were established at national level (youth, the long-term unemployed and those receiving sickness benefit), the local job centres were found to have considerable freedom to choose more specific target groups and to use their budgets to implement a variety of different measures (counseling, training, wage subsidies and specific job referrals), either keeping the services in-house or outsourcing them. Local employment councils took a significant role in deciding on appropriate local policies and job centres also received a financial envelope which they could spend how they wish (though they receive separate funding for ALMP and staffing costs). In the United States, in large measure, state and local areas may also design their own employment programmes consistent with federal and state laws. The Workforce Investment Act allowed states a relatively high degree of freedom to decide how to spend 15 per cent of their funding allocation among a wide variety of state-wide employment and training activities. Local Workforce Investment Boards could move limited amounts of funds within budgets for adults and dislocated workers, and could provide varying levels of services to individuals in industries according to their importance to the local economy. In New Zealand Regional Commissioners for Social Development had discretionary budgets to spend on local issues and were, for example, involved in national policy design through an internal consultation process.

In Italy and Canada, while there was considerable flexibility in the delivery of employment policy at the regional scale (being two devolved administrations), this did not translate into high levels of flexibility in local offices. In the Southern European countries of Portugal and Greece the system was much more centralised, with Greece being particularly inflexible – here most decisions were taken by central officials. Similarly, among those countries not included in the OECD 2008 analysis, in Bulgaria employment policy was found to be both rigid and highly centralised in relation to programme design and funding, with a limited role for local offices. Further,

Table 1.3. **Policy flexibility in labour market policy at the local level**

	No flexibility	Are consulted	Design strategies	Can choose mix	Involved in design	No flexibility	Special funding	Can move funding	Block grant	No flexibility	Some freedom to decide	Set criteria	N/A	No flexibility	Negotiate targets	Set targets	Outsourcing	Collaboration
	Programme design					Budgets				Eligibility				Performance management				
Bulgaria	-	-	-	-	-	-	-	-	-	-	-	-	-	-	-	-	-	-
Canada[a]	●							●		●					●		●	●
Croatia	-	-	-	-	-	-	-	-	-	-	-	-	-	-	-	-	-	-
Denmark			●		●		●	●			●				●		●	●
Greece	●					●				●			●					●
Italy	●							●			●			●			●	●
New Zealand		●					●				●				●		●	●
Poland					●				●	●					●		●	●
Portugal	●						●			●					●		●	●
Romania	-	-	-	-	-	-	-	-	-	-	-	-	-	-	-	-	-	-
United States		●			●[b]		●				●				●[c]		●	●

Notes: a. Results for co-managed provinces only.

b. In addition to delivering national programmes.

c. Local offices also set additional targets for their own offices.

Source: Giguère & Froy, 2009.

some discrepancy was identified between needs at the local level and the design of interventions at the national level. In Croatia and Romania employment policy was also highly centralised in terms of the ability of local actors to influence the design of programmes, the delivery of budgets, and the type of people to assist.

Flexibility in other policy areas

For local policy to become more integrated it is not just labour market policy which needs to be delivered flexibly. Other partners around the table also need to be able to be able to adjust their policies to priorities agreed in partnership. Taking a broader look at all three policy areas under examination, this study has analysed flexibility in four main areas: (1) the framework for designing policies and programmes, (2) the legal framework, (3) the budgetary framework, and (4) the performance management framework. Overall, out of the three policy areas employment policy was found to be the most rigid and economic development perceived to be the least rigid.

Figure 1.9. **Which policy area was felt to have most flexibility?**

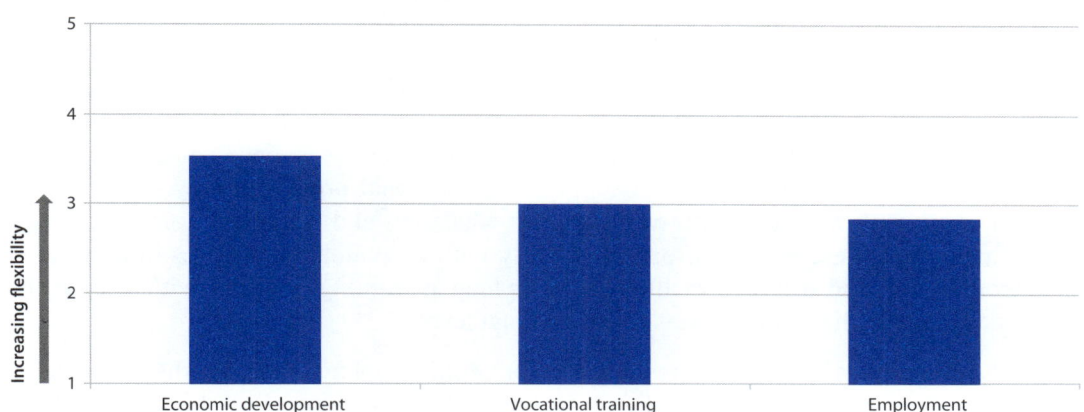

Notes: 1. This constitutes an average of the views expressed at the local, state (where applicable) and national levels.
2. Where 1 is very inflexible and 5 is very flexible.

Vocational training policy

In vocational training the main factor restricting flexibility appears to be the time which it takes to update curricula and alter training and education programmes. Institutions also have a duty to take into account demands from the local student population which limits responsiveness to business and wider community needs. A further inflexibility in some countries can be found in students' ability to transfer between different training strands, and adapt and build on their training during their adult life. This was evident in Croatia where it was not possible for students to transfer from vocational training strands to academic strands and build on their generic skills as adults. While this study has only been able to undertake a broad assessment of the degree of flexibility available to local officials, the perceptions of flexibility in vocational training policy by country (taking into account the views of both national and regional stakeholders) were as follows:

Figure 1.10. **Flexibility of training policy by country**

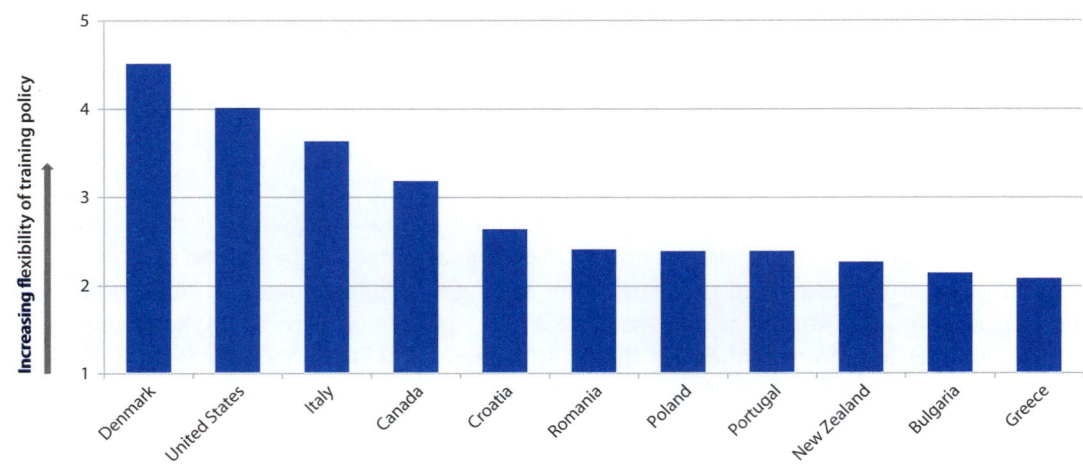

Notes: 1. This constitutes an average of the views expressed at the local, state (where applicable) and national levels.
2. Where 1 is very inflexible and 5 is very flexible.

In Denmark the education system was recently decentralised in terms of delivery to the local level. Officials of the educational system felt they had a relatively high degree of freedom to design programmes and meet the demands of specific enterprises; once education and training institutions have been authorised to supply an educational programme by the Ministry of Education, they were free to decide what specific education and training to offer. Since 2004 training institutions were free to co-operate closely with individual enterprises in order to customise programmes and still receive allowances, as long as training complies with a competency framework agreed with social partners at the national level.

In Italy the regions are entirely responsible for training policy, although the provinces and local areas receive variable amounts of flexibility depending on the province. In the United States education and training institutions have a strong degree of freedom because this policy area is particularly decentralised. Federal level funding for Career and Technical Education represented only 5 to 7 per cent of total funding, with the rest coming from state and local funds. There is great variation in the degree to which the states then exert control over localities and most see themselves as occupying a leadership role, particularly as 84 per cent of resources were required to go to local educational agencies and post-secondary institutions at the time of study. Texas has a particularly decentralised education system and is funded through the local tax base, with more than 50 community colleges, each reporting to an elected governing board funded by local tax revenues.

The ability of local officials to influence the design of training programmes (and *i.e.* curricula) is perceived to be particularly low compared with other policy areas, limiting responsiveness to local needs. However, in the case study focus areas of Texas and Bornholm, colleges were required to indicate local labour market demand for training prior to programme approval; in Texas if local advisory board members articulated a need for a new programme they could get approval rapidly (usually within a month) if it was classified as a "local needs" course (although no funds are made available for new programme development). After three years this would be assessed to ascertain whether there was a state-wide need.

As mentioned above, in some countries training institutions were being given more flexibility to co-operate directly with other local actors on the delivery of vocational policy. Denmark and New Zealand have effectively "re-centralised" the strategic design of policy while providing flexibility to local institutions. While this meant considerable flexibility at institutional level, education policy risks becoming a missing link when it comes to making strategic decisions to influence the delivery of policies and programmes across a locality or region. In New Zealand, despite the high level of co-operation, interviewees in the Bay of Plenty expressed a concern about a relatively low level of integration between regional economic development strategies and training strategies. This meant that the medium to long-term impacts of training policy were not being considered. As one local actor pointed out, "the skills gaps identified by regional stakeholders for long-term economic development may require a different alignment of labour resources than that required to address medium-term skills shortages". It was also indicated that the "bigger picture" of a lack of productivity, good quality employment and attractiveness in local industry, which had led to the labour shortages, was not being addressed despite being a concern for economic development officials, who felt that it was important not to suppress signals to employers to raise productivity.

It is not just strategic presence which is important, but also the ability to influence the system at a high enough level to have critical mass at the regional level. This is demonstrated in the region of Timisoara in Romania (see Box 1.11 below and Romania country chapter), where strong strategic planning in the field of vocational training has failed to have an impact due to the inability of stakeholders to have any significant traction to influence skills provision regionally.

Box 1.11. Influencing vocational training policy at the regional and local levels – the case of Timisoara

In Timisoara in Romania local stakeholders used a European pre-accession programme, PHARE, to try and influence local curricula during a period of skills shortages. Under this nationwide programme, regional consortia (including representatives of development agencies, county councils, county employment agencies, school inspectorates and local universities) identified and established priorities for vocation training (VET), and developed local and regional action plans for VET (PRAIs and PLAIs). These action plans were based on analysis of current labour market trends, strategic forecasts and a set of measures proposed for implementation, with targets attached. However, the only entry point at which these plans could influence training curricula was at the individual school level, and only at this level did the whole hierarchy of strategies comes into contact with the budgetary process and with concrete decisions on resource allocation. The plans were sometimes used as the basis of discussions between schools and the local government in the process of budgetary planning, however since local governments participated very little, if at all, in the production of the VET strategies, there was no guarantee that they would be reflected in the resulting financial allocations. Consequently, while the strategies developed within the PRAIs and PLAIs were far sighted and useful, there was very limited power available to back them up, since those who actively participated in their formulation only had advisory power regionally and locally.

Economic development policy

Economic development policy was judged to be the most flexible of all the three policy areas.

Figure 1.11. **Flexibility of economic development policy by country**

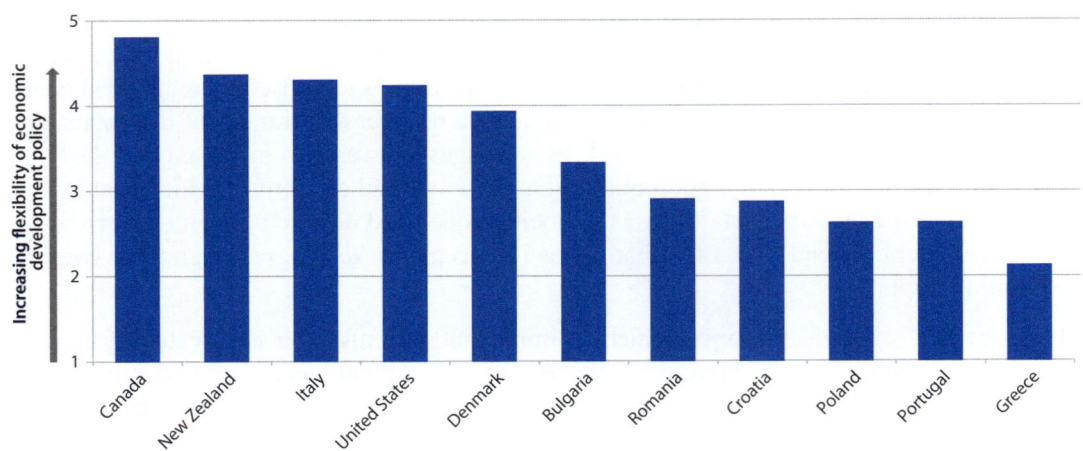

Notes: 1. Where 1 is very inflexible and 5 is very flexible.

2. This constitutes an average of the views expressed at the local, state (where applicable) and national levels.

The countries where economic development was perceived to the most flexible were Canada, New Zealand and Italy. In the east of Canada ACOA had no specific programme activity or budget targets for specific geographic areas by region or province; programme delivery was in response to demand and driven in large part by the strategic plans of regional development agencies and the private sector. Each regional development agency was independent in terms of the development of its strategic plans and its budget allocations for core and programme activities. These were aligned with ACOA and provincial, wider objectives because field staff are often ex-officio members of regional development agency boards. New Zealand Trade and Enterprise officials and regional economic development advisors also had a great deal of discretion in encouraging local initiatives within national policy guidelines.

In Southern and Eastern European countries economic development is in some cases far more centralised. In Croatia, for example, local project approval was usually obtained through "lobbying the Ministry of Finance" and budgets were generally only reallocated to account for changes in inflation. Economic development officials in Europe can also find themselves themselves constrained when delivering European programmes, particularly where regional programmes are designed at the national level. In Greece the regional operational programme budget was decided centrally, and regional actors had the freedom to only move five per cent of funds. In Italy it was the regional level which controlled funds, being able to decide on the timing and the budget of nearly all activities, including those planned within specific decentralised or local initiatives such as the PITs. Local actors generally applied for funds through a regional tendering process (see Box 1.12), and while there were a large number of potential activities which could be supported, the limited size of the resulting projects frequently led to local level fragmentation.

Box 1.12. **Tendering and grants programmes: a recipe for fragmentation?**

In many European countries, local actors compete for funding by bidding for projects within tendering processes. In Puglia, Italy, local stakeholders bid for funding under the *bandi territoriali* which are essentially long lists of potential actions identified at regional level. Financial resources are allocated along different budget lines with limited reference to other priorities, leading to a lack of focus on potential synergies or trade-offs between different actions. At the same time, bidding based funding exercises were found to reward those localities with the highest capacities and ability to generate matched funding in other countries, meaning that those localities in real need were often not the ones to receive the most help.

Relative flexibility of different management tools

When management tools were compared, the perceived difference in the flexibility associated with each tool was relatively low. Overall, budgetary management was found to be the most restrictive in terms of allowing local actors to co-operate with other actors and adapt their programmes and policies, with the legal framework the least restricting. Performance management was seen as relatively inflexible when "management by objectives" were applied. Local actors also found that they had more freedom in some aspects of policy management than in others. National policy makers perceived less variation than local policy makers, suggesting that they were not fully aware of the particular impact that some management frameworks may have on the flexibility available locally.

Figure 1.12. **Flexibility by management tool**

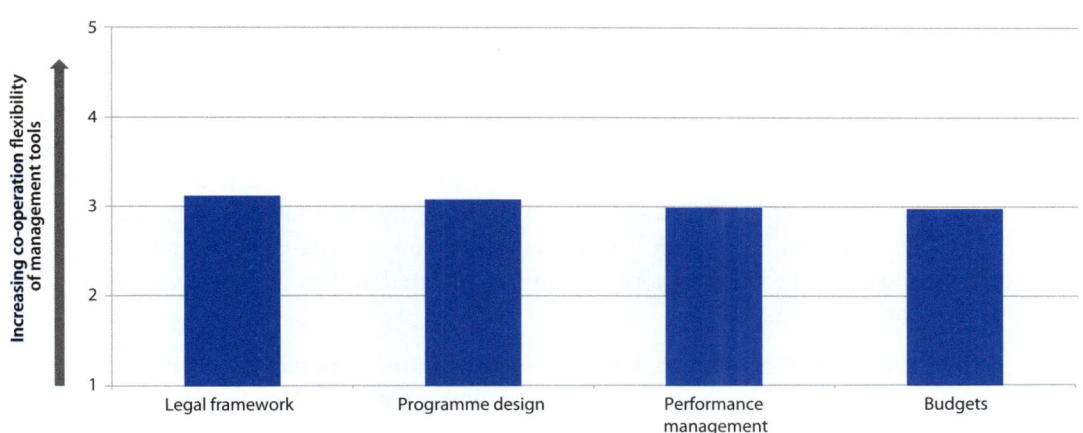

Notes: 1. Where 1 is very inflexible and 5 is very flexible.

2. This constitutes an average of the views expressed at the local, state (where applicable) and national levels.

Design of programmes

As noted above, local stakeholders frequently have a low level of input into the design of policies and programmes locally, particularly in relation to employment and vocational training policy. In labour market policy Mosley (in Giguère & Froy, 2009) points out that, at minimum, local actors should be given considerable leeway in shaping their local programme mix and be allowed to allocate a portion of their resources to innovative programmes not foreseen in the national programme portfolio. While such flexibility existed in Denmark, Poland and the United States, in the other participating countries local actors were either consulted when programmes were being developed nationally (New Zealand) or not involved at all. Likewise, it is rare for local or regional actors to be strongly involved in curricula design for vocational training policy, even if local training institutions are being given more flexibility to decide on the courses they deliver in some countries.

Legal framework

Overall, the legal framework was found to pose the fewest restrictions to local policy makers, largely because its importance in determining actions and initiatives at local level is felt to be relatively low. The United States is perhaps one exception to this rule, as arguably the legal system provides a mechanism for the federal level to be able to influence the actions of states and localities beyond the rather limited operation of federally funded programmes. In recognition of the potentially restrictive influence that this could have on local and state flexibility, a "waiver" system was set up by the Department of Labor to allow states to apply for certain provisions of the law to be waived and for additional flexibility in implementing innovative workforce strategies and initiatives. Many states have taken advantage of this provision in the Workforce Investment Act, following active encouragement from the Department of Labor, and 439 waiver requests and 331 were approved as of summer 2006. Waivers were also one of the tools used by local agencies in the Lower Rio Grande Valley to increase their flexibility to respond to local priorities.

In other countries local agencies did not consider themselves particularly restricted in their local engagement by the legal powers, suggesting that the legal framework is, for the most part, sufficiently broad to allow local agencies to co-operate towards attaining economic development goals. Local stakeholders in the Bay of Plenty case study region, New Zealand, did not identify any serious legal barriers to their work and one person noted that it would not be too difficult for the agency's minister to amend any legislation that was found to be inhibiting. In addition, there was often more legal space for decentralisation in participating countries than was actually carried out, as seen in Bulgaria, for example, where more authority could be delegated to the local level within the current framework if felt appropriate.

Programme eligibility is also an area where the legal framework can have a particular impact on local flexibility. This was seen in Poland where employment policy is highly decentralised but local implementation was restricted by the fact that the target groups for active labour market policy were strictly defined at the national level at the time of study; labour market policy only targeted recipients of unemployment insurance (EI) and could not provide assistance to other at-risk groups such as the economically inactive, youth, elderly and disabled. In Canada tight eligibility criteria also meant that certain types of individual "fell through the cracks" between institutions, and could not be helped by local programmes and eligibility criteria have limited the extent to which local labour offices can undertake pre-emptive action to support people at risk of losing jobs. However, a new fund was introduced in Canada to fund provincial and territorial labour market programmes and services that focus on skills development for both the employed and unemployed with no high school diploma or recognised certification, or with low levels of literacy and essential skills. CAD 500 million has been made available at national level annually to allow local agencies to offer a more seamless service and, in particular, better respond to the economic crisis through helping at risk workers.

Budgets

In New Zealand local actors felt that the ability to commit resources was the key to effective participation in regional partnerships. However, overall, the budgetary framework was felt to be the most inflexible accountability mechanism at the local level in all the participating countries. Budget lines for economic development were felt to be the most flexible, followed by employment budgets, and then vocational training budgets. In many cases local actors are allocated pre-defined budgets with a very limited possibility to move funds between budget lines. In only limited cases were local agencies allocated a "financial envelope" which they can use as they see fit, despite the fact that Mosley (Giguère & Froy, 2009) argues that budget flexibility can be conceded to local employment agencies without posing serious accountability problems, as long as other checks – such as "management by objectives" – are in place.

Performance management

Eggers and Goldsmith (2004) identify accountability as "one of the most difficult challenges of networked government". Performance management is one way in which governments attempt to retain control over local actors, particularly in more flexible overall systems. "Management by objectives" was fully in operation in less than half of the participating countries. In particular, it appears to function relatively weakly in Southern and Eastern European countries, where specific performance targets for local government offices either do not exist or have only recently been introduced. In Greece employment policy was managed almost 100 per cent through programme rules and regulations until recently, with, at one stage, only one output target set – for all registered unemployed to go through the individualised approach; in 2006 performance targets were set for each Centre for the Promotion of Employment for the first time. In Poland local labour offices provide indicators to regional administration but this varies between regions and a standardised approach to data collection and evaluation is lacking at the national tier. Nevertheless, some countries are working to introduce more targeting; in Romania comparative benchmarking now exists on targets and performance indicators between the 42 sub-regional employment service offices. In Portugal a new emphasis on targets, organisational rationalisation and search for efficiency formed the backbone of a recent national plan to reform the public sector.

In Canada, Denmark, New Zealand and the United States, performance management and "management by objectives" was more widely used, with policy makers in each of the three policy areas generally reporting back on the achievement of objectives set by national and regional levels. It is more frequent for local offices to be judged on output indicators (the number of people advised, the number of people trained, number of events, volume of time spent on counseling), with outcome indicators (impact on local conditions, such as unemployment, skills levels etc.) used rarely. Denmark was regarded as highly innovative in basing the management of local job centres on the achievement of outcome indicators.

Where "management by objectives" is in use, the increased ability to evaluate local interventions can be accompanied by perverse effects. In the United States, with the multiple funding programmes existing at state and local levels, incentives which promote counterproductive behaviours and activities can result. Targets are also largely restricted to a particular sector meaning limited incentives for cross-working. As identified above, at the national level participating countries had a low level of experience when it came to introducing cross-sector performance targets which might encourage policy integration. Texas went some way in tackling this through merging different programmes and funding streams, and through applying for a waiver from the US Department of Labor to allow greater flexibility when contracting performance measures with local Workforce Investment Boards. When the Texas Workforce Commission merged 28 agencies over a decade ago, there were 350 different performance measures for which the different agencies were responsible; that has been streamlined considerably to 72 measures.

The state of Texas also introduced a two tier system of formal and less formal measures. Formal measures are consistent across workforce programmes and include mainly output targets, for example, entered employment, retention, educational achievement and customers served. Less formal measures are not collected across all boards but are judged critical to the work of one or more agencies to achieve an objective in their strategic plan. These are often outcome based and include, for example, impact on recidivism, youth transition and school drop-out rates. Interestingly, certain workforce development boards have broader targets to contribute to local economic development. This was the case for the Gulf Coast Workforce Development Board which included more competitive employers, more and better jobs, and higher incomes within their informal targets.

Mechanisms for increasing horizontal accountability

In Denmark, Poland and the United States the fact that employment agencies are governed by local boards, comprising employers and other stakeholders, allowed a certain degree of relaxation in relation to vertical performance targets. By creating a situation whereby local agencies respond to other local agents in addition to national stakeholders, vertical accountability is supplemented by horizontal forms of accountability. As local actors work with other actors to achieve locally agreed objectives, horizontal feedback loops start to balance out the "vertical feedback loops" through which officials communicate their actions to their national counterparts (see the Figure 1.13 below).

Figure 1.13. The relationship between vertical and horizontal accountability

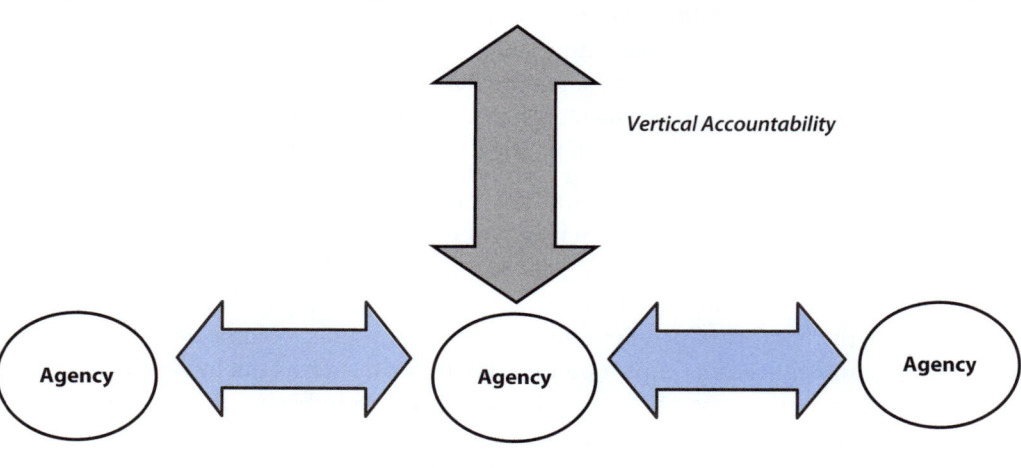

Evidence from the case study areas shows that in addition to cross-sector boards, there are a number of other ways in which local areas can tackle the "perverse effects" of conventional performance indicators and introduce new forms of horizontal accountability locally:

Negotiated targets: Greater flexibility can be achieved by consulting the local level when setting government targets, thereby also allowing government officials to ensure that sector performance is compatible with broader area-based strategies. In Denmark, Canada, New Zealand, Poland, Portugal and the United States targets for employment policy were negotiated with local offices. Strengthening horizontal accountability relationships by encouraging social partners and economic development stakeholders to scrutinise and comment on the targets proposed, would further contribute to policy co-ordination locally. As demonstrated in Texas, encouraging local and sub-regional actors to set additional targets to those set as a baseline by the national level, can also help.

Outcome targets: Setting outputs and outcome targets rather than input targets permits governments to retain control over results while allowing local entities to determine the best way to administer services to achieve them, including experimenting with innovative approaches. Outcome targets can also encourage local agencies to become more cross-sector and long-term in their approach. However impact data is often hard to capture, particular when data availability at the local level is low.

Cross-sector targets and community score cards: Governments can provide incentives and structures for local agencies to develop joint targets with other government agencies to co-ordinate a range of services for businesses and individuals. Friedman (2005) argues that localities should focus on a two tiered approach to performance management, measuring not only the effectiveness of "performance accountability" (*i.e.* catering for clients/customers, which would generally involve a single sector approach) but also "population accountability" (*i.e.* catering for whole populations such as cities or regions, generally a cross-sector process). The latter approach is increasingly common in countries such as the United States, where local communities use a "community report card" approach to (1) agree on community wide objectives, (2) translate these into outcomes, (3) develop the outcomes into achievable outputs deliverable by identified agencies, and (4) measure them annually or biannually.

Local scrutiny panels: Allowing a wider group of local actors to scrutinise and report on the overall performance of local branches of national agencies (*i.e.* not just participate in target setting) can lead to more horizontal systems of mutual accountability.

Cross-sector public appointments: In the United States it was shown that having other agencies involved in recruitment panels creates staff allegiances to more than one agency. In Poland and Portugal, however, the fact that there was local involvement in the recruitment of the heads of local labour offices seems to have had a limited effect on encouraging their independence.

Customer-led approaches: Customer led approaches such as providing local people with individual training accounts, which they can decide how to spend, can raise the degree to which local agencies look outwards as opposed to upwards when monitoring their performance. This approach is weakened by the fact that it can prevent agencies from thinking more strategically about community level needs.

Flexibility can be awarded incrementally. The United States "waiver" system described above, for example, was successful in granting greater flexibility to local Workforce Investment Boards experimenting with new activities and with a proven capacity to deliver. This can be seen as an efficient way of building capacities, whilst also promoting innovation and awarding flexibility to those most able to make good use of it.

Perceptions of flexibility

Overall, local level actors felt that they had less flexibility in the implementation of policies than was assumed by national policy makers, who were relatively confident across the board that policies could be adapted to local conditions. This highlights a problem identified in wider research that national level policy makers often have a looser understanding of the rules and regulations imposed in their management structures than local level actors do themselves. National policy makers frequently expressed the opinion that while rules and regulations were important, they would be tolerant of locally occurring transgressions if this was seen to have a positive impact on the policy delivery, and, indeed, in many cases where local actors managed to develop strong and integrated approaches, this was due to a relatively loose understanding of their responsibilities to other levels of the system. However, while many regions will go against the system to produce meaningful actions, there are many more timid regions which spend their time "toeing the line". This is not helped by the fact that when national policy makers develop policies and programmes with a relatively loose sense of compliance to rules, they do not necessarily communicate this to other actors at the national tier, particularly auditors. The report on the United States identified a degree of confusion and contradiction between federal and state leadership which promoted a more creative, flexible vision of programme co-ordination, and progamme auditors who interpreted Congressional intent and Executive branch prerogatives very narrowly. Some

---

Box 1.13. Summary of key issues regarding flexibility

1. Flexibility in the management of government policies (in relation to budgets, performance targets, the legal framework and programme design) was found to be the most important factor affecting policy integration at the local level.

2. OECD research shows that flexibility in labour market policy varies considerably across countries, but that both centralised and decentralised systems can offer flexibility to their labour offices. However, generally employment policy was found to be the most rigid of the policy areas.

3. Flexibility in education policy largely relates to the ability to influence the content of curricula locally and was generally found to be low. In some countries more flexibility has recently been granted to individual training institutions to decide on programme content locally.

4. Economic development policy is the most flexible policy at the local level, although in some countries, particularly in Central and Eastern Europe, it remains relatively centralised.

5. It was not perceived that there was a strong difference in flexibility between the array of management tools, although local actors perceived more variation than national actors. Actors felt they were most constrained in the management of their budgets and least constrained by their legal framework.

6. Management by objectives was only used to any great extent in under half of the countries under study. It can have a distorting effect by encouraging policy officials to meet their own sectoral targets and neglect strategies agreed in partnership with other actors. Some countries are finding ways around this through negotiating targets further with their local offices and developing more horizontal forms of accountability, including local monitoring boards. A focus on cross sector targets and outcome targets, for example through a community score card approach, can be helpful.

7. Perceptions of flexibility vary between national and local levels, with some local actors being unnecessarily "timid" when it came to interpreting the flexibility available to them.

8. Flexibility can be awarded incrementally.

national policy makers stated that they would be broadly positive about local actors "pushing the boundaries" of their legal and management frameworks if this would lead to good results. In contrast, locally many officials are relatively timid about breaking the rules when implementing policies and programmes, which may be wise given that national policy makers often fail to communicate their more relaxed perspective on rules and regulations to their auditing bodies.

Capacities

Co-operation and flexibility will not produce policy integration unless they are accompanied by adequate skills and resources at the local level. A "chicken and egg" situation exists in relation to local capacities; national governments fear that local capacities are low and, consequently, are reluctant to offer new responsibility and new resources. However, without gaining responsibility and a degree of control over policy implementation, local actors have little capacity to build their competences and capacities. As a result they often feel relatively powerless faced with the complex issues that exist. A further complicating factor is that national and regional policy makers often feel that there is less capacity on the ground than actually exists; national policy makers perceived a lower level of capacity than local policy makers. Indeed, perceptions of capacity between different government levels are often negative, as evident in Italy where "the perception of a capacity deficit is often reciprocated between regional and sub-regional levels".

Capacity at the local level can be broadly divided into skills (the competences which government officials and other stakeholders have to carry out their work) and resources (the financial resources and other assets which make local action possible). Local actors in the case study regions were asked to rate their own levels of resources and skills, and also those of their partner institutions and other local stakeholders. Local stakeholders in all the case study regions considered their level of skills and resources to be relatively low, except in the United States, Denmark and Canada. Interestingly, in the majority of cases local actors felt that their skills were higher than or equal to the resources available to them, while in Italy, Portugal, Romania and Greece this was reversed, due perhaps to the influx of European funds into these regions.

Figure 1.14. **Levels of skills and resources in the case study areas**

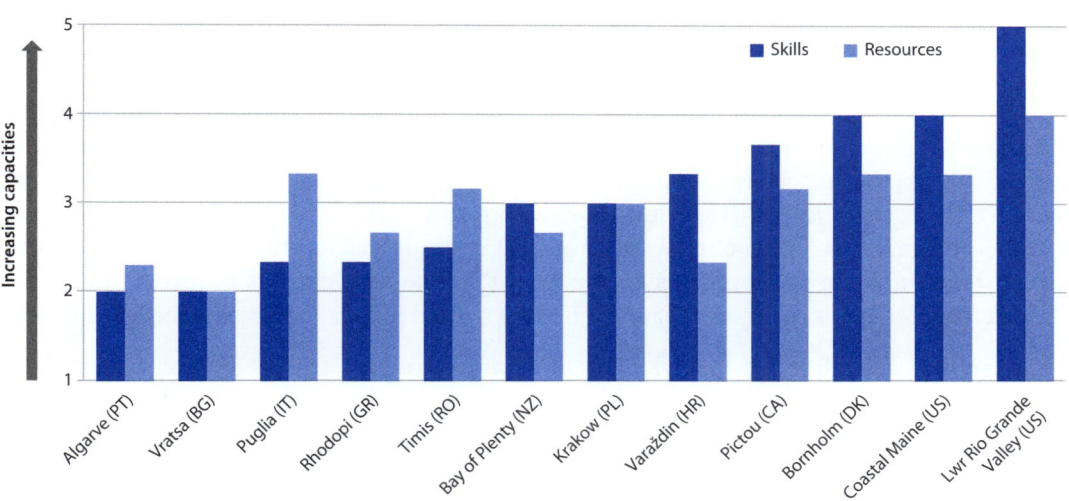

Note: Based on an assessment of all local stakeholders of their own capacities and the capacities of their partners where 1 is non-existent and 5 is very strong.

Local actors considered capacities to be broadly similar across the three policy areas, although slightly higher in the field of economic development. The employment service often has the highest number of resources locally, even if these are tied to specific national programmes. In Bulgaria the economic development sector was the only policy area with real capacity to act, with resources in other policy areas more limited. The public employment service was seen to lack the human resources and skills necessary to engage fully in co-operation and joint initiatives at the local level. In Greece employment service staff, like other public sector actors, were felt to be risk averse and given the lack of a staff evaluation system there were limited incentives for staff to achieve. Interviewees recognised that the majority of staff in the public employment service had limited qualifications and there was a lack of strategic planning and management skills, although it was noted that injections of new graduates and staff training on core skills were helping to turn things around. In Croatia a drive to recruit newcomers was moving things forward within the public employment service, although remuneration systems had not yet been redesigned to reflect the amount of responsibility new, young workers were shouldering.

Capacity issues also exist in the vocational training sector. The post-communist countries covered in this research have had particular problems adapting an outdated VET system to the modern day challenges of globalisation. In each of these countries, traditionally very close links existed between vocational training institutions and state owned enterprises but these have since fragmented and particularly low levels of adult training are now evident. For example, in Croatia only three per cent of adults participated in education as opposed to 40 per cent during the communist era. The slow pace of reform of the VET sector has been blamed for creating a bottleneck for development and in Poland investment in vocational training declined still further following reduced demand in the context of the knowledge economy. Privatisation has to some extent been building capacities in recent years in post-communist countries. In Southern Europe VET reform has also been taking place, with strong efforts to better recognise and offer credentials for training in Portugal and Greece. However, a continuing lack of focus on the generic skills important to today's economy (*e.g.* analytical skills, problem solving, creativity, innovation), were noted.

Resources for regional development are low in many countries, meaning an increasing reliance on European structural funds in the case of European countries. Indeed, in the case study region of Puglia, Italy, more than 90 per cent of regional expenditure went through the European funded regional operational programme at the time of study, while in Greece "the EU structural funds are seen as the main tool for developing the region, rather than one tool to get the region to where it wants to go" (Manoudi, submitted). Regions receiving significant European structural funds can quickly find themselves with the problem of surplus resources and difficulty absorbing them. In Romania the effort to plan and utilise these funds absorbed all the strategic and administrative capacity of the public sector, leaving limited capacity for wider actions to promote regional development. In Greece and Italy difficulties in delivering structural fund projects on time has meant that strategic intentions are quickly abandoned. In Greece it was found that a "trade off emerges between the need to spend money versus the need to make hard choices to invest in more complex, selective and intensive projects that are better targeted to local needs" (Manoudi, submitted).

The degree of funding for specific tiers of government can strongly impact on their ability to co-operate with other actors. This was seen in Bulgaria where a lack of budgets for regional development at NUTS II and NUTS III levels (regional and provincial levels)[7] impeded their participation in strategic development, while in Croatia the county councils were particularly poorly funded, undermining their ability to work in partnership and act as leaders for the integration of other policy areas.

Skills

Strategic skills

A skill often lacking at the local level – and yet key to policy integration – is the ability to develop sound local strategies. In the best of circumstances a coherent strategy can provide a "regional lens" through which local officials see their policies and programmes, but this appears rarely to exist. In many of the case study areas local strategies took the form of long lists of potential actions, with very limited prioritisation. In the region of Vratsa in Bulgaria, for example, the first regional development plan (2000-2006) represented a wish list for funding relatively short-term projects of different sizes and scope, including 50 projects in the field of infrastructure, 40 in the field of economic development, 15 in social infrastructure, and ten environmental projects. While local actors across the different policy fields were involved in, or consulted on, the creation of the strategy, the more difficult discussions which would lead to a review of the trade-offs between different actions had not taken place.

In many cases, local strategies do not refer to the means for their implementation. In Romania it was found that "strategies are written without a great deal of regard for the competences and tools of intervention that sub-national authorities actually have" (Ionita, submitted), and "since employment and vocational training are both policy areas still to be decentralised, and the local /regional governments are either not involved at all (employment) or implement strict national mandates (education), the progressive agenda for negotiating and drafting strategies for these domains at sub-national levels is in good part void of content". In contrast, in Portugal while regional strategies were well regarded and based on extensive consultation, the lack of guidance on implementation meant that were barely referred to in practice.

Part of the problem is that local agencies are often not required to think strategically or in the long-term either on an individual agency basis or in partnership. The public employment service, for example, often encourages local officials to focus their actions towards individuals as opposed to communities, which inherently creates a short-term timescale for their actions. In addition, while employment service staff often receive relatively specific training in relation to programme implementation and claim management, they rarely receive guidance on the broader policy framework for labour market policy and on other policy fields such as economic development and innovation. This is changing in some countries, with employment agencies and workforce investment boards in New Zealand and the United States being encouraged to think strategically through the production of strategies and work plans.

Employment agencies are not the only ones within limited strategic capacities. In Greece and Portugal local development agencies had limited possibility to galvanise integrated strategies locally despite their cross-cutting focus, because they were low level, had very limited resources and generally ended up focusing on keeping their own organisation afloat through access to European grants and programmes. Likewise, the business community appeared to have very little capacity to think strategically in many of the case study regions. In Canada it was found that "the business community, as a whole, is not adequately engaged in strategic planning as it relates to the skills agenda" (Bruce, submitted). In Pictou chamber and regional development agency members tended to be thinking more of "member services" rather than development and productivity of the business sector on a collective basis.

Generic and leadership skills

The analytical and planning skills required to build an effective strategy are not the only skills important for developing integrated policy at the local level, with communication and net-working skills likewise particularly important, as is local leadership. Indeed, training schools for generic local development skills have been on the rise in recent years, such as the Academy for Sustainable Communities in the United Kingdom, for example. In the case study regions it was clear that local leadership was a key factor in producing integrated working. In Greece it was found that "the role of charismatic individuals who care for their locality and who make things happen is very important", allowing local regions to achieve things "despite the challenging insti-tutional context" (Manoudi, submitted). In the United States case study region of the Lower Rio Grande Valley the importance of leaders who can "prod" other stakeholders to act, earn people's trust, and have an alternative vision for the future was emphasised.

Political leaders are obviously important in this respect, though the nature of the political system in many European countries means that local mayors are not always the most likely fig-ures to encourage long-term integrated approaches, despite their ability to generate loyalty and activity at local level. In Central and Eastern European countries, much local activity in the case study regions appeared to be based on "implementing the ideas of the mayors" and the need to maintain visibility in the relatively short-time scales of political office meant that, in many cases, these ideas were focused on short-term infrastructure projects. Longer-term investment in "soft issues" such as education and training whose impact would be harder to demonstrate were more difficult to justify. Political concerns can influence the selection of local projects; in Italy it was found that local actors appeared to have an incentive to perpetuate policy fragmentation in order that the interests of individual "parties and clans" continued to be satisfied, whatever the impact for the community as a whole. Where public appointments are influenced by political allegiances this can also create problems of frequently changing personnel at local level, while competing allegiances between different layers of the administration can prevent joined up working. Political pressures can also side-track integration efforts due to the need to disperse investments in the interest of apparent equality. In Maine, for example, political pressures were identified as cen-trifugal and they tend to spread resources widely to satisfy constituents. With a "one man – one dollar" approach limited resources are spread thinly and there is a lack of critical mass to generate projects which will have a real impact on the ground and potentially generate multiplier effects.

Resources

While skills were generally thought to be more lacking than resources, in countries with more advanced systems in place to support flexibility and co-operation (United States, Canada, Denmark) the paucity of resources was considered a more important factor explaining variation in policy integration. In Denmark a lack of resources was a key factor undermining a high degree of flexibility and potential co-operation. Danish public institutions felt that they had too few resources to become involved in partnerships as much as they would like, and a lack of staffing at the Job centre in the island of Bornholm curtailed their focus to their own objectives as opposed to playing an additional role in regional development. In the United States, similarly, a lack of resources undermined the ability of the Workforce Investment Boards to co-operate locally, although the Workforce Investment Act gave them broader responsibility to work not only with disadvantaged groups but also with local employers during an extended period of budget cuts. In Canada field offices often found themselves stretched to the limit, meaning limited contact between officials even if co-located. In New Zealand, also, the barrier to effective working cited most frequently was financial constraints.

Information and data

Information and data availability is a critical local issue. To a large extent local strategies can be evaluated on whether they focus on pressing and unique issues which affect a locality, and, in the case of the Lower Rio Grande Valley, a key role for local leaders was to ensure that all stakeholders fully realised the severity of the local situation. However these issues are difficult to spot when there is a dearth of local level data available. For the Italian region of Puglia it was stated that "although proximity to local labour markets should ideally induce co-ordinated and integrated local policies around particular local issues, this is not generally the case" because "many local and regional institutions have a superficial and insufficient knowledge of labour market dynamics" (Fadda, submitted).

In the absence of disaggregated national data, local actors are often forced to resort to expensive and ad-hoc local surveys. In the best cases, such studies can result in a shared local knowledge base which galvanises the development of a strong local strategy for change (as in the case of the Lower Rio Grande Valley). In the worst, and more frequent, cases such information is collected separately by different government agencies and the practice of limited sharing means that it is difficult for any one agency to get an overall picture of what is going on. A data short-fall also makes it difficult to evaluate the outcomes of local policies, particularly at community level. For this reason a growing number of experts (Eberts et al, 2006) recommend focusing on a "dashboard of key indicators" which all local actors can monitor over time. In the Lower Rio Grande Valley, for example, local actors supported their strategy by commissioning a major local data survey, with those involved coming together to review their performance against an agreed set of indicators every two years.

National governments are starting to take the problem of local data collection more seriously. In Greece a regional observatory of labour market has been set up which is aiming to produce annual reports on labour market needs in each region, including prefectures. The reports will be analytical and the priorities of local economies taken into account during the design of individual studies. In New Zealand the emphasis is not just on statistics but on the need for "an authentic blend of wide-ranging local knowledge with robust statistical analysis". Local actors recognised the need for local data that was ideally:

- Owned or commissioned by a credible partnership of relevant regional actors
- Reliable as a result of using advanced and robust analytical methods
- Disaggregated at least to city council and district level
- Informed by regional long-term economic development strategic plans
- Updated regularly
- In a form useful for guiding decisions of all stakeholders.

At the time of the study, the New Zealand Department of Labour was working on annual reports for regional labour markets and analytical tool sets customised to regional needs.

Building capacities while allocating new responsibilities

It is important for governments to build capacities more generally at the local level, including personnel capacities (technical, managerial), organisational capabilities (governance and management structures, information technology systems) and fiscal capabilities (adequate resources to carry out responsibilities). However, local actors will only significantly gain in skills if they are at the same time given more responsibility in their various policy fields. Many national governments are nervous about trying to tackle the "chicken and egg" problem of low capacities and low responsibilities, however, ultimately local capacities will be built through learning by doing. Sennett (2008), for example, demonstrates the advantage of people learning to solve problems as they go along, accumulating skills as opposed to merely implementing a blue print developed at a higher government level. This points to the need for a new era of professionalism at the local level, with actors empowered to learn the "trade" of local development by trial and error and requiring not only the allocation of new forms of flexibility but also increased tolerance for risk taking. Building capacities in this way takes time, and it will require strong structures and technical support from other governance levels. In Poland, where policies are now particularly decentralised, local policy makers believed to know their fields relatively well still have a tendency to turn to the national level for guidance, and therefore do not fully take advantage of the freedoms available to them.

Box 1.14. Summary of key issues regarding capacities

1. There is a "chicken and egg" situation when it comes to capacities at the local level – national governments fear that capacities are low and are therefore reluctant to allocate new responsibilities and flexibilities to local actors. At the same time, without such responsibilities it is difficult for local actors to build their skills and develop a professional problem-solving approach to local issues and challenges. Local actors rated their capacities higher than was perceived by national actors.

2. A lack of skills was generally felt to be more important than a lack of resources at the local level. However in countries with relatively strong systems of co-operation and policy flexibility resource shortfalls tended to play a stronger role.

3. Across each of the policy areas a lack of staff with the generic skills to participate in integrated working locally was perceived as a problem. In some countries the public employment service was perceived as a relatively passive institution, with low-trained staff and a lack of rewards for innovative action. In Central and Eastern European countries the vocational training system has been particularly slow to adapt to new economic realities, providing out-dated training and acting as a bottle neck for economic development.

4. The ability to design concise and targeted strategies is particularly lacking at the local level, with a tendency to produce long "wish lists" for action as opposed to strategies which both reflect the pressing and unique issues affecting a given locality and provide a coherent plan on tackling these.

5. Leadership skills are important locally. However, political factors can sometimes act to the detriment of policy integration through (1) short-termism, (2) political allegiances affecting the selection of projects, and (3) a tendency to spread resources too thinly in an attempt to guarantee equality of opportunity.

6. Information and data is particularly lacking at sub-regional levels, undermining a good understanding of the local context. In many countries information is only weakly disaggregated, particularly in the field of skills and productivity, leading to expensive and ad-hoc surveys by local organisations which are not always shared effectively. Where good information and data is accessible, this can provide an effective tool for galvanising local action.

In European countries the structural funds have provided an important degree of learning in practice, with the report on Romania, for example, finding that the pre-accession programme PHARE functioned as a "crash course in new public management" (Ionita, submitted). However this has lead to a cleavage at the local level between those implementing routine tasks in public institutions (who have, in fact, become more isolated) and those implementing tasks for European programmes. More work therefore needs to be done in mainstream policy areas to further train local people and give them a wider ability to problem solve locally.

Labour market conditions

The study controlled for labour market conditions to verify whether these have an important influence on the level of integration, whether the other factors are present or not. Overall, labour market conditions were not felt to have a significant impact on policy integration when compared with the other factors under consideration. However, an analysis of the case study regions illustrates that extreme labour market conditions, either in terms of high unemployment or skills shortages, have acted as catalysts for bringing people together in order to tackle a common issue. In Pictou in Canada, for example, the greatest degree of policy integration was found around the response to the closure of a major local plant, Trenton Works, where a transition team was set up involving many different stakeholders. Such plant closures were also responsible for stimulating much of the joint working apparent in Puglia and in Maine (which has been particularly vulnerable to closures by the defence industry). In Maine the severity of the economic threats of plant closures "mitigated the potential for conflict among agencies over roles, responsibilities, credit, and contributions because all involved realised the devastating nature of the potential loss of jobs and income if they didn't act accordingly".

Conversely, several of the case studies found that in times of growth, tight labour markets are likely to drive forward a policy integration agenda. In the case study regions in Poland, Denmark and New Zealand local labour shortages and loss of skills to emigration were behind much local co-operation. Emerging skills shortages in Poland in the last decade have given a significant boost to national and regional efforts to integrate skills and vocational training policies with labour market policies while in the island of Bornholm, Denmark, the immediate threats posed by high emigration were felt to create a "burning platform" for action.

In more stable economic conditions, however, serious labour market challenges can exist without necessarily leading to policy integration. Arguably, only conditions which threaten the current status quo usually stimulate actors to accept change in their working conditions in this way. In regions of low skilled equilibrium, for example, where a lack of skills in the labour market is met by a low demand for skills (as faced by the Algarve and Pictou regions) there is limited compulsion to act, and policy makers often continue in a situation of "business as usual" without confronting the major challenge facing their region.

In this light, the recent global economic slowdown may have provided an opportunity for new forms of locally based integrated working which have not been seen before.

Conclusions and recommendations

The "Integrating Employment, Skills and Economic Development" study has found that despite the significant number of cross-cutting, complex issues which challenge our local economies today, real policy integration is relatively low in the OECD countries studied. Despite the relatively high degree of co-operation and governance locally, especially in the more advanced economies, this level of co-operation is not matched by the degree of flexibility and capacity available locally, which suggests that partnerships may only be working at face value. This echoes the findings of various studies, including the OECD Study on Local Partnerships (OECD 2001a, 2004) which showed that partnerships are generally more effective at defining ad-hoc projects to address specific local issues as opposed to co-ordinating policies and adapting them to local conditions.

Policy integration, it appears, is a tall order. It requires the acceptance of conflict and the management of change out of "old working practices". Responsibilities need to be accurately mapped and information shared. Local agencies also need to be convinced that the extra costs and potential conflict associated with working closely with others will ultimately be worth it when real change becomes visible at the local level. Strategies must be long-term: the Lower Rio-Grande Valley, while producing impressive outcomes today, took over 20 years to turn itself around.

The study has revealed that policy flexibility is the most important issue in determining whether local actors can effectively work together but to make a difference it must be accompanied by good local governance and growing local capacities. The recent global economic crisis has seen many countries building up local capacities to respond to rising unemployment; however this will need to be accompanied by new forms of flexibility and accountability if localities are really going to develop the innovative approaches which will support their re-emergence as growing and successful regions longer term.

Recommendations for the national and local levels follow:

Table 1.4. **Creating a supportive environment at the national level**

Flexible policy areas with broad mandates	In order for local actors to effectively tackle local problems, it is time for **a re-professionalisation of employment and vocational training policy** so that local agencies have the chance to learn by doing and get engaged with other actors in active problem solving. National power can hinder the "culture of creativity" to address problems at the local level. A more sensible approach to risk management locally is required, with more tolerance for actors that take risks when trying to develop approaches to local problems in partnership with other actors.
	As demonstrated by previous research (Giguère & Froy, 2009) flexibility in policy management is often not available at the sub-regional level (*i.e.* NUTS 3 or below). Local government agencies in many countries remain restricted in the degree to which they can influence the design of policies, move funding between budgets lines, negotiate performance objectives and choose local target groups. Mosley (*op. cit.*) points out that, at minimum, local actors can be given considerable leeway in shaping their local programme mix and be allowed to allocate a portion of their resources to innovative programmes not foreseen in the national programme portfolio. International evidence also shows that budget flexibility can be conceded to local public employment service actors without posing serious accountability problems, as long as other checks (through "management by objectives" for example) are in place.
	At the same time, the complexity of the issues being faced at the local level mean that **broad mandates are needed for government agencies locally, particularly in the field of employment policy** (Giguère, 2008). Employment agencies need to look beyond helping disadvantaged groups to helping other policy actors create the high skilled local workforce which will lead to economic growth within the knowledge economy. At the same time, **vocational training policy needs to keep longer-term community level outcomes in mind**, and economic development agencies need to include human resources and skills in their regional development strategies.

Table 1.4. **Creating a supportive environment at the national level** *(continued)*

Set cross sector targets and working methods at the national level	The study has shown that there is no straightforward relationship between national co-operation and integrated policy at the local level. For national co-operation to have a real impact, it must lead either to new structures for co-operation at the local tier (as in the case of the Danish Globalisation Strategy), or **cross sector targets which will require joint working**. The latter is a new area for national governments but one that would merit further research and investment.
Institutional change is not required	Policy integration does not necessarily require institutional change at the local level – indeed **too much institutional change can be self-defeating**. In countries such as the United Kingdom, Italy and the United States, many years of institutional reform to achieve different policy objectives has often lead to a complex multi-layering of organisations, partnerships and initiatives and a confusion regarding roles and responsibilities at the local level (Giguère & Froy, 2009), detracting from, as opposed to consolidating, policy integration. What is needed across the board is rather a change in working practices and supporting a **"refocusing of government"**.
	In addition, it may be that achieving separate but focused institutions at the local level is better in the longer-term than creating too many joint institutions locally. While it makes sense for employment institutions to merge with institutions focusing on social welfare when dealing with significant problems of worklessness, for example, a new strategic alliance between employment institutions and economic development institutions may be more appropriate in trying to kick start local economies into growth. It makes sense for institutions to be able to form and reform multiple alliances at different governance levels to tackle different types of problem.
Horizontal forms of mutual accountability are a vital supplement to national policy management	In order to allow local actors more flexibility, **new forms of horizontal accountability** are required. A major factor restricting the ability of national actors to decentralise flexibility to ground level is the need to retain accountability within the delivery of policy. Indeed, this is one of the most difficult challenges faced by decentralised frameworks. True decentralisation implies a sharing of responsibility for decision-making among a number of actors, however, a missing link in the majority of the participating countries was a local accountability relationship among the public sector, private sector and NGO groups. There is a need to **create systems of mutual accountability** where all local actors have a vested interest in the outcomes of the work of other agencies. At the very least, incentives and targets which are set for deconcentrated bodies need to take local strategic priorities into account.
Locally disaggregated information and data is essential	Good local information and data is essential if policy makers are to tackle both the pressing and longer-term issues which affect their localities. Co-ordinating labour market policy with economic development beyond the fulfilment of short-term business needs requires an understanding of both the local and global conditions for the local industry and an ability to help business managers to avoid future bottlenecks, skills gaps and deficiencies, and to improve productivity. Joint and integrating planning requires locally-assembled data and expertise which can support the establishment of common strategic objectives and facilitate decisions on policy trade-offs. Thus, for government the **provision of disaggregated data** should be central elements in their strategy to ensure policy integration.

Table 1.4. **Creating a supportive environment at the national level** *(continued)*

Build capacities while awarding responsibility	**Responsibilities should be incrementally increased** in line with growing local capacities. In particular, experience suggests that greater flexibility should first be allocated to those local areas which have the highest capacity to use it. Tools such as "waiver" schemes and pilot schemes can be useful here. National and regional governments need to be prepared to provide technical assistance during this process while creating real incentives and bonuses for local/sub-regional and regional self-governments that better co-ordinate and integrate policies locally. Through **sharing experience and promoting peer review nationally**, governments can also help local actors with weaker skills and resources to improve their working practices, thereby contributing to improved capacities across the board.
Reward prioritisation at the local level	**Prioritisation is key at ground level.** The most successful local strategies are those that decide upon a limited number of areas for attention and investment, as opposed to those which provide a scatter gun approach. National tendering schemes do not always help, as they encourage local actors to construct "wish lists". At the same time, political pressures mean that local institutions feel obliged to ensure that funding is spread across many different stakeholders. It is therefore critical for national programmes to reward and give incentives to those local areas that are able to come together and agree on a more limited set of achievable joint objectives based on pressing local needs.
Getting traction at the right governance levels	In some countries the **sub-regional level needs to be reinforced with strong policy platforms** that involve *all* the relevant policy players. Travel to work areas, in particular, appear to be a strong level for planning effective employment, skills and economic development policy, while also allowing strong contact with business leaders and other stakeholders

Table 1.5. **Actions to be taken at the local level**

Ensuring clear prioritisation	**Local strategies must be made more concise and more realistic**. They should be based on (a) a sound understanding of the local context, (b) a real discussion of the trade offs and synergies between different policy interventions to respond to threats and opportunities in the longer-term, and (c) a clear understanding of the real competences of local actors. In addition, a good balance is needed between the three policy areas to ensure sustainable growth in the context of the knowledge economy.
Supporting informal relationships and social capital as important as formal partnerships	While creating properly aligned strategies is important, **developing a strong network of informal relationships** will be key to policy integration in the long-term. This study has shown that is not necessarily formal partnerships which will make the difference, indeed, evidence from Italy, Greece and South East Europe show that formal partnership and committee arrangements can serve to further dissipate energies. The case of the Lower Rio Grande Valley in the United States demonstrates that what is important is developing an agreed perception of local opportunities and threats on which basis local actors meet informally as and when they need to, to achieve results. What is important is mutual trust between actors, the ability to galvanise support on new initiatives when needed, and a common vision of the key opportunities and challenges for an area based on shared information and data. At the same time, procedures need to be put in place (such as memoranda of understanding) to ensure that relationships are built between institutions and not only individual personalities. Industry can serve as a good model for the public sector in how to further build network governance locally.

Table 1.5. **Actions to be taken at the local level** *(continued)*

More clarity on roles and responsibilities	A first step in developing a coherent local approach is to **map the competences and responsibilities of local actors** in any given locality. As these competences and actions will inevitably overlap and also diverge in some respects, policy officials need to be prepared for a degree of conflict during the process of policy integration which, though painful, may be necessary to developing real local priorities and agreeing on the means of approaching them. The global economic crisis may provide a degree of opportunity here, in that local actors are no longer prepared to tolerate "business as usual" and have been required to make some brave decisions in the face of diminishing local resources.
Support cluster and sector based strategies	The case studies illustrate that **basing co-operation around clusters and sectors** can be particularly effective in generating joined up working locally which also involves employers. The national level can provide the framework for this type of action, as for example in the United States where cluster based strategies were promoted by both the Department of Labor, the Department of Education and also state governors working in the field of economic development.

Areas for consideration by country

This study has highlighted an important degree of variation between countries in terms of the relative importance of the different factors in enabling or restricting integration. In the Eastern European economies of **Romania, Bulgaria** and **Croatia** it is clear that capacities, level of co-operation and flexibility were all considered to be areas needing considerable attention if policy integration is to be improved. In Romania it is policy flexibility which requires the most attention, whereas in Bulgaria both capacity and flexibility need to be upgraded. In Croatia roughly equal investment is required in all three areas. **Portugal** and **Greece** also clearly need investment in all three areas, with local regions suffering a lack of capacity, flexibility and meaningful co-operation in the context of strongly centralised governments. Despite the significant investment from the European Union in both countries in the last decades, with its associated emphasis on capacity building and the development of the partnership principle, the public sector is only just opening up to change.

Denmark and the **United States** scored fairly highly on all aspects of co-operation, capacity and flexibility. In both cases, however, capacities were thought to be particularly important in achieving overall policy integration. In the context of the recent restructuring of the Danish governance system, the relevant actors are also still adapting to their new roles and responsibilities. In the United States, where local leaders have the capacity to take advantage of the flexibility available to them, the results were impressive. However, local actors equally go relatively un-penalised for failing to take co-ordinated action, and the largely "carrot-based" approach to fostering co-ordination and local capacity building has resulted in a situation where the degree of integration achieved varies a great deal, state-by-state and region-by-region.

Local capacities are also of key interest in **New Zealand**, where local officials often have a degree of flexibility and co-operation but lack the critical resources to back this flexibility up with concrete actions, is undermining the potential to integrate policies in practice. In **Italy**, similarly, flexibility is felt to be particularly high but the ability of local officials to take advantage of this is reduced by lower levels of capacity and a lack of effective co-operation. The level of flexibility within the employment, training and economic development systems in **Poland** is found to be strong in what is a relatively decentralised system; however this is not matched by local capacities or the degree of local co-operation and governance. In **Canada** all three factors are seen as relatively strong, but capacities and flexibility do not match the level of co-operation visible locally.

Notes

1. A Foreign Trade Zone (FTZ) is a "free port" (under U.S. laws and NAFTA provisions) through which raw materials and/or finished goods may be brought from another country duty-free and then may be stored, assembled, repackaged, graded, manufactured, or re-exported without payment of U.S. Customs duties.

2. Financial assistance from the European Union to resolve structural economic and social problems.

3. The partnership principle was formally introduced as part of the 1988 reforms and strengthened in 1993. It has played a fundamental role in European cohesion policies.

4. The Lisbon Agenda, also known as the Lisbon Strategy or Lisbon Process, was an action and development plan for the European Union. Its aim was to make the EU "the most dynamic and competitive knowledge-based economy in the world capable of sustainable economic growth with more and better jobs and greater social cohesion, and respect for the environment by 2010". It was set out by the European Council in Lisbon in March 2000.

5. LEED research using this comparative indicator highlighted that the flexibility granted to local labour offices could be linked with employment outcomes. An increase of 1 point in the flexibility index (for an index that ranges from 0 to 5.0) is related to an increase in employment rates of 1.64 percentage points.

6. Bulgaria, Croatia and Romania were not covered in this analysis. For Canada the results were based on analysis for co-managed provinces.

7. According to the European Nomenclature of territorial units for statistics (NUTS).

Bibliography

Bruce, D. (2007, submitted), "Integrating Employment, Skills, and Economic Development in Canada", OECD, Paris.

Coyle, D (2001), Paradoxes of Prosperity: Why the New Capitalism Benefits All, Texere, New York.

Crnkovic-Pozaic, S. (2007, submitted), "Integrating Employment, Skills, and Economic Development in Croatia", OECD, Paris.

Dalziel, P. (2007, submitted), "Integrating Employment, Skills and Economic Development in New Zealand", OECD, Paris.

Eberts, R W., Erickcek, G A. and Kleinhenz, J (2006), "Dashboard Indicators for the Northeast Ohio Economy: Prepared for the Fund for Our Economic Future", FRB of Cleveland Working Paper No. 06-05, available at *SSRN: http://ssrn.com/abstract=1022345*

Eggers, W.D., and S. Goldsmith (2004), "Government by Network: The New Public Management Imperative", Deloitte Research and the Ash Institute for Democratic Governance at the John F. Kennedy School of Government at Harvard University, US.

Fadda, S. (2008, submitted), "Integrating Employment, Skills and Economic Development in Italy", OECD, Paris.

Friedman, M (2005), *Trying hard is not good enough,* Trafford Publishing, Canada.

Froy, F., S. Giguère and A. Hofer (2009), *Designing Local Skills Strategies*, OECD Publishing, Paris.

Giguère, S. (2008), *More than Just Jobs: Workforce Development in a Skills-based Economy*, OECD Publishing, Paris.

Giguère, S. and F. Froy (2009), *Flexible Policy for More and Better Jobs*, OECD Publishing, Paris.

Gorzelak, G. and M. Herbst (2007, submitted), "Integrating Employment, Skills and Economic Development in Poland", OECD, Paris.

Henriques, J.M. (2008, submitted), Integrating Employment, Skills and Economic Development in Portugal", OECD, Paris.

Ionita, S. (2006, submitted), "Integrating Employment, Skills and Economic Development in Romania"", OECD, Paris.

Klassen, T.R. (2006), "Can decentralization alleviate labour market dysfunctions in marginal jurisdictions? Active labour market policies in Nova Scotia and Saxony-Anhalt", Canadian Public Policy. 32.3: 317-337

Manoudi, A. (2007, submitted), "Integrating Employment, Skills, and Economic Development in Greece", OECD, Paris.

Mosley, H. (2003) "Flexibility and Accountability in Labour Market Policy: A Synthesis" in *Managing Decentralisation. A New Role for Labour Market Policy*, OECD Publications, Paris.

New Insight (2008, submitted), "Integrating Employment, Skills and Economic Development in Denmark", OECD, Paris.

OECD (2001), *Local Partnerships for Better Governance*, OECD Publishing, Paris.

OECD (2003), *Managing Decentralisation: A New Role for Labour Market Policy*, OECD Publishing, Paris.

OECD (2004), *New Forms of Governance for Economic Development*, OECD Publishing, Paris.

OECD (2005), *Local Governance and the Drivers of Growth*, OECD Publishing, Paris.

OECD (2006), *Skills Upgrading: New Policy Perspectives,* OECD Publishing, Paris

Putnam, R., R. Leonardi and R. Nannetti (1993) *Making Democracy Work: Civic Traditions in Modern Italy,* Princeton University Press,

Stoyanovska, A. (2006, submitted), "Integrating Employment, Skills and Economic Development in Bulgaria", OECD, Paris.

Troppe, Mark *et al.* (2007, submitted), "Integrating Employment, Skills, and Economic Development in the United States"", OECD, Paris.

Treasury Board of Canada Secretariat (2006), "From Red Tape to Clear Results: Report of the Independent Blue Ribbon Panel on Grant and Contribution Programmes", Ottawa, Canada.

Annex A

The study team

Table A.1. **The study team**

Country	Expert
Bulgaria	Antonina Stoyanovska, Foundation for Entrepreneurship Development, Sofia
Canada	David Bruce, Mount Allison University.
Croatia	Sanja Crnkovic-Pozaic, Director of the SMEs and Entrepreneurship Policy Centre (CEPOR), Zagreb
Denmark	Peter Plougmann, Peter Lindstrøm and Allan Wessel Andersen, New Insight
Greece	Anna Manoudi, Consultant
Italy	Sebastiano Fadda, Faculty of Economics, University of Rome
New Zealand	Paul Dalziel, Agribusiness and Economics Research Unit (AERU)
Poland	Grzegorz Gorzelak and Mikolaj Herbst, University of Warsaw
Portugal	José Manuel Henriqués, Instituto Superior de Ciências do Trabalho e da Empresa (ISCTE)
Romania	Sorin Ionita, Romanian Academic Society (SAR)
United States	Mark Troppe, Mary Clagett, Robert Holm, Tim Barnicle, National Center on Education and the Economy (NCEE).

Annex B

The case study regions

Table B.1. **The case study regions**

Country	Region	Case Study Areas
Bulgaria	North West	Vratsa
Canada	Nova Scotia	Pictou County
Croatia	North West	Varaždin
Denmark	Employment region Copenhagen & Zealand	Bornholm
Greece	Eastern Macedonia & Thrace	Rhodope (Western Thrace)
Italy	Puglia	Nord Barese
New Zealand	Bay of Plenty	Western Bay of Plenty
Poland	Małopolskie	Krakow
Portugal	Algarve	Algarve
Romania	West region	Timiş county
United States	Texas	Lower Rio Grande Valley
	Maine	Coastal Maine

Part II

Country synopses

BULGARIA[1]

National policy integration and co-ordination

The Ministry of Labour and Social Policy (MLSP) leads employment policy in Bulgaria, shaped by the National Employment Strategy 2004-2010. National Employment Action Plans (NEAPs) are the main instruments for delivering employment policy, which is implemented by the National Employment Agency. The Ministry of Education and Science (MES) is responsible for education policy and, in conjunction with the MLSP, is tasked with policy formulation and delivery in vocational education and training (VET), in tandem with regional counterparts.

Institutional framework

The Ministry of Economy and Energy (MEE) leads regional and economic development, and industrial policy. The Ministry of Regional Development and Public Works (MRDPW) oversees the development, co-ordination and implementation of regional policy. State policy for regional development is set out in the Regional Development Act, and includes, inter alia, priorities such as decentralisation of management and the enhancement of partnerships with local authorities.

Figure 2.1. Bulgaria: Institutional framework map at national, regional, sub-regional and local levels

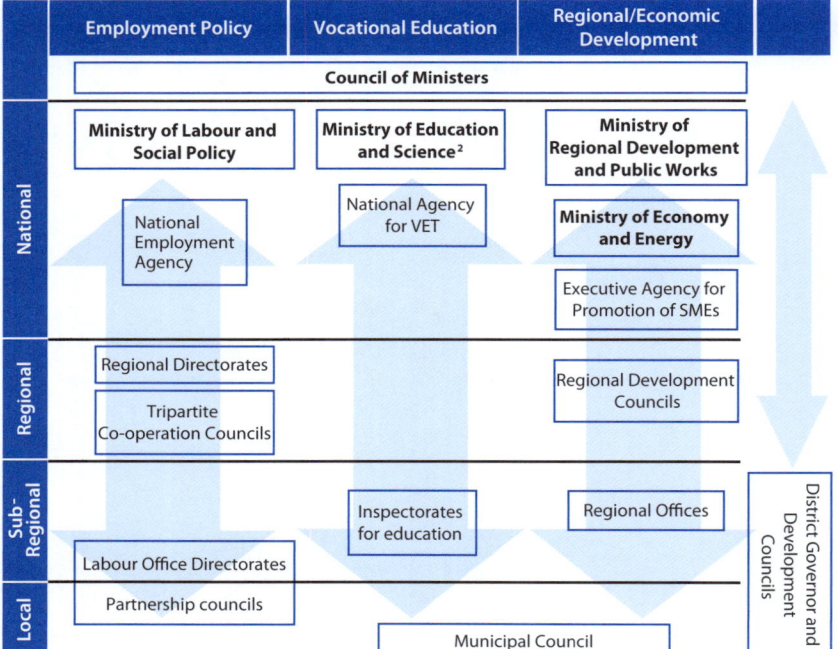

Integration and co-ordination

The Bulgarian Government is highly centralised, with policies being delivered vertically along sectoral lines. At the time of the study, different ministries were found to pursue priorities and objectives in isolation and policy integration at national level was still at a rudimentary stage. This had led to the duplication and overlapping of programmes by different state bodies. For example, attempts to tackle cross-government issues through the Strategy for Poverty Reduction and Strategy for Roma Integration failed to succeed, despite well-formulated objectives, as they went against the grain of existing departmental policies and programmes.

MLSP and MEE have established new consultation mechanisms in recent years. Social partners have taken an increasingly active part in consultative bodies such as the Economic and Social Council and National Employment Promotion Council, allowing them to have a role in the design and monitoring of policy implementation. The input of non-governmental stakeholders has also been widened by the subcontracting of many government tasks, such as the preparation of development plans and strategies, and project management.

Nevertheless, it was perceived that this drive towards consultation had spawned a large number of different committees, each requiring substantial resources and heavy stakeholder time commitment – indeed, one representative of an employer's organisation commented that they had to provide experts for 126 different consultative bodies, resulting in overlap and inefficiency. Another common complaint was the lack of transparency on the criteria for inclusion in some of the nationally led working groups and lack of knowledge sharing prior to meetings, making the social partners feel that their involvement was a "token gesture".

Flexibility

Policy in the three sectors of employment, economic development and skills development in Bulgaria was found to be highly centralised, with local offices being delegated little flexibility to adjust or alter programmes content. Flexibility was assigned by allowing local authorities to select measures from a "menu" of national programmes which could be feasibly implemented in their respective regions, and by providing feedback on how successfully policies were implemented to improve future national programme design.

Figure 2.2. **Local flexibility**

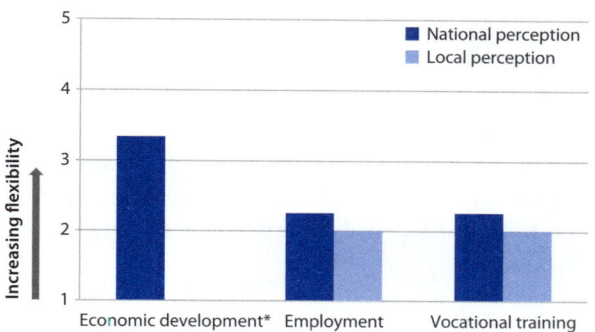

Note: No data was available for economic development at the local level.

As seen in Figure 2.2, local flexibility in the case study region of Vratsa was graded low both nationally and locally. National players rated the policy area of economic development as having "average" flexibility, and awarded employment and vocational training a ranking slightly above "inflexible". Local participants were more negative in their assessment of the two policy fields, ranking them as "inflexible".

As can be seen in Figure 2.3, each of the four management tools was perceived to be "inflexible" in Vratsa.

Flexibility in financing local intervention programmes was severely restricted at the time of study. Funding for regional development initiatives and active employment measures came mainly from the central budget and EU

Figure 2.3. **Vratsa: Flexibility of management tools**

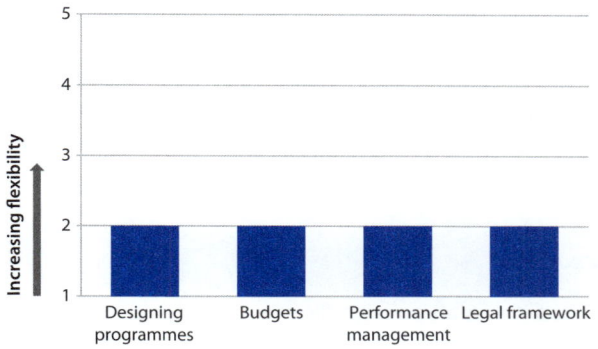

projects and representative structures of central government were very limited in the extent to which they could determine local budgets, having to comply with centrally developed priorities and eligibility criteria. Budgets were pre-divided into specific funding streams and funds could not be moved from one stream to another. There was a lack of financial stability, due in part to a lack of multi-annual programming, and districts faced continual uncertainty as to future funding.

At the municipal level, much available funding was aimed at projects with short-term objectives, and few avenues were open to regional departments for self-financing. In recent years a process of fiscal decentralisation has been initiated but until this process has been completed, municipalities will continue to be dependent on central government budget allocations. There was also a lack of trust at the national level that local authorities had the experience and know how to spend budgets appropriately, emanating in part from the weak accountability structures in place, leading to tighter financial control from above.

A significant proportion of local funds were used to co-finance participation in nationally structured initiatives through grant scheme arrangements. While this gave a degree of flexibility to local players to design and propose projects tailored to local needs, often funds did not end up in regions where they could be most beneficial: projects were not implemented according to need, but according to which municipalities had the capacity to lobby for grant schemes and allocate matched funding resources. The legal framework was, for the most part, sufficiently broad to allow local agencies to co-operate towards economic development goals. In fact, it was noted that there was capacity within the law to allow further authority to be delegated to the local level.

Co-operation and policy integration at the regional and local level

Partnership working at the regional and local level appeared to operate less effectively than at central level in Bulgaria due to weak administrative units, limited devolved responsibilities, and competition for resources. Bulgaria's 28 administrative districts were once the traditional units for regional planning, but in the transition to a market economy they have become a much less dominant force. While remaining the main units with the autonomy to plan and implement local projects, the impact of their interventions on national policy is reduced as a result of scarce resources and a centralised government structure. Some interviewees were hopeful that changes in policy management arrangements would bring a greater delegation of responsibilities to regional and local structures.

Figure 2.4 illustrates that integration between policy areas was perceived to be relatively weak in Vratsa, particularly between regional development and the other two policy fields. The employment and vocational training sectors were seen to be slightly more integrated, with integration identified as "average".

Figure 2.4. **Vratsa: Integration between policy areas**

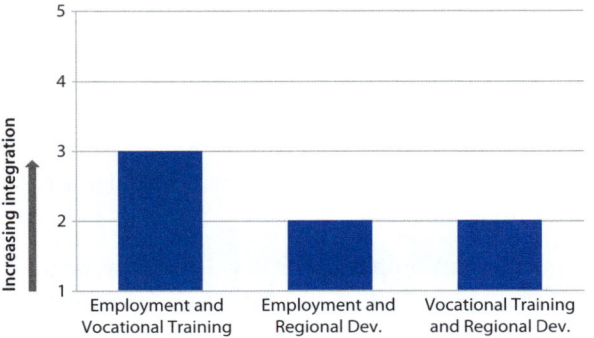

The study found there to be little vertical coherence between national and regional strategies and objectives, particularly with regard to employment policy. Under these conditions, regional stakeholders stated that the successful attraction and delivery of programmes was highly dependent on the lobbying skills of regional governors and party affiliation, rather than the appropriateness of the programmes for the needs of the locality. Only a small percentage of the long list of measures included in regional strategies materialised into local initiatives.

Figure 2.5. **Extent of engagement in cooperation at the local level**

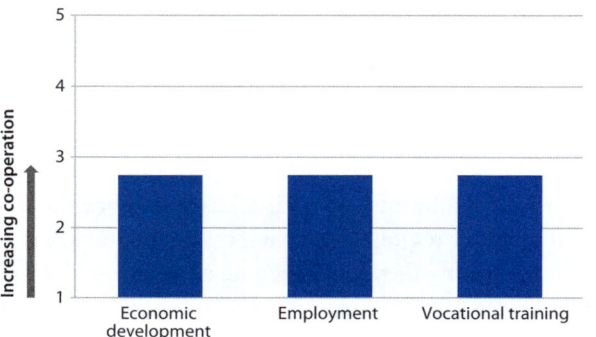

Engagement in co-operation in the case study region was perceived to be below average for all three policy areas, indicating that information sharing, multi-stakeholder partnerships, and substantive collaboration were present but relatively embryonic. "There is no understanding of the benefits of partnership, besides we also lack capacity and resources", commented a representative of one of the labour confederations. Institutions saw themselves as competitors for scarce resources rather than potential partners, an outlook intensified by the uneven and selective distribution of information. Stakeholders identified the development of public private partnerships as a valuable tool in building up financial resources and encouraging more collaboration locally, but the legal framework for establishing these had not yet been developed at the time of the study.

> *"There is no understanding of the benefits of partnership, besides we also lack capacity and resources".*
>
> Labour confederation representative

Encouraging examples do exist, however, of concrete collaboration, particularly within the field of employment policy. In the district of Vratsa, local employment agencies have been collaborating regularly with the private sector to better identify needs and advise on relevant programmes and services.

Permanent Employment Commissions (PEC) are a further example of useful structures for district co-ordination and partnership, notwithstanding that their role is mainly consultative. PECs bring together an array of regional players (including mayors, directors of labour offices, social partners) to monitor the outputs and impacts of employment measures, review projects designed to stimulate employment, issue recommendations and approve VET programmes. Nevertheless, their efforts are hampered by capacity shortfalls, ad-hoc processes and skepticism among the business community as to the value of such collaborative efforts.

Capacities

The average capacity of organisations in Vratsa in all three policy areas was regarded as limited, with both skills and resources perceived as "weak".

Resources

Funding for all policy areas was considered to be severely limited. Employment policy was identified as receiving the most funding but, nonetheless, the public employment service was felt to lack the human resources and skills necessary to engage fully in local joint initiatives.

Figure 2.6. **Vratsa: Average capacity of organisations**

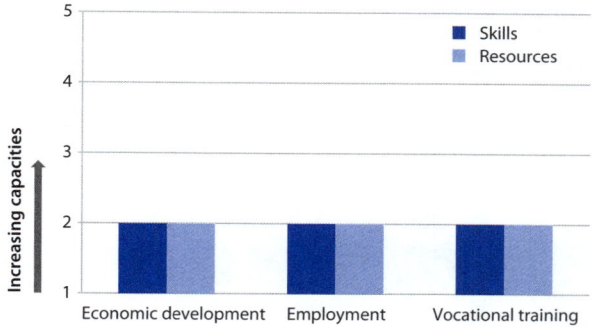

This lack of capacity was outlined as a key barrier to the effective participation of local stakeholders in implementing EU structural funds, despite EU support for the training of local officials. At the level of the NUTS II regions officials described a lack of financial capacity, a lack of experience when it came to applying programmes, and a lack of human resources as major barriers to further joint working.

Another prevalent weakness was the lack of up-to-date data on the labour market. Local officials in the Vratsa region found that nationally commissioned surveys produced results which were not always compatible with their local knowledge of the region. In addition, while the MLSP regularly collected monitoring information and compiled data on output indicators, this was perceived to have little influence on policy formulation.

Skills

A skill commonly lacking at the local level was the ability to develop sound local strategies. While a coherent strategy can provide a lens through which officials can develop a shared view of key local priorities, regional development plans in the case study region were found to be essentially wish lists for short-term projects of different sizes and scope. The potential trade-offs and synergies between different actions had not been considered. This lack of prioritisation was identified as a common shortcoming, partly emanating from the perception that the greater the number of priorities listed, the greater the likelihood of receiving national funding.

Box 2.1. **Case study region: Vratsa**

Responding to an outdated skills structure and developing human capital

The Vratsa district is located in North-West Bulgaria and has a population of 201 200 (2008). It includes 10 municipalities and is a predominantly rural area. Vratsa has witnessed steady population decline in recent years at a rate higher than the national average, as a result of natural population decline and out-migration.

STRENGTHS AND CHALLENGES	
STRENGTHS	CHALLENGES
• Regional unemployment rate dropped to national average; • Significant restructuring and modernisation of local economy; • Educational attainment in line with national average.	• Limited foreign investment; • Large number of small subsistence farms; • Low employment rate and declining labour force participation rate; • Skills shortages in emerging sectors.
OPPORTUNITIES	THREATS
• New trade clusters emerging in recent years; • Agriculture development potential; • Tourism development potential due to rich natural environment.	• Rate of population decline higher than national rate; • Unfavourable population age structure; • Intra-regional disparities; • Persisting long-term unemployment.

The region's economy has undergone significant shifts in recent decades. Prior to 1990 it was dominated by large scale, heavily state-subsidised industrial enterprises in the energy and chemical sector, but transition to a market economy triggered significant industrial decline. Today the industrial sector provides almost 50 per cent of regional gross value added, while services contribute over one third and agriculture accounts for 17 per cent.

Vratsa had the fourth highest rate of long-term unemployment in the country at the time of study, at almost 66 per cent, perhaps reflecting a mismatch between skills supply and demand and the poor qualification levels of the labour force. The skills structure of the labour force still reflected demand of the pre-1990s, with a significant share of the population possessing energy, textile and heavy industry related skills and lacking skills increasingly required, particularly in tourism, finance, management and marketing.

Links which traditionally existed between employers and VET schools in pre-transition times have also largely been broken, partly because many employers fear that investment in staff training is counter-productive as up-skilled workers are more likely to move company or migrate to a more prosperous region or abroad. The low educational status of the Roma minority in the region was also identified as a serious problem, which made it more difficult to integrate this ethnic group into the labour market.

> *"In recent years the number of organisations licensed for provision of vocational training in the district has increased. A training centre has been set up, for example, by the Regional Chamber of Commerce in Vratsa with a special focus on training women, in skills relating to the clothing sector."*
>
> Bulgaria Country Report

The National Regional Development Strategy 2005-15 outlines the long-term priorities for the region, one of which is the development of human resources. In keeping with this, the district has begun to place greater emphasis on vocational training for adults. For example, the Regional Chamber of Commerce has set up a training centre with a special focus on training women on skills in the clothing sector and the initiative has been highly praised locally. Business support centres have been established to support SMEs by organising specialised training courses, providing information and financial leasing. There have also been attempts to set up a business incubator in a joint effort between the municipality, regional governorship, Chamber of Commerce, NGOs and businesses. Initiatives such as these encourage local collaboration and create regionally managed, targeted responses to the specific regional context of Vratsa.

Conclusions

It was clear that capacities, levels of co-operation, and flexibility were all areas needing attention in Bulgaria if policy integration was to be improved. This was supported by the low overall ratings awarded to policy integration in Bulgaria based on the combined responses at national and local level; 2.0 for capacity, 2.5 for flexibility and 2.8 for local co-operation from a maximum of 5.0, as highlighted in Figure 2.7.

Figure 2.7. **Attention Areas**

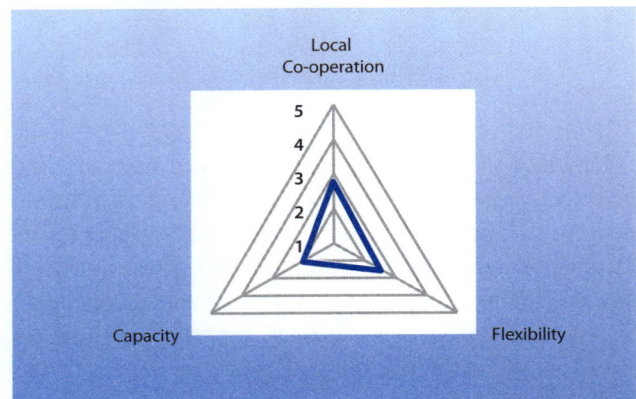

Policy integration at the regional and local level would be strengthened if local actors were granted more responsibilities and greater flexibility to make decisions. At present, employment, education and economic development policy delivery remains highly centralised. Awarding greater flexibility incrementally to those local areas that have proven capacity to deliver is one possible path, while building trust between national and local actors will also be crucial.

Recommendations

- More flexibility should be provided to sub-regional and local level authorities. At the same time capacities will need to be built, and greater transparency established to build mutual trust between actors at all governance levels.

- When allocating national funds to local development activities, it will be important to favour initiatives which are long-term, involve multiple partners and are broad in scope. This would encourage prioritisation, reduce fragmentation and make interventions more effective and sustainable.

- Allocate regional quotas to national programmes. This means that funds will be spread more fairly to localities which have till now lacked the capacity to tender effectively for national programmes.

- Systems for ongoing evaluation and monitoring of the effectiveness of national and local programmes need to be introduced, alongside greater flexibility to define target groups and priorities at the local level.

- Reinforce structures and systems at the local and regional level, including capacity building and allocation of adequate resources at all stages of policy formulation and implementation.

- Greater resources need to be allocated for data analysis, development and evaluation of regional plans and programmes and project preparation.

Notes

1. This synopsis is based on the following country report: Stoyanovska, A., "Integrating Employment, Skills and Economic Development in Bulgaria", submitted 2006.

2. The Ministry of Education and Science became the Ministry of Education, Youth and Science in 2009.

CANADA [1]

National policy integration and co-ordination

The overarching national government direction for improving the quality of life for Canadians by building a stronger economy is found in Advantage Canada. Each province and territory also plays a role in policy development and delivery in these policy areas, with municipal government playing a more limited role. In most cases the federal government transfers funds for programmes, with the role of provinces and territories being to deliver these programmes while ensuring they adhere to broad national outcomes.

The Atlantic Canada Opportunities Agency (ACOA) is the federal agency responsible for co-ordinating economic development interests across the four Atlantic Canadian provinces in the eastern part of Canada, where the case study province of Nova Scotia is located. Set up in 1987 to increase economic development opportunities, it seeks to build a link between economic development and other policy areas by playing a co-ordinating role. With an office in each province and field offices throughout the region, it oversees partnership and cost-sharing arrangements in local development projects and partially funds regional economic development organisation.[2] The Office of Economic Development drives provincial interests in economic development and, in conjunction with the ACOA, chairs provincial committees to bring together players from different departments and agencies to encourage information exchange.

Labour force and skills development are administered by Human Resources and Skills Development Canada (HRSDC) and Service Canada. HRSDC has a broad social and economic mandate and offers a range of employment skills programmes, which seek to integrate economic, skills and employment development policies, as illustrated by the Youth Employment Strategy. Canada has been going through a steady period of decentralisation of labour market policy and since 2009 all provinces have acquired responsibility for designing and implementing employment policy, though a set of labour market development agreements.

Institutional framework

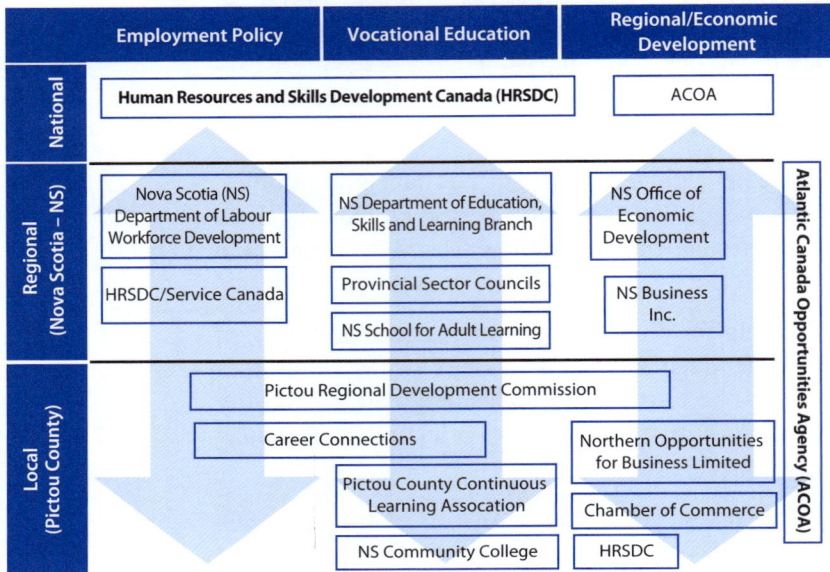

Figure 3.1. Canada: Institutional map at national, regional and local levels (Maritime provinces)

Integration and co-ordination

The study found a high degree of policy integration and co-ordination at the federal level in Canada. Horizontal co-operation was well developed: HRSDC and ACOA are well integrated and a Memorandum of Understanding has been developed between them to ensure policy objectives are aligned. ACOA senior officials interact daily with other departments on an informal basis and there are a variety of formal structures in place to facilitate planning and implementation.

There was also evidence of a fairly high degree of federal-provincial vertical co-ordination and consultation. In Nova Scotia federal staff regularly engage with their provincial counterparts in response to major issues and potential opportunities, or as part of a defined project – the Canada-Nova Scotia Skills and Learning Framework, for example. At the provincial level, policy co-ordination was also relatively frequent, with regular interdepartmental meetings held at senior level. The Office for Economic Development, Nova Scotia Business Incorporated, the

Department of Education (Skills and Learning Branch) were found to communicate at least once a week.[3]

Flexibility

Generally speaking, the major agreements between the federal and provincial governments are sufficiently flexible to allow for local variation in how programmes and services are delivered. Local stakeholders perceived the flexibility available to them to be significantly higher in all policy sectors than their federal counterparts.

Figure 3.2. **Local flexibility**

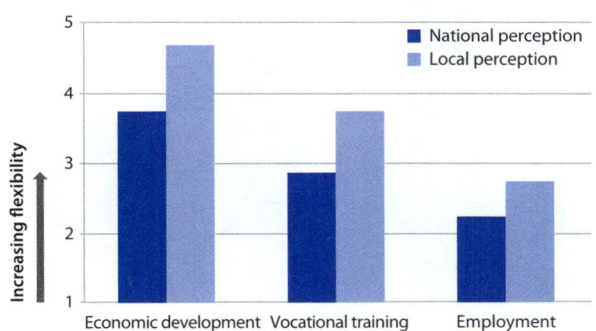

Amongst all the countries studied as part of the "Breaking out of Policy Silos: doing more with less" project, Canada was perceived as having one of the most flexible regional economic development frameworks by both national and provincial participants, achieving a scoring not far off "very flexible" (see Figure 3.2). Economic development programme delivery in Nova Scotia is driven in large part by the strategic plans of regional development agencies and demand from the private sector. Each development agency is independent in terms of the development of its strategic plans and its budget allocations for core and programme activities – budgets are allocated to programmes and services most closely in line with the objectives of regional strategic plans.

Vocational training was rated as highly flexible by regional players, but received a lower rating by federal policy makers. The Nova Scotia Community College, for example, is an active player at the local level which is able to provide customised training programmes (see Box 3.1), while the Nova Scotia Skills and Learning Framework represents an attempt to better adapt training to local and regional needs.

Box 3.1. **Nova Scotia Community College**

With almost 10 000 students and 13 campuses located throughout the province, Nova Scotia Community College (NSCC) plays a critical role in promoting skills and labour force development to meet the needs of the provincial economy, and the flexibility of its core curriculum means it can respond quickly to labour force and skills needs.

Each local campus has a Business Development Manager who actively seeks out opportunities to customise training for large and small local businesses. For example, tailor-made training has been provided in the energy sector and health services in the past. Some of the largest companies in the region have made use of NSCC's custom training programme options, including Michelin and Convergys. In partnership with Service Canada, the NSCC has also developed a customised welding programme for young African Nova Scotians needing vocational training.

The employment policy area was perceived as the least flexible by both national and regional participants (see Figure 3.2). At the time of study this responsibility was shared between the provinces and HRSDC within a co-management structure, and the local Service Canada office was perceived to have little room for manoeuvre to adapt federal and provincial programmes to local conditions in Pictou County.[4]

All four management tools in the case study region of Pictou County, Nova Scotia, were highly rated in terms of the flexibility they provided to local officials (see Figure 3.3). Programme design was the most highly ranked, performance management and legal framework received the same scoring at a slightly lower flexibility rating, with budgets receiving the lowest rating.

Figure 3.3. **Pictou: Flexibility of management tools**

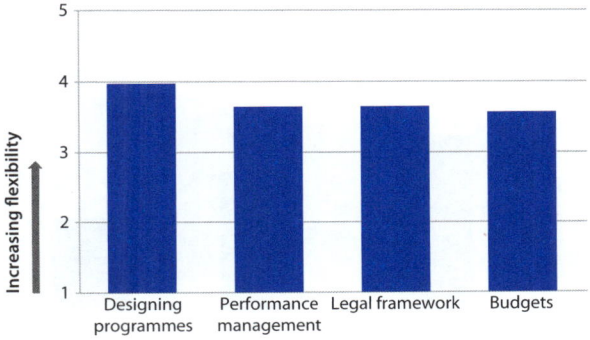

One area where the legal framework was seen as relatively inflexible, however, was in relation to programme eligibility. Tight eligibility criteria within local programming meant that certain types of individuals "fell through the cracks" and could not be helped by local programmes. Since the end of the 1990s, an ongoing tightening of administrative requirements and eligible expenses introduced in response to the need for appropriate financial documentation at the federal level, has been seen to dilute flexibility and add to bureaucracy at the local level. A 2006 Blue Ribbon Panel report on grant and contribution programmes pointed to a management culture in government where fear of criticism or blame had "permeated so deeply that it has begun to undermine effective administration". As a result "people are less forgiving of honest mistakes grounded in good intentions, today, than in the past" and individuals working in the public sector were seen to have a "diminished tolerance for risk taking". However, a number of best practices were identified by the Panel and improvements are being implemented across government.

Local labour offices were also found to have limited options to undertake pre-emptive action to support people at risk of losing jobs at the time of the study. In order to rectify this, a new national annual fund of CAD 500 million has been introduced to fund provincial and territorial labour market programmes and services that focus on skills development for both employed and unemployed individuals who do not have a high school diploma or recognised certification, or with lower levels of essential skills.

Co-operation and policy integration at the regional and local level

Collaboration at the federal and provincial levels does not necessarily trickle down to the local level in Canada. The study found a gap in communication between senior

Figure 3.4. **Pictou: Integration between policy areas**

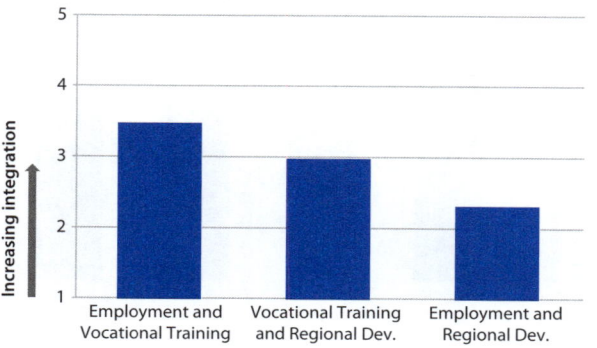

government, government field officers working on the ground, and other local actors. Activities at the local level are considered to be generally fragmented, with weak and ad-hoc collaboration. As seen in Figure 3.4, of the three policy sectors under examination, the employment and vocational training sectors displayed the highest degree of joint integration in Pictou County, followed by the vocational training and regional development sectors.

Figure 3.5. **Extent of engagement in cooperation at the local level**

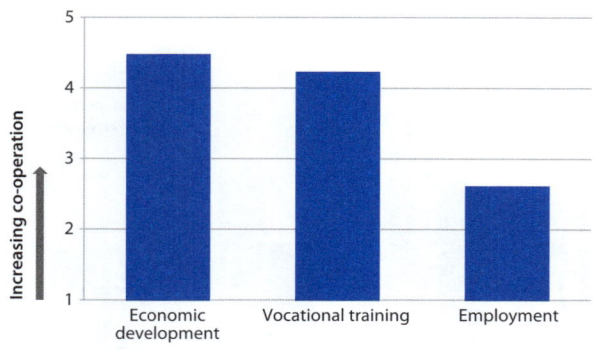

Figure 3.5 illustrates the extent of local engagement in co-operation in Pictou. According to the views of regional participants, there was a "strong" level of engagement in co-operation in both the economic development and vocational training sectors, indicating substantive collaboration on policy development and programme delivery, participation in multi-stakeholder partnerships and a strong level of information sharing. The employment sector was perceived as significantly less engaged in co-operation.

In Pictou there are a wide range of agencies, committees and partnerships operating at ground level, often sharing premises or closely located, thereby encouraging informal contact. However, despite the number of structures in place to facilitate dialogue and co-operation, interviewees commented that they did not always seem to achieve real policy integration. The "maze" of programmes and initiatives being taken forward made it almost impossible to develop effective, efficient and comprehensive local strategies. Personality clashes between local participants, and time constraints were also mentioned as barriers to policy integration, as were inflexibilities in the management of individual policy areas (particularly employment), with frustration at the lack of local responsibility for decision making. The sheer number of municipal units (five towns and a county government serving fewer than 50 000 people) was also seen as a barrier, creating a climate of competition among local authorities, who were mainly interested in business development occurring within their own administrative area.

In addition, department and programme mandates were perceived to be narrow and there was a lack of commitment to a shared vision. Pictou's strategic economic development plan was drawn up by RDAs and was mainly confined to business development and infrastructure investment, not taking broader obstacles to sustainable regional prosperity into consideration. The local skills and labour force development agenda, in particular, was not well integrated into the plan (see Box 3.2 below). A general short-termism was also apparent; for example, tackling labour shortages was generally limited to activities promoting new immigration to the region, rather than devising a broader strategy addressing other structural weakness such as youth out-migration, low wages and the need for investment in productivity and new forms of work organisation.

> *"... sometimes the private sector is reluctant to talk to us or seek our help as a government department ... Once the private sector comes forward ... we find we can often position their concern and we all benefit..."*
>
> Canada Country Report

A "disconnect" was also seen to exist between the business community and local public sector, with the former tending to by-pass the latter and attempt to influence strategic planning at the federal or provincial level. Local enterprises appeared to be unaware of programmes and services available to them, and according to one Pictou stakeholder from a government department, the private sector was reluctant to engage in communication.[5] Efforts were underway to buck this trend and encourage the private sector to participate more fully in apprenticeship and skills investment locally.

Box 3.2. Case study region: Pictou county

STRENGTHS AND CHALLENGES

STRENGTHS	CHALLENGES
• Diverse economic base; • Home to international businesses' head offices; • 2nd most competitive community in which to do business (2006 International KPMG Competitive Alternatives study).	• Labour market shortage & skills gaps; • Lower labour force participation rate; • Higher unemployment rate than province; • Municipal units compete; • Workforce educational attainment below provincial average.

OPPORTUNITIES	THREATS
• New opportunities in active recreation, tourism, hospitality and energy; • Export opportunities from interests in establishing an "Atlantic Gateway"; • New potential labour source from those currently not in labour force.	• Aging workforce; • Continued out-migration of young in search of better employment prospects; • Expectation of continued labour force shortages; • General lack of immigration.

Greater partnership working triggered by a labour market crisis

Pictou County is located in North Eastern Nova Scotia and has a population of 46 631 (2008). The region has a diverse economic base and growing tourism, energy and export sectors, but faces labour force structural weaknesses, including lower levels of education and skills shortages. The primary agency responsible for implementing economic development activities in the region is the Pictou Regional Development Commission (PRDC). A non-governmental agency, it does not develop policy per se but is in charge of leading the creation and implementation of projects and programmes in partnership with governmental departments, agencies and NGOs. It has two core activities; strategic planning and business counseling, and is flexible enough to adjust to new issues as they emerge. Its operating budget is cost-shared by three levels of government (national, provincial and municipal) and it retains complete control over spending. The PRDC identifies and works with companies that could potentially relocate to the county, supports entrepreneurship efforts and plays a role in coordinating regional development and infrastructure projects. There is a reasonable amount of cooperation between the PRDC and other regional players and the Strategic Plan 2005–10 was informed by extensive consultation with a wide variety of stakeholders. However, local, provincial and national stakeholders do not necessarily consider the Strategy to be "their plan" and the PRDC has no mandate to put in place a mutual accountability system and hold contributors accountable for broad community economic development outcomes. In addition, the plan is largely focused on a broadly defined concept of economic development, meaning that some elements of labour force and skills development activities such as skills inventories and workplace programmes are not explicitly linked to economic development. Where they have been addressed it is largely triggered by a crisis brought about by firm closures – as evident in the response to the closure of a local manufacturer, Trenton Works.

A well known manufacturer of railway cars, Trenton Works had been an integral part of Pictou County since the late 1870s and employed approximately 1,100. With the announcement of down-sizing in 2005, the PRDC responded by setting up a steering committee to explore product diversification, comprised of representatives from the Commission itself, Trenton Works management, Office of Economic Development and ACOA, inter alia. When closure was announced two years later, the Department of Education, Service Canada and the Pictou Campus of NSCC were added to the steering committee in order to provide workers with workforce transition information and services such as job searching skills and career counseling. A worker transition needs assessment was also carried out to determine existing workforce skills and learning needs to help plan future workforce transition activities.

Capacities

As seen in Figure 3.6, the average capacity of organisations in Pictou County was perceived to be relatively high for economic development and vocational training in terms of skills and resources; in both cases skills were considered to be greater than resource levels. The policy area of employment was bottom ranked with capacity rated between "weak" and "average" for both skills and resources.

Figure 3.6. **Pictou: Average capacity of organisations**

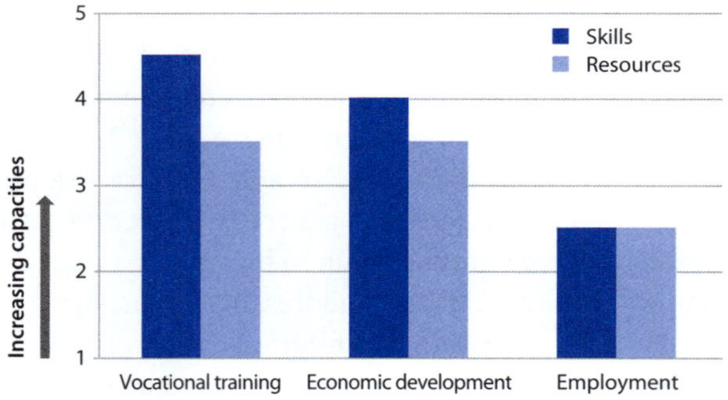

Resources

The ratings in Figure 3.6 indicate that a lack of resources was seen to be a more prominent factor in explaining variation in policy integration than inadequate skills. Many interviewees expressed dissatisfaction with the extent of human resource capacities in government bodies, which were seen to jeopardise the effectiveness of some working arrangements and action plans. In many cases there were too few people, too thinly spread across a large geographic area and with responsibility for supporting several regional development authorities simultaneously. Other factors identified as hampering efforts at local co-operation and integration were insufficient financial capacity, and the limited presence of key federal and provincial departments and agencies on the ground.

A significant capacity issue experienced in Nova Scotia was poor data and knowledge banks. While there were a number of data sources available on labour market conditions, timely market information at county or municipal level was generally not available, preventing more concrete analysis and focused programme intervention. Stakeholders called for more financial and human resources to improve the quality of information, thereby allowing them to better identify and understand the implications of local economic and employment trends.

Skills

A skill found lacking at local level was the ability of the private sector, public employment service and local agencies to work together to develop sound local strategies and share responsibility for outcomes. Presently, regional development agencies are held accountable for the outcomes of strategic plans, even though they depend on input from many other stakeholders, and a strengthened local and mutual accountability framework among the three primary groups is the "missing link". The business community, in particular, "is not adequately engaged in strategic planning as it relates to the skills agenda and its integration into the broader strategic plan for the county". In Pictou, even chambers of commerce and regional development agencies tend to be thinking more of "member services" rather than working with the private sector to support longer term economic development.

Conclusions

Figure 3.7. **Attention Areas**

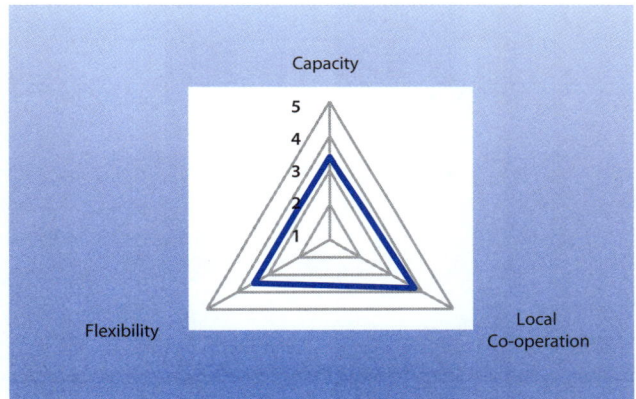

As seen in Figure 3.7, the combined responses at the national, local and provincial level on flexibility, local co-operation and capacity return relatively strong scorings and are one of the highest sets of results from all participating countries in the IESED study: 3.5, 3.8 and 3.4 respectively. At the national and provincial level there is an ongoing evolution of roles and responsibilities among various departments and agencies. The degree of co-operation, co-ordination and consultation at the federal and provincial levels is relatively high, however this did not seem to be trickling down effectively to the local level, which saw greater levels of fragmentation.

In the case study area of Pictou County, local actors were initiating many positive activities in the three policy areas but lacked a shared vision for the direction of regional development. In particular, human resource and skills issues did not feature in local economic development plans. A tight accountability framework combined with the lack of local responsibility for programme decision making and a shortage of resources also constrained co-operation and integration at ground level. Since the study, the devolution of labour market policy to all the Canadian provinces may well have increased the flexibility and policy integration in the Nova Scotia province.[6]

Recommendations

- Devise more incentives for civil servants to participate in joint strategic planning exercises locally with other local stakeholders (for example private sector and NGO).

- Ensure that targets set for each local area for the implementation of labour market programmes are negotiated with local stakeholders. This would increase the need and potential for local employment officials to co-operate more fully on local projects and strategies and to have a vested interest in the outcomes.

- Local strategic plans require a stronger consideration of skills and human resource issues within broader economic development strategies in order to strengthen local outcomes. This includes fully exploring the links between low wages, wage competition, private sector investment in skills and apprenticeships, immigration and labour force attraction, and economic development plans.

- Improve the quality of data and information and make it more available to local players, thereby allowing them to better understand the implications of local trends. This must be done in tandem with capacity building to enhance overall local analytical and strategic capacities.

- Provide scope for greater local accountability and "mutual accountability" and introduce sensible risk management for grants and contributions. This can be aided by altering the accountability framework to simplify administration.

Notes

1. This synopsis is based on the following country report: Bruce, D., "Integrating Employment, Skills and Economic Development in Canada", submitted 2007.

2. In Nova Scotia these agencies are known as regional development agencies (RDAs).

3. Since 2008 a new Department of Labour and Workforce Development was created in the province to administer labour market policy (see *www.gov.ns.ca/lwd/*).

4. Since then the province has acquired full flexibility for designing labour market policy, although it remains to be seen how far this flexibility will have been devolved to the local level. The management of flexibility and accountability post-labour market development agreements in Canada has recently been reviewed in the provinces of Alberta and New Brunswick (see Wood, 2010).

5. In the Canada-Nova Scotia Labour Market Agreement and the Canada-Nova Scotia Labour Market Development Agreement, the province agrees to consult with stakeholders while developing their annual plans to ensure provincial services are tailored to meet local and regional needs.

6. The impact of the labour market development agreements on local flexibility and co-operation in Canada has recently been reviewed in the provinces of Alberta and New Brunswick (see Wood, 2010).

CROATIA[1]

National policy integration and co-ordination

Institutional framework

Figure 4.1. **Institutional map at national, regional, sub-regional and local levels**

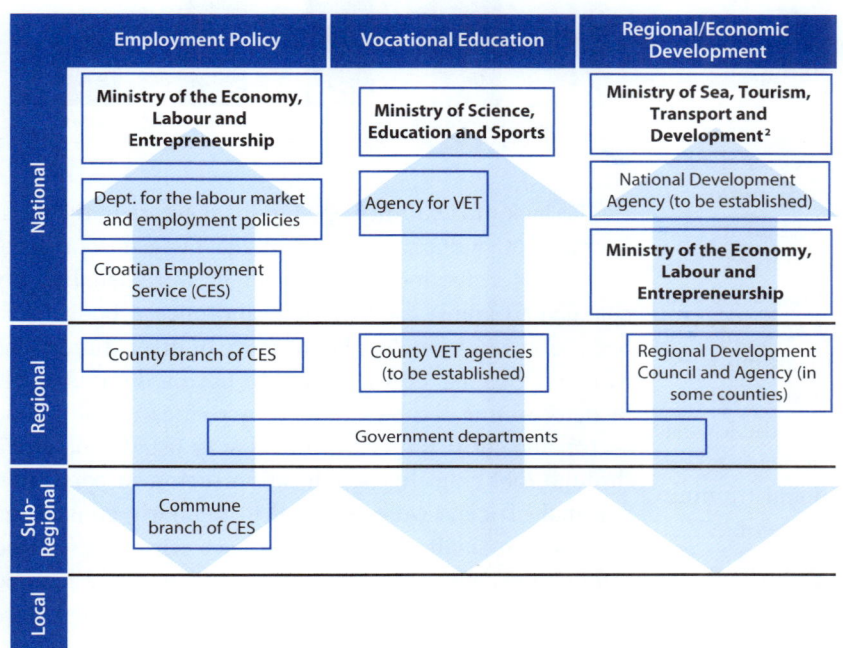

The principle ministry for structural policy and regional development in Croatia is the Ministry of the Sea, Tourism, Transport and Development (MMTPR). The MMTPR is also responsible for co-ordinating inter-ministerial working groups dealing with regional development and activities related to harmonisation with EU regional policy. The Ministry of Science, Education and Sport (MSES) is responsible for defining the legal framework for all levels of education in Croatia. The Ministry of the Economy, Labour and Entrepreneurship (MINGORP) has responsibility for vocational education and training (VET). The Croatian Employment Service (CES) is the national employment service, a mainly centralised organisation with some regional co-ordinating bodies.

Integration and co-ordination

The management of policy in Croatia is relatively centralised and sector-based. Ministries and their adjacent institutions have a great deal of autonomy in designing and implementing policies in their specific sectors and rely on relatively little inter-departmental communication to inform policy design. The degree of co-ordination between departments is at the discretion of the respective ministers, often resulting in conflicting or overlapping objectives. When ministerial interests clash, a higher political authority – usually the Prime Minister – intervenes, a situation sometimes exploited by lobbying factions for political purposes. The Government Office for Strategy has taken over the process of national development and planning and is growing in expertise and financial support.

At the time of this study, the greatest degree of horizontal co-operation was evident between the ministries responsible for employment and vocational training policy (MSES and MINGORP). Regional development policy was viewed as particularly fragmented with respect to the preparation and implementation of structural and regional development plans. A plethora of institutions and bodies were involved (for example, the Government Office for Strategy, Ministry of Finance, Central State Office for Administration), each retaining its own mandate. A Government Central Co-ordination Unit is designed to play a co-ordinating role but no one institution has an overview of the policies, instruments and measures implemented at any one time.

Flexibility

Croatia's centralised governance system means that the national level "has a dominant influence in all policy areas" (Crnkovic-Pozaic, submitted), while the sub-regional level appeared to have few decision making powers and play a mainly consultative role. This study estimated that over 86 per cent of all decisions relating to policy, programme and service design were taken by central government in 2007. The county level is granted greater say in choosing which projects to implement. It was expected that greater local flexibility and local autonomy would be granted as a result of forthcoming amendments to the legal basis for regional development.

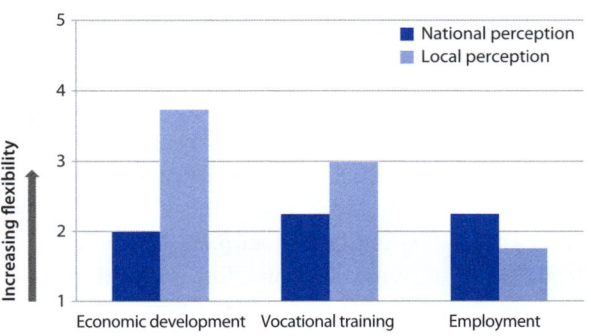

Figure 4.2. **Local flexibility**

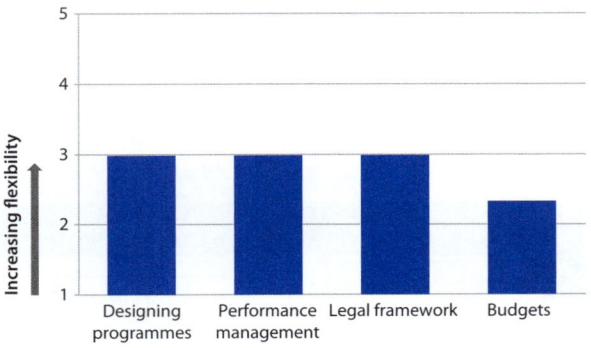

Figure 4.3. **Varaždin: Flexibility of management tools**

Figure 4.2 illustrates how national and regional participants perceived flexibility in the case study region of Varaždin County. It is interesting to observe that in two of the three policy areas, national players perceived flexibility to be lower than their regional counterparts, and there was no consensus as to which policy area was the most flexible. Employment and vocational training were equally scored at national level as slightly above "inflexible", whilst economic development was given the lowest rating as "inflexible". Economic development was ranked most flexible by local stakeholders, vocational training was seen as "mixed", and employment as "inflexible".

Interviewees identified the VET system as particularly constrained and unresponsive to labour market demands. The centralised nature of the system prevented rapid change to meet local needs, and by the time curricula, training and education programmes had been updated, skills demands had often shifted. Because of the inability of VET schools to adapt and develop programmes in skills growth areas, much adult training took place in the private sector. Students wishing to transfer between educational strands were confronted with an unwieldy system which made it almost impossible to switch focus to an area not within their initial career path; this was particularly the case for "three-year schools" which did not enable students to progress to higher education and blocked careers for those forced to select a particular education path at an early age. There was little dialogue between schools and companies, marking a change from pre-transition times when strong links were maintained.

As seen in Figure 4.3, the flexibility of programme design, performance management and legal framework management tools were scored as "mixed", with budget management receiving the lowest rating.

The lack of flexibility open to local actors in the management of budgets was one of the biggest sources of frustration at the local level. Budgets were usually only changed to adjust for inflation, and once a budget had been set it was very difficult to move or divert funds. The Ministry of Finance was found to have a dominant role in determining the outcomes of activities in the public sector and local project approval was usually obtained through lobbying. In the education sector, in particular, regional officials were required to regularly consult the ministry on small budgetary changes. Any funds raised through the commercial activity of schools partly accrued to the ministry, reducing their motivation to become more financially independent and participate in local community partnerships. As a positive spin off, however, local stakeholders had been spurred on to seek out alternatives sources of funding, creating a new and more entrepreneurial climate in public institutions.

The employment service was also found to be constrained by a legal framework which discouraged innovative policy intervention at the local level.

Co-operation and policy integration at the regional and local level

In the case study area of Varaždin, integration was identified as "average" between regional development and the other two policy areas. Employment and vocational training, however, received a poorer scoring of "weak" integration.

The degree of local co-operation was found to very much depend on the relations between local actors: "… all it requires is that a critical mass of people of a certain

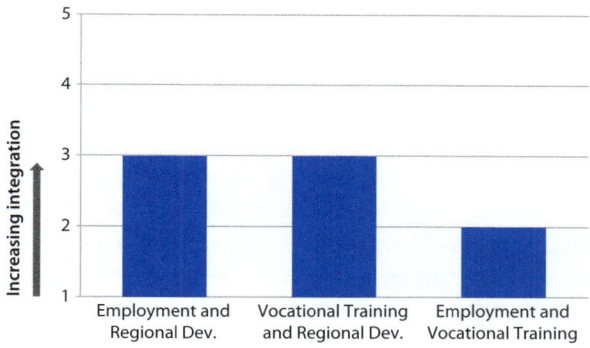

Figure 4.4. **Varaždin: Integration between policy areas**

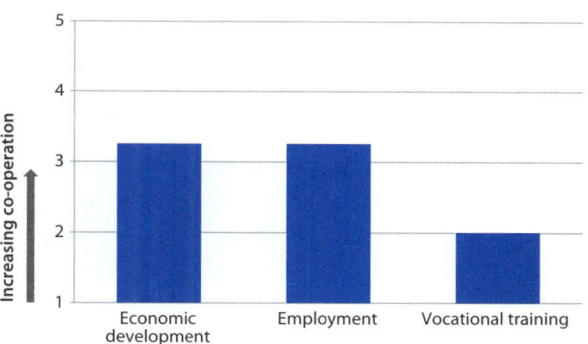

Figure 4.5. **Extent of engagement in cooperation at the local level**

kind and with adequate mutual trust decides that they want to achieve something" (Crnkovic-Pozaic, submitted). In Varaždin, for example, the existence of good informal relations had spurred good co-operation particularly in the field of entrepreneurship policy. The *župan* (head of regional administration) belonged to a different political party from the mayor, yet they usually managed to set their differences aside to support useful projects.

> *"... all it requires is that a critical mass of people of a certain kind and with adequate mutual trust decides that they want to achieve something".*
>
> Croatia Country Report

However, such co-operation was heavily dependent on the personality of individuals and their agendas. It was also politically driven, with new project ideas usually coming from political leaders, with other regional stakeholders being tasked with an implementation role.

Figure 4.5 indicates that the extent of engagement in co-operation in Varaždin was considered to range from average to low. Economic development and employment policy sectors engaged in an "average" extent of co-operation, while co-operation by the vocational training sector was considered "weak".

Integration between business organisations and the public sector was also identified as weak. In particular, employment policy makers were commonly seen to focus mainly on disadvantage and equity issues, and as a result employment policymakers were not seen as an "equal partner in development" by a private sector which was looking for modern skills and high potential workers.

It was apparent that vertical national – regional co-operation was relatively weak in Croatia at the time of the study. Many policy directions instigated at the national level had not filtered down to the regional level, with the result that counties felt that work carried out "above" them in the governance scale was relatively abstract and irrelevant; stakeholders commented that central institutions were tied up with their own problems and did not have time for regional challenges.

A number of further policy initiatives and partnerships have been developed to increase integration, strengthen county critical mass and pave the way for a more innovative and entrepreneurial society. The pre-European accession regional operative programme (ROP) process is an attempt to integrate employment, education and economic development programmes at design stage and has provided a new mechanism for more inclusive economic development and policy design, with the potential to raise strategy survival rates beyond election periods (see Box 4.1). Partnership Councils have also been established as advisory bodies for the preparation and implementation of regional development policy. They bring together development stakeholders (public, private and civil sector representatives). Regional Development Agencies (RDAs) co-ordinate regional development, operating as a stepping stone towards a more integrated economic development support system while County Development Agencies co-ordinate county level activities and monitor regional development policy implementation.

Capacities

Resource and skills capacity levels were found to be low at the local level in Croatia. Figure 4.6 outlines the average capacity of organisations in Varaždin. The policy sector most highly rated in terms of skills and resources was economic development, with skills capacities perceived as "strong". Employment and vocational training both received an equal "average" scoring for skills and a "weak" scoring for resource levels.

Resources

Financial resources across the board were considered to be insufficient and to negatively impact on the ability of government institutions to co-operate with other actors. County councils were seen as especially poorly funded, undermining their ability to work in partnership and push for substantial policy integration. Meanwhile, those regions experiencing robust economic growth expressed the view that they were subsidising poorly performing regions, and that any increase in their GDP (gross domestic product) per capita jeopardised their own eligibility for central funding.

Figure 4.6. **Varaždin: Average capacity of organisations**

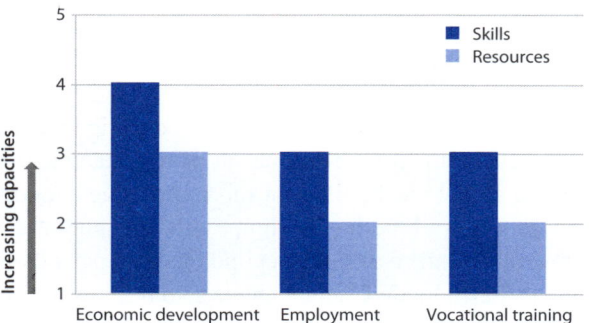

Resource levels within the vocational training sector were identified as particularly low by interviewees. GDP invested in the sector is less than the European Union average and most of the funding was spent on wage costs as opposed to the upgrading of facilities or teacher training. A country-wide network of Open Community Colleges exists, which work with employment services at county level to provide courses for the unemployed. However this network has had little impact on reversing a dramatic decline in participation in adult training since the communist era. Reform of the VET system has commenced in response to the challenges of globalisation, but the pace of reform was seen to be slow and was being blamed for creating a bottleneck in economic development.

The national employment service was not considered active enough or broad enough in scope to lead change in this respect, in that it limited itself to mainly administering unemployment benefits and providing counselling.

Capacities were also found to be low in the area of data collection and analysis. An absence of accurate data on the local context was blamed for a mis-identification of problems and the implementation of outdated policies. Monitoring and evaluation of project results was also relatively rare and not always made available for public scrutiny.

Skills

Policy makers, particularly at the regional level, often do not have the necessary experience and skills to put together submissions for funding and create viable strategies. For example, in Varaždin County only 3 per cent of the 282 project proposals which were received in relation to the initial regional operative programme were found to comply with the Terms of Reference. Often it is those local authorities which are most adept at applying for funding that received the most financial support, rather than those most in need; over the long-term this has reinforced rather than diminished regional differences. However, there was optimism that the ROP process will foster new skills and greater knowledge among public sector workers and that the wave of new, younger employees entering the profession is slowly introducing a more pro-active and entrepreneurial attitude. The EU accession process was also rated positively at raising motivational levels and improving human resource capacities.

Box 4.1. **Case study region: Varaždin County**

STRENGTHS AND CHALLENGES	
STRENGTHS	CHALLENGES
• One of fastest developing counties in Croatia;	• GDP per capita below national average;
• Unemployment rate below national average;	• Labour market supply & demand mismatch;
• Good transport connections to capital;	• Uneven spread of economic growth & development throughout region.
• One of the country's most successful "free zones".	

OPPORTUNITIES	THREATS
• Consolidating a strong entrepreneurial spirit & developing support infrastructure; • Potential to attract further FDI; • SMEs relatively well developed & represent dynamic economy; • New tourist portal being developed.	• Declining traditional industries. • Lack of basic competences for new economy, e.g. IT. • Weak business to educational institution links and knowledge transfer; • Inadequate education provision for life-long learning framework.

Varaždin County is situated in North-West Croatia and has six towns and 22 communes, with a total of 182 600 inhabitants (2008). The GDP of the region was only 86% of the national average in 2006 (Croatia Central Bureau of Statistics), but the county has made great strides in recent years in promoting entrepreneurship and attracting FDI to its region.

The region has a particularly well developed SME sector, representing the most technologically dynamic and innovative part of the economy; 98 per cent of all enterprises belong to this sector and it produces over 50 per cent of total income and jobs created. Local players have successfully collaborated to win government tenders for SME support, and have built a substantial entrepreneurial infrastructure over the last decade, led by two Regional Development Agencies.

The region also hosts one of Croatia's eight "free zones", which grants custom and tax exemptions to businesses located in it, and it has attracted more than 100 million euro in FDI in the last few years. Also present are 28 entrepreneurial zones (with 70 planned in total), a business park orientated primarily towards manufacturing, and a technological park which serves as the nucleus of a renewable energy and bio-technology knowledge cluster, emphasising innovation and scientific research activities.

The region's success in nurturing and attracting SMEs is in large part a result of consensus among the different parties in power at city and county level on the need to collaborate in the interests of community and economic development. To a large extent politics were put on the back burner to enable forums without political legitimacy to work effectively and deliver on promises, and to forge a unified vision.

However, four key challenges remain to further developing Varaždin's SME sector; a lack of trust between entrepreneurs making it difficult to establish hubs and clusters; inadequate financial support for new businesses; the uneven distribution of economic development throughout the region; and, most importantly, a skills shortage in developing fields such as management, IT, marketing and sales.

Tourism is also a strategic development focus in the region, leading to several tourism development programmes. Most of the tourist services are concentrated in the City of Varaždin and Varaždinske Toplice, a well known spa. The challenge is in unifying the existing fragmented offer of tourist services and better marketing the whole county as a tourist destination. With this in mind, a new tourist portal is being developed.

Given the increased demand for skills being brought by business growth and FDI, a key priority for the region in the coming years will be building an effective skills and training infrastructure. A main objective of the 2006 regional operative programme was to "develop human resources", however the region received few requests for financing in this area, meaning that more work will need to be done to raise regional capacities to bid for funds in the future.

Conclusions

In Croatia it is clear that levels of co-operation, flexibility, and capacities are all areas needing considerable attention if policy integration is to be improved. Based on combined responses at national, local and state (where appropriate) level, Croatia received a low to medium overall rating; 2.8 for capacity, 2.8 for local co-operation and the lowest rating of 2.5 for flexibility.

At the national level, government is seen to be overly bureaucratic, characterised by a hierarchical structure and autonomous working practices within different ministries.

Figure 4.7. **Attention Areas**

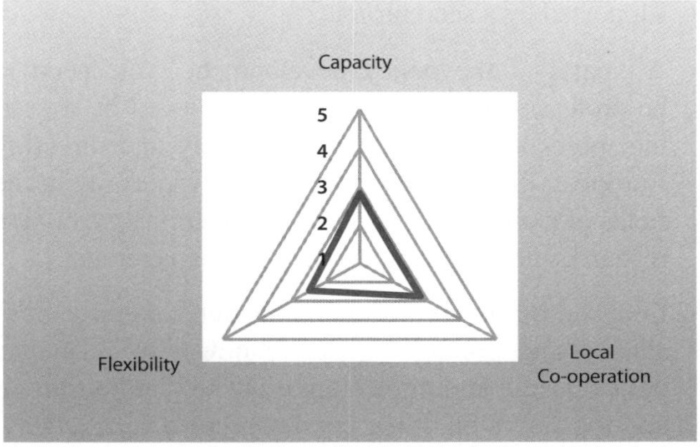

This has contributed to policy which is fragmented and unfocused, and serves as a barrier to more effective regional and national partnership working. Co-operation at the regional and local level is more commonplace and there are many examples of successful bottom-up activities, aided by European pre-accession programmes, but these activities are often reliant on informal networks and personal relationships.

Flexibility is visible in certain sectors and emerges strongly in the case study region of Varaždin, a region in which local players had enough freedom and initiative to strengthen an already evident entrepreneurial spirit and construct an impressive SME sector. However, the lack of financial flexibility is proving to be a major impediment to economic development and policy integration, and national policies are implemented uniformly regardless of regional characteristics. The capacities of local actors are growing but still too low to undertake all the responsibilities of decentralised policy making and its implementation. National and regional authorities lack the monitoring and evaluation skills and data required of them to introduce a more decentralised, integrated system.

Recommendations

- The governance of employment and education policy should be further decentralised, allowing local players to have greater influence on policy design and implementation, whilst ensuring that monitoring and evaluation is sufficiently robust.

- Systems need to be put in place to increase the amount of labour market information available locally.

- Better co-ordination between labour market policy, training and economic development could be achieved through the establishment of a local strategic platform, supported by a secretariat.

- All parts of the policy development cycle need to be professionalised. This can be achieved by investing more in human resource capacity and directing European funding towards this aim, especially in the fields of management, information technology, human resources development and project management.

- Local administrators should be given clearer responsibility and greater legislative power to influence policy design and implementation, so that bottom-up and top-down planning can be better integrated.

Notes

1. This synopsis is based on the following country report: Crnkovic-Pozaic, S., "Integrating Employment, Skills, and Economic Development in Croatia", submitted 2007.

2. The Ministry of Sea, Tourism, Transport and Development has since been replaced by the Ministry of Regional Development, Forestry and Water Management.

DENMARK[1]

National policy integration and co-ordination

Denmark has a unique "flexicurity model" in which low barriers in hiring and firing (flexibility) is the foundation of the model and is supplemented by a high level of compensation (security) to the unemployed. This model constitutes a central element in the Danish welfare state model and has a strong influence on the design of employment, skills and economic development in the country.

Figure 5.1. **Denmark: Institutional framework map at national, regional and local levels**

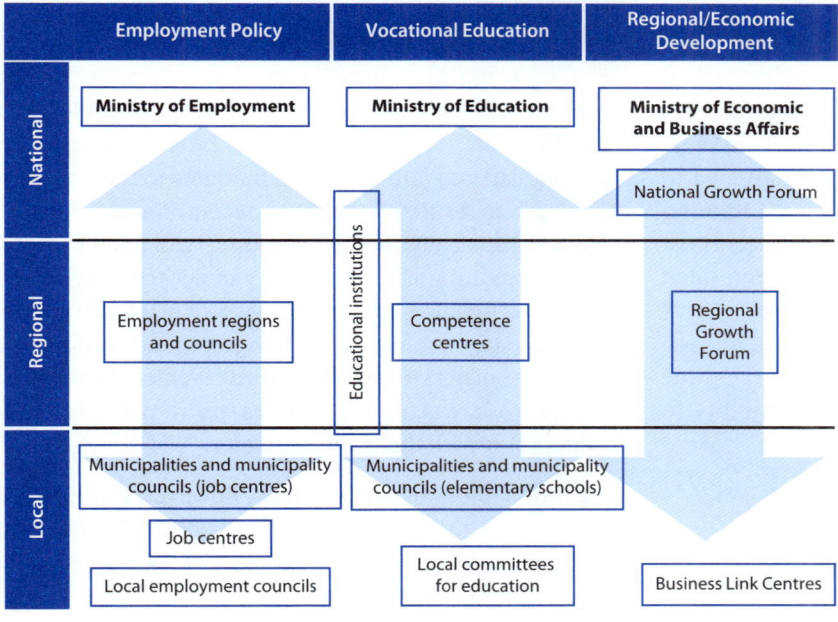

Institutional framework

Major structural reform in 2007 significantly altered the institutional landscape in Denmark for employment, vocational education and training (VET) and regional development, and shifted power from the regional to the local level. Municipalities were merged from 271 to 98 units and granted greater powers, with the expectation that they would be better able to deal with strategic challenges by regionalising strategies and bringing different policy objectives into line. In relation to employment policy, 14 regions were replaced by four "employment regions" and county labour market councils have been dismantled. The public employment service was reorganised to create job centres which functioned as a single gateway for all unemployed, with municipal run services under the same roof. In August 2009, the municipalities obtained full responsibility for managing local job centres.

Integration and co-ordination

A high level of policy integration and co-ordination is evident at the national level in Denmark, and social partners play a strong role in the development and implementation of policy in "consensual" politics. Co-operation at ministerial level takes place both through institutionalised structures and informal networks and there is generally an awareness of what initiatives are in place in related policy areas.

In 2006 central government presented a new Globalisation Strategy outlining an overall vision and initiatives to ensure that Denmark could maintain a healthy economic position in a globalised economy. The strategy called for further co-operation between relevant stakeholders, in particular the integration of business demands and education supply, and was developed through tripartite co-operation between the government and social partners. It has been implemented through a series of mutually binding regional partnership agreements.

A National Growth Forum has been established to aid the development and co-ordination of the growth strategy and its principle goal is the creation of more partnerships between large businesses, social partners and public administration. Six regional "growth forums" have also been established.

Government officials have reinforced the horizontal dimension of the Globalisation Strategy by ensuring that the objectives of the relevant ministries were correlated, while also maintaining institutionally separate systems with clear definitions of responsibility. The regional partnership agreements contribute to vertical integration with the regions, aligning the Globalisation Strategy and regional business development strategies to consistent goals.

However, at the time of the study regional growth forums reported that they had found it difficult to communicate with central government departments, other than the Danish Enterprise and Construction Authority, on implementing the strategy in practice. In this respect it was felt that regional growth forums and regional development as whole would have benefitted from an increased commitment from all the relevant ministries to the Strategy at the national level.

Flexibility

It was generally considered that a high level of flexibility was available to local actors in Denmark and this had strengthened the degree of local policy integration. As can be identified in Figure 5.2, national and regional players from the three policy sectors were closely aligned in how they perceived flexibility levels. Vocational training received the highest flexibility rating from both levels of the hierarchy, followed by economic development, rated as slightly less than "flexible". Employment policy was posited as the least flexible, identified as below "mixed" by national and regional participants. In two of the three policy sectors, the national level perceived flexibility to be higher than the local level.

Figure 5.2. **Local flexibility**

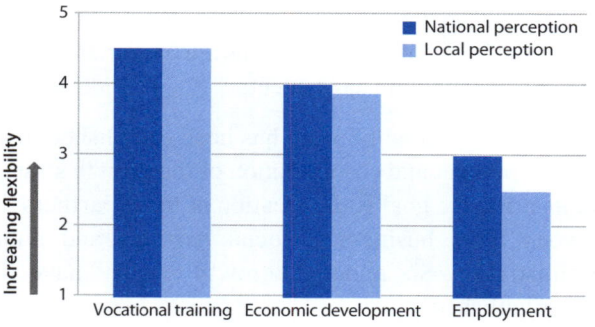

Figure 5.3 indicates that the flexibility of management tools in the case study municipality of Bornholm, located within the Copenhagen region (see Box 5.2), was considered to be quite high, and all four management tools received similar ratings between "mixed" and "flexible".

Figure 5.3. **Bornholm: Flexibility of management tools**

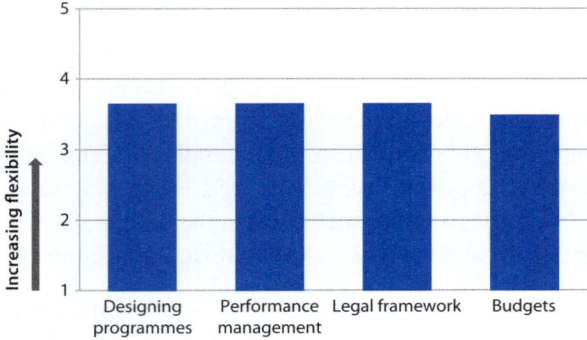

Officials working within the education system at all governance levels felt that there was a high degree of freedom available. Education programmes were becoming more flexible and modular with the aim to allow students to create their own education programmes, and to allow industry to tailor training modules to their specific needs. As a result of the new decentralised education model and a relaxation in regulation – with local tripartite councils having greater autonomy under the "taximeter" system – efficiency has also improved; VET institutions must regularly evaluate their programmes, forming the basis for ministerial/stakeholder involvement in identifying problem areas, and incentives are in place for close co-operation with the business sector.

As pointed out by stakeholders, however, limiting factors remained: the taximeter system offered little room for manoeuvre and placed a high risk on developing new training programmes which would not attract enough participants. Institutions identified that they were unable to offer education that was not general in its objective and that did not fall under agreed national competence descriptions; it was also suggested that education institutions needed to be more active in listening to the business sector when designing courses.

In the field of labour market policy, targets were set by the employment regions for local job centres at the time of the study.[2] The four employment regions entered into a contract with the Ministry of Employment outlining overall targets which had to tie in with the national strategic objectives of reducing unemployment, implementing the A New Opportunity for Everyone scheme (aimed at the long-term unemployed) and targeting young people. Local job centres were generally free to arrange initiatives as they pleased as long as they met overall targets, with the flexibility to decide which groups to focus on within the target areas and which active labour market programmes to employ. They received a financial sum which they could spend as they sought fit and were offered extra funds to target bottlenecks, reduce imbalances and offer training programmes which allow for regional flexibility.

Performance was measured in a national benchmarking system, the results from which formed the basis for setting more specific objectives or establishing new initiatives in local job centres. Thus, although regional objectives remained subordinate to national objectives, due to the general character of national objectives this was not felt to limit regional initiatives.

However, in the municipality of Bornholm most local players desired more flexibility in the implementation of employment policy, and felt that the government did not sufficiently take the special needs of regions into account when negotiating partnership agreements with growth forums. There was a view that the policy framework and legislation prevented local actors from being more active in helping themselves, and left little room to experiment.

In addition, labour market policy was not seen to offer long-term strategic solutions which were adapted to local contexts, and employment and training service provision remained guided by short-term needs. This was seen as a reflection of the government priority of supporting rapid labour market adjustments in the context of the "flexicurity" system. Access to training for the unemployed was regulated by tight criteria in terms of eligibility and funding that hampered adaptation to local conditions, and risked under-investment in longer term human resource development. It was felt that there was a risk of the development of a low skills equilibrium in Bornholm associated with decreasing productivity, high turn-over and low wages and benefits if people were only guided into shorter-term, lower quality employment without investment in their skills.

Co-operation and policy integration at the regional and local level

Integration and co-operation at the regional and local level was felt to be quite high in Denmark. The policy areas of regional development and VET were considered to engage in a "strong" degree of integration, while integration between employment and regional development, and employment and VET was rated as "average". It

was felt that there was room for further integration, in particular between employment and VET which were characterised has having "silo behaviour".

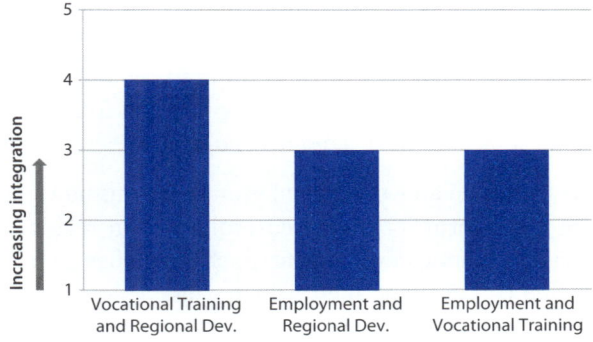

Figure 5.4. **Bornholm: Integration between policy areas**

Figure 5.5 illustrates the extent of engagement in co-operation in the case study municipality of Bornholm. According to the views of local participants, the sectors most likely to participate in multi-stakeholder partnerships, be involved in substantive collaboration and in a strong level of information sharing were economic development and vocational training. Employment received a slightly weaker scoring.

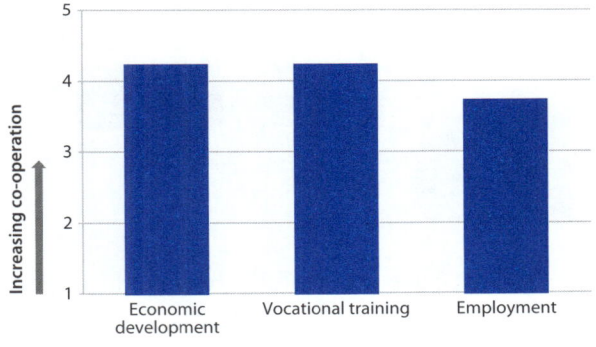

Figure 5.5. **Extent of engagement in cooperation at the local level**

Employment and regional development co-operation generally occurred within regional and local committees, with the same organisations frequently represented in different forums. Employment councils exist at the regional and local level, bringing together social partners, trade union representatives, municipalities and employers. These councils had been given enhanced powers in recent reforms to monitor and influence the implementation of policy locally, advise local job centres and develop training initiatives.

As shown in Figure 5.5, the Danish VET system is also characterised by a high degree of stakeholder involvement. Social partners, enterprises, teachers and educational committees are involved in a continuous dialogue on how to develop the system and the Ministry of Education has established local competences centres in educational establishments to strengthen training and competence development in SMEs. The centres work closely with local and regional businesses on their training needs and assist educational institutions in managing the shift from course supplier to becoming a "competence partner".

As identified above, regional growth forums now operate as a platform for policy co-ordination in relation to regional economic development. Each forum has 20 members (see Box 5.1) and their primary task is to develop a regional business development strategy which corresponds with the Globalisation Strategy.

Box 5.1. **Partners to the regional growth forum**

The forums have successfully brought local people together to deliver a common strategy to improve the relevance of skills to the local economy. For example, the forum in Bornholm has drawn up the region's business development strategy and established business clusters – a cornerstone in the strategy – resulting in improved co-operation between relevant policy areas and more understanding of shared interests, particularly between VET and the business community (see Box 5.2 below). They have also "provided local stakeholders with a sense of common direction, togetherness and not least interdependency" and created a desire among islanders to "do something for themselves" (New Insight, submitted).

Despite the positive results shown by some regional growth forums, there is concern that there has often been a focus on devising EU funded initiatives rather than improving the integration and effectiveness of mainstream policies at the local level. It was also suggested that there were limited links to other local forums, such as the employment councils and the tripartite councils which make strategic decisions regarding education policy.

Capacities

Skills and resources

Realising the full potential of recent institutional reforms requires considerable capacity at local and regional levels. Local actors in Bornholm considered skills levels as "strong" in all three policy sectors. Resource levels were as highly rated for economic development and VET, but received a significantly lower "weak" scoring for employment. Stakeholders considered there to be few limitations to institutions' possibilities to enter into partnerships, but that low resource levels in public agencies prevent them from becoming as fully involved in partnerships as they would hope.

Figure 5.6. **Bornholm: Average capacity of organisations**

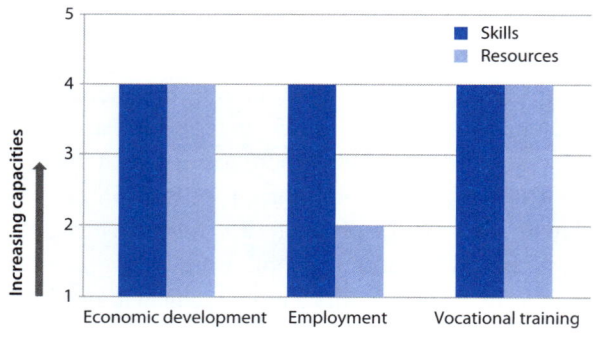

In Bornholm the job centre identified that it lacked human resources, limiting its ability to go beyond its operational objectives and play an additional role in the business development strategy. Budget cuts at local government level were also an obstacle as they reduced resources available for horizontal projects. Local stakeholders are able to carry out useful initiatives through applying for European funding, however this came with a significant administrative and technical burden and tended to lead to the development of short-term initiatives, as opposed to more mainstream adaptation of policies and programmes.

Better information gathering and analysis was seen as critical to enabling regional forums to assess vocational training needs and accurately forecast future demand. A number of stakeholders in Bornholm also expressed the need for a skills audit that would gather information on local businesses, and for a shared knowledge base to make it easier to identify shared objectives.

Box 5.2. Case study region: Bornholm

STRENGTHS AND CHALLENGES	
STRENGTHS	CHALLENGES
• Strong sense of identity and safe environment for all; • Cohesion between public and private bodies and civic population; • Specialised and competitive businesses.	• Poor accessibility; • Low level of formal qualifications and lack of educational institutions; • Relatively high unemployment rate; • Large share of sectors with low employee productivity/requiring higher skills level.
OPPORTUNITIES	THREATS
• Economically more attractive than Copenhagen; • Growth in outsourcing and subcontracting; • Potential to develop industry based on experience and lifestyle; • Location and safety levels make region more attractive.	• Diminishing employment opportunities for unskilled; • Lack of job opportunities and declining workforce; • Distance between growth industries and knowledge institutions; • Reduced regional funding.

The "burning platform" – population decline, youth exodus, and a diminishing workforce

As an island situated in the Baltic Sea, Bornholm provides an interesting and unique case study locality. Quite far from the Danish mainland and relatively close to Sweden, it has a relatively small population (42 800 in 2008). Bornholm is part of the Copenhagen region but has been allowed to develop its own regional development strategy and establish its own growth forum in recognition of its relative economic isolation. Ahead of the structural reforms, in 2003 its five municipalities and one region merged to form a combination of two administration levels.

The island has a low employment participation rate, a relatively high unemployment rate and many of its enterprises are occupied in low productivity sectors. The average level of formal qualifications remains low and there is a lack of educational institutions, constituting a severe weakness in progressing towards a knowledge economy. The net outflow of human capital has contributed to a skills shortage in the island and Bornholm has a higher share of medium, low and unskilled labour than Eastern Denmark.

Bornholm is experiencing population decline, the mass exodus of young people, and a diminishing workforce. These have merged to become a "burning platform", which has been the biggest enabling factor in encouraging cooperation and policy integration: all actors in the region are aware of the underlying context and the challenges they face. The Bornholm Growth Forum produced a vision for the region built upon reversing these trends, based around developing the existing industrial knowledge base, expanding the tourism sector and promoting entrepreneurship.

Working towards these objectives there has been a continual effort to optimise cooperation between VET and local businesses to better meet the demand for more skilled labour. The Forum has contributed to internal cooperation by engaging regional enterprises in strategic thinking relating to educational needs. It has also institutionalised collaboration between the public and private sectors, and driven the establishment of regional business clusters (such as the Iron and Metal Cluster described below).

The forum's success highlights the importance of involving relevant local actors early in the process, and the inclusive process of drawing up the regional business development strategy has resulted in a sense of shared ownership.

"... it could be argued that many of the actors would have been forced to do something without the introduction of Bornholm's new Growth Forum. However ... [it] has undoubtedly provided local stakeholders with a sense of common direction, togetherness and not least interdependency".

Denmark Country Report

Bornholm's Iron and Metal Cluster

The Bornholm Growth Forum has resulted in the establishment of cluster working groups that secure coordination in specific lines of trade and develop shared strategies through regular meetings, overseen by a coordinator who pushes the cluster work forward. Bornholm's Iron and Metal cluster has engaged with Bornholm's Jobcentre to jointly recruit unskilled labour to the metal sector, as well as participating in a joint advertising campaign to attract new labour and, in particular, more young people to the sector. Representatives within this cluster have also worked together to identify and address long-term training and education needs, such as planning the number of apprentices needed and relevant courses within vocational training provision.

Conclusions

Figure 5.7. **Attention Areas**

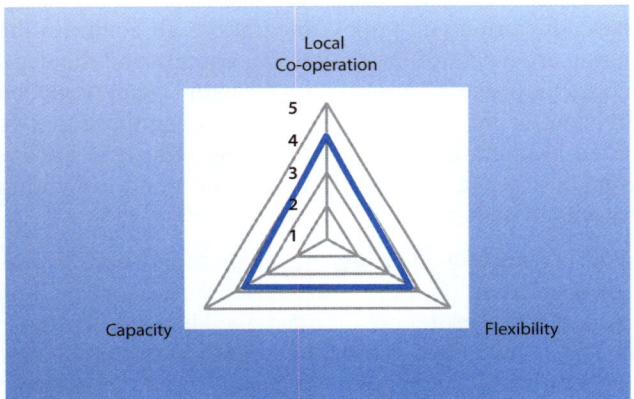

Denmark scored highly on all aspects of co-operation, capacity and flexibility. As seen in Figure 5.7, the combined responses at the national, local and state level (where appropriate) return 3.7 for capacity and flexibility, and 4.1 for local co-operation from a maximum of 5.0. The recent restructuring of the Danish governance system has brought about fundamental change and at the time of study the relevant actors were still adapting to their new roles and building capacities.

Stakeholders considered that in the face of future technological developments and shifting demands, retaining Denmark's qualities of flexibility in a demand-led system is positive. However there was uncertainty as to whether local stakeholders were fully exploiting the institutional flexibility that is available. There was a need for closer co-operation between regional and national actors on longer-term strategic plans adapted to local conditions.

While good collaboration mechanisms have been set up in the fields of employment, skills and economic development, there needed to be better linkages between these governance mechanisms. The relevant policy fields need to work towards common targets at the local level rather than only following targets set vertically.

There is a need to move away from short-term thinking in relation to skills development and adopt a longer term approach within local and regional collaboration with the private sector. In addition, it needs to be considered how initiatives developed using European structural funds can be better mainstreamed into normal policy delivery.

Recommendations

- Build more effective bridges between current collaboration mechanisms such as the training councils, regional employment councils and the growth forums. One example would be that local and regional training plans are reviewed by the local employment councils and growth forums.

- Give policy makers incentives to act strategically and with a long-term perspective by making the participants in the various collaboration bodies mutually accountable for each other's activities (*e.g.* by establishing cross-sector targets).

- Modulate flexibility in employment service and training provision regarding financing and eligibility, responding to the size of the region and the scope of the problems faced locally, such as skills shortages, unemployment, talent flight and low wages.

- Better link growth forums to the regional business development process to avoid duplication at the local level.

- Develop a way of evaluating the successes and failures of growth forums and other collaborative bodies, and holding members accountable.

Notes

1. This synopsis is based on the following country report: New Insight, "Integrating Employment, Skills and Economic Development in Denmark", submitted 2008.

2. Since the study the system of management has changed with municipalities being responsible for running local job centres.

GREECE[1]

National policy integration and co-ordination

The state in Greece remains relatively centralised. The Ministry of Employment oversees employment policy through the Organisation for Manpower Development (OAED), the Greek public employment service.

Institutional framework

Figure 6.1. Greece: Institutional map at national, regional, sub-regional and local levels

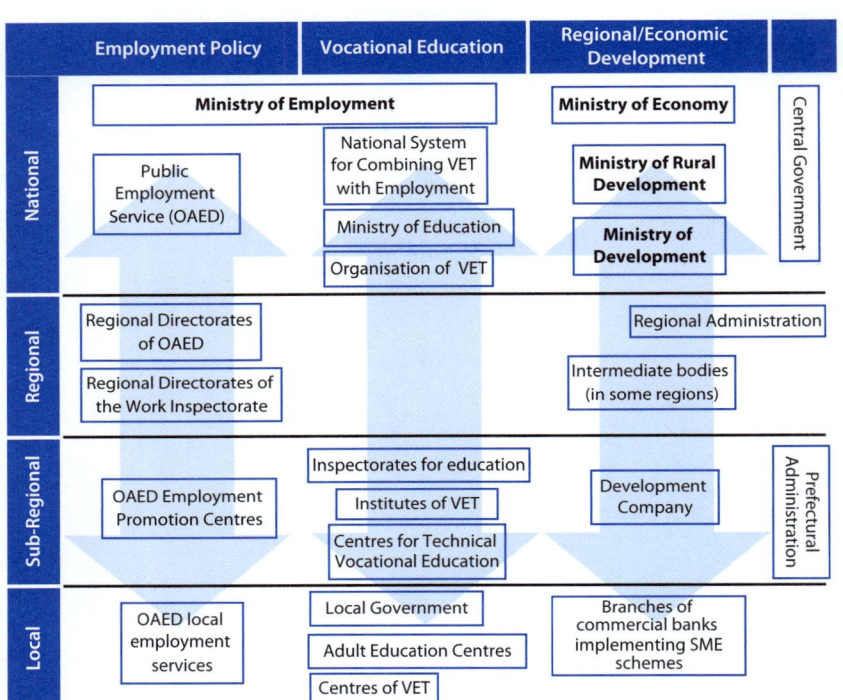

The organisation implements central government employment policy and its key responsibilities include registration of the unemployed and labour market vacancies, and collecting information on labour market trends. At sub-national level the OAED is divided into regional offices, local services and local employment promotion centres and also has representatives in municipalities. Responsibility for vocational education and training (VET) was shared by the Ministry of Education and the Ministry of Employment at the time of the study. The Ministry of Education was responsible for general education and initial vocational training while the Ministry of Employment delivered continual vocational training and OAED planned vocational training programmes for the employed and unemployed. Regional and economic development is promoted by the Ministry of Development, with the Ministry of Rural Development also playing a role.

Integration and co-ordination

Partnership working at national level has been strongly promoted over the last two decades, largely as a result of the partnership principle which informs the implementation of the European structural funds.

However, the study found that this had more rarely translated into national policy integration in practice. Policy interventions were found to overlap and the channels of communication between ministries appeared limited, with synergies occurring mainly in the design phase of programmes. A lack of clarity regarding ministerial responsibilities and roles was also evident, particularly within employment and active labour market policy.

The overlap and duplication between ministries could be seen clearly in the field of vocational training: the fact that VET was split between two different ministries at the time of the study resulted in two separate vocational training centres operating at the local level, creating confusion amongst clients. Similarly, poor collaboration between the Ministry of Development and the Ministry of Employment led to various programmes aimed towards the same target groups (such as graduates or women), while other groups remain unaddressed, demonstrating "a lack of truly integrated planning at national level that could be remedied through increased co-operation".

Greater policy integration has been encouraged by the National Reform Programme 2005-08 (NRP) and the National Strategic Reference Framework 2007-13 (ESPA). The NRP was developed in response to requests from the European Commission to set out a pathway of reforms and establish more extensive dialogue between ministries. The ESPA process has encouraged an integrated framework design for the use of European structural funds. In 2003 a law was passed on the development of a National System for Combining Vocational Education and Training with Employment to exploit synergies and promote collaboration among the various ministries and agencies active in the field of training and employment. Another significant step for policy integration was a new law on Co-ordinating Lifelong Learning, constituting the first such integrated strategy at national level.

National government has also sought to strengthen social partner participation in planning, financing, implementing and evaluating labour market policies. For example, an Employment and Vocational Training Fund was set up to systematise in-company training, supervised by the social partners. Social partners were also closely involved in the process of designing "accredited job profiles". The profiles cover a multitude of emerging professions, and provide a basis for training curricula. This was seen as a significant initiative for Greece and illustrated the involvement of social partners in an effort to advance training and labour market integration.

> *"These [job] profiles will subsequently be accredited and training institutions will then be expected to adapt their curricula in accordance ... This is a significant initiative for Greece illustrating the involvement of the social partners in an effort to improve the link between training and the requirements of the labour market."*

> Greece Country Report

Since 2009, both initial and continuing VET have come under the supervision of the newly renamed Ministry of Education, Lifelong Learning and Religious Affairs, reflecting the emphasis now being placed on lifelong learning within this Ministry, and reducing duplication in programme delivery.

Flexibility

The design, co-ordination and delivery of policy remains top-down in Greece, particularly with regard to employment policy. The trend towards centralisation has increased in recent years and fewer central institutions have agencies at local level; the SME support agency EOMMEX, for example, contracted its services into one central office.

As illustrated in Figure 6.2, both national and regional stakeholders perceived overall levels of flexibility in

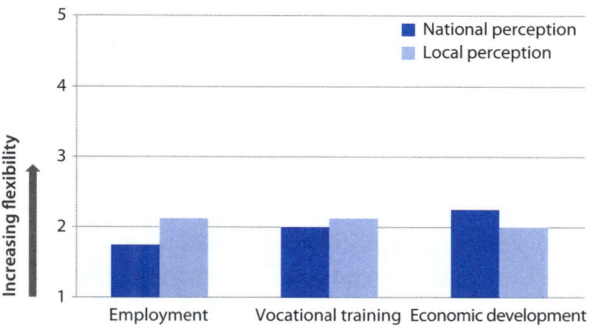

Figure 6.2. **Local flexibility**

the case study region of Rhodope to be low, with scores in or around "weak". In two of the three policy sectors (employment and vocational training) national players classed flexibility as slightly lower than their regional counterparts. Economic development was ranked most highly by the national level, at slightly above "weak", but received the lowest local rating.

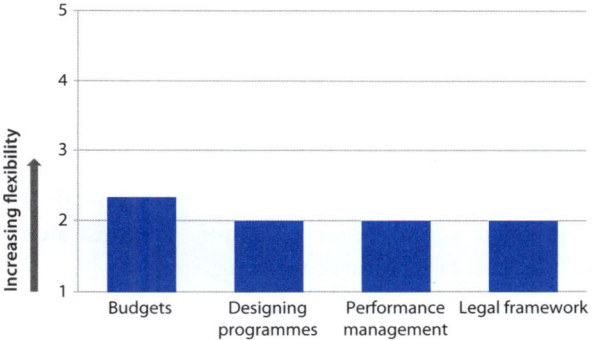

Figure 6.3. **Rhodophe: Flexibility of management tools**

Figure 6.3 indicates how flexible four different management tools were perceived to be in Rhodope (in the region of Eastern Macedonia and Thrace). Overall, the tools received a poor scoring, with programme design, performance management and legal framework awarded an "inflexible" rating. Budget management achieved a slightly higher rating. Performance management was seen to function relatively weakly and specific performance targets for local government offices either did not exist or had only recently been introduced.[2] As most decisions on regional budgets and the allocation of EU funds were taken centrally, regions were seen to have little financial autonomy, with flexibility only available for an estimated five per cent of the European regional development budget.

The inflexibility of the policy framework was reflected in the rigidity of training programmes on offer. Designed at the national level, it was felt that they frequently did not meet local business needs and were considered by employers to be unresponsive to market forces; when demands for new skills emerged it took so long to alter training programmes that by the time they were in operation they were already rendered obsolete. Such delays also led to last minute decisions to abandon the more complex projects within European regional strategies and implement "quick fixes" to ensure that the available finances were spent.

Interviewees suggested that improving local policy adaptability lay not in the creation of new agencies but in better exploiting existing structures and processes, such as the regional government planning division which is currently under-used. Making regional administrations more accountable to citizens by, for example, democratically electing the regional governor would also reinforce local autonomy. Currently the governor is appointed by national government.

Co-operation and policy integration at the regional and local level

Perceptions of policy integration in the Rhodope prefecture ranged from "weak" to "average" (see Figure 6.4). Vocational training and regional development policy areas were perceived to be the least integrated, while employment and vocational training demonstrated the greatest level of integrated working.

Figure 6.4. **Rhodophe: Integration between policy areas**

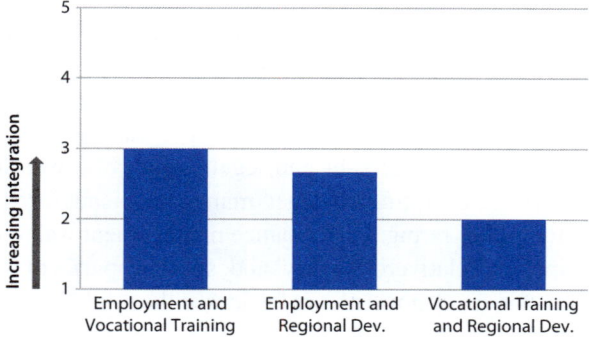

The level of co-operation between agencies in the Rhodope prefecture was also considered to be relatively weak (see Figure 6.5). According to local actors, the strongest level of co-operation occurred in the economic development and employment sectors, rated at slightly less than "average".

Vocational training was perceived to be engaged in the lowest level of co-operation, indicating weak participation in stakeholder partnerships, little information sharing, and unsubstantial collaboration on policy development and programme delivery.

Figure 6.5. **Extent of engagement in cooperation at the local level**

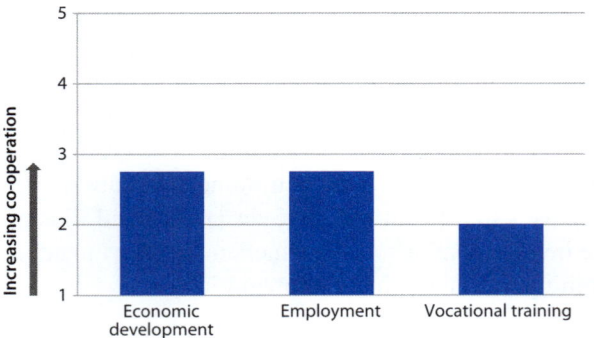

The relationship between local authorities, local social partners and the OAED public employment service was also seen to be limited in the province of Rhodope. The OAED was a frequent participant in local partnerships but was rated by local participants as inflexible, slow to act and not active enough in sharing local labour market data. It was hoped that recent restructuring by the OAED and the establishment of local "one stop shop" job centres would help change this.

The impact of local collaboration was seen to be undermined by a low capacity for strategic planning and the fact that strategic aims agreed in partnership were mostly non-binding. However, local leaders were seen as important in helping to overcome such challenges to produce concrete results. Charismatic individuals who care for their locality and can make things happen were seen as very important, and were mentioned by nearly all interviewees as a factor contributing to the effectiveness of individual projects. Such leaders could help local regions to achieve things "despite the challenging institutional context".

Local development companies also have a strong local presence in Greece. Their role is to co-ordinate and implement local development initiatives. The local development companies were identified in Rhodope as positively influencing local economic development due to their dynamism and broad representation local government and social partners act as shareholders in these agencies. However due to a lack of resources, they have developed an inward looking perspective, focused on keeping afloat and winning European funding bids, and currently have little flexibility or mandate to go beyond this.

It was considered that if restructured to operate in a less ad-hoc manner, and on a larger scale, development companies offered great potential for integrating activities from the different policy fields in a more effective manner.

Capacities

As can be seen in Figure 6.6, the average capacity level of organisations in Rhodope for both skills and resources was felt to range from "weak" to "average"; in two of three policy sectors skills and resources were rated at the same level. Economic development was the most highly rated, with skills and resource levels "average". Vocational training received the same scoring for resources but a "weak" allocation for skills, while in the employment sector skills and resources were both rated as "weak".

Figure 6.6. **Rhodophe: Average capacity of organisations**

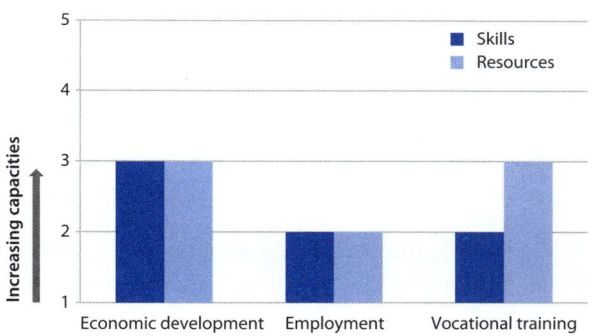

Resources

Local actors felt that the degree of resources available was greater than the average skills levels, in large part due to the influx of European funds. It was identified that regions which are used to receiving significant European structural funds can show signs of "EU-induced syndrome"; passive and process driven strategic planning which is powered by the need to spend money rather than a response to pressing local issues.

Box 6.1. **Case study region: Eastern Macedonia and Thrace**

STRENGTHS AND CHALLENGES	
STRENGTHS	CHALLENGES
• Strategic geopolitical position close to the Balkans and Middle East; • Significant primary sector and mineral resources which are largely unexploited; • Rich environment and ecology.	• Difficulties in governance framework and slow responses to regional needs; • Remoteness from capital and poor transport infrastructure; • Small scale landownership and industrial production.
OPPORTUNITIES	THREATS
• High value agricultural products; • Promote financial services and tourism and food processing industry; • Diverse multi-cultural population; • Planned improvements to transport infrastructure.	• Competition from neighbouring countries; • Agricultural restructuring and decline; • Relocation of industry; • Inadequate human resources; • Poor regional marketing strategy.

The region of Eastern Macedonia and Thrace (REMTh) occupies North Eastern Greece and borders Turkey, Bulgaria and Macedonia. It comprises five prefectures, including Rhodope, and has a population of 606 700 (2008). It is markedly agricultural and the poorest region in Greece. The Regional Operational Programme of Macedonia-Thrace 2007-2013 (ROPREMTh) for the implementation of the European structural funds is the main policy document outlining the regional strategy.

During the early 1990s, the main focus of the regional strategy was on infrastructure development, with an aim to reduce the region's geographic isolation and make fuller use of natural resources. From 2000 to 2006, the core aim shifted to retaining the local population and slowing out-migration to competing regions by improving quality of life. The latest planning period (2007-13) has seen economic convergence as the strategic aim, with the rationale being that infrastructure is now at a satisfactory level and it is time to foster commerce, entrepreneurship and develop human resources.

The ROP has proved to be a uniting force within the region and is the most visible integrative strategy incorporating elements of employment, training and local development. From 39 ROP measures, four specifically attempt to integrate these policy sectors.

One measure, in particular, focuses on local initiatives for employment and involves the greatest number of stakeholders, with a total of 120 people from across the region closely involved in the design of individual projects. The measure aims to guide unemployed people back to the labour market through access to targeted advice and training. It was implemented by local training centres and development companies, monitored by a cross-sector partnership.

The prefecture of Rhodope also benefitted from a European Commission Urban II programme from 2000-6 which focused on urban regeneration in Komotini (the capital of the Rhodope prefecture). Approx EUR 8 million European funding was matched by EUR 2.7 million from the public sector and EUR 1.7 million from the private sector, creating a total investment of approximately EUR 12 million. The focus was on the regeneration of a derelict neighbourhood of the city around a landmark building. The renovated building was then used to house a centre offering support services for local disadvantaged persons. The centre was also staffed by local people.

Such over-reliance on external funding has resulted in a situation whereby grants and subsidies are commonly seen as the main tool for developing the region, rather than "one tool to get the region to where it wants to go".

It was suggested that the weak institutional framework and emphasis on party politics also caused local government to push forward populist, short-term projects rather than advancing longer term projects which involved more risk. Central government has taken this problem seriously and a regional labour market observatory of labour market (PAEP) has been set up to produce annual reports on labour market issues in each region in Greece, including prefectures.

Skills

Capacity levels within public institutions at both the national and local level have been a cause for concern. In the past, staff within the public sector at the local level were seen to lack strategic planning and managerial skills, and those who had the necessary skills and qualifications usually left the region or moved into the private sector.

Public sector actors were felt to be risk averse, and as staff evaluation was largely absent, those who took responsibility and showed initiative were rarely rewarded. The more innovative employment initiatives funded by the European structural funds have also had a limited influence on the public employment service. As so many different local bodies implement European projects (*e.g.* local development companies and training organisations), it is rare for any learning gained to be transferred back into the OAED system.

However, the OAED has recently been attempting to address these shortcomings, with staff quality improving thanks to injections of new graduates, more staff training on core skills, and greater experience of working with EU funding frameworks.

Conclusions

Figure 6.7. Attention Areas

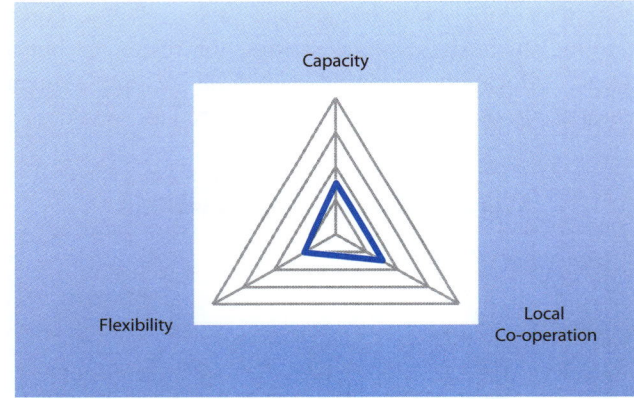

As seen in Figure 6.7, the combined responses at the national, local and state level (where appropriate) returned a low set of results for Greece; capacity and local co-operation received 2.5 and flexibility totalled 2.0 from a maximum score of 5.0. In the context of strongly centralised government, local regions were seen to suffer a lack of capacity, flexibility and meaningful co-operation. Investment was required in the three policy areas of employment, VET and economic development, and synergies between the policies at the national level were identified to be low, trickling down to local level as a lack of integrated approaches. The current challenging labour market conditions are mobilising local actors to take action to a certain point but their overall impact on policy integration is perceived to be negligible.

Co-operation and integration between national departments and agencies is slowly increasing, largely thanks to the requirements of the structural fund planning process and significant investment from the European Union. With its associated emphasis on capacity building and the development of the partnership principle, EU funds and policy guidelines have helped social partners to become more involved at both national and local level. More improvements are expected as the public sector opens itself up to change. Recent economic difficulties may complicate this process, however.

Recommendations

- More direct channels of communication and clearer mandates are required between national ministries to avoid duplication of efforts at the local level.

- A trade-off exists between the need to spend European money versus the need to make hard choices to invest in more complex, selective and intensive projects which are better targeted to local needs.

- Local actors should increase their prioritisation, for example through focusing on one or two strategic cluster areas (such as tourism). This would act as a hook for wider policies and a means of better targeting different training and employment actions around a common goal.

- As enterprises increasingly look for skilled labour, training will be a critical tool to lifting living standards in the regions. To ensure that training meets local labour market needs, greater local flexibility in programme design will be essential.

- Labour market intelligence is necessary for well targeted local strategies. Regional labour market observatories would be one step towards addressing this issue, but it will be important that local actors are involved in analysing data so that they "own" it and use it to collaboratively identify priorities.

- In the area of Thrace, the establishment of a regional development agency would assist in creating a common vision for development and mobilise local actors behind this.

- Training should be improved for public sector staff, particularly in partnership working and problem solving among public employment service workers.

Notes

1. This synopsis is based on the following country report: Manoudi, A., "Integrating Employment, Skills and Economic Development in Greece", submitted 2007.

2. Employment policy was managed almost completely through programme rules and regulations; performance targets were set for each employment promotion centres for the first time in 2006.

ITALY[1]

National policy integration and co-ordination

Institutional framework

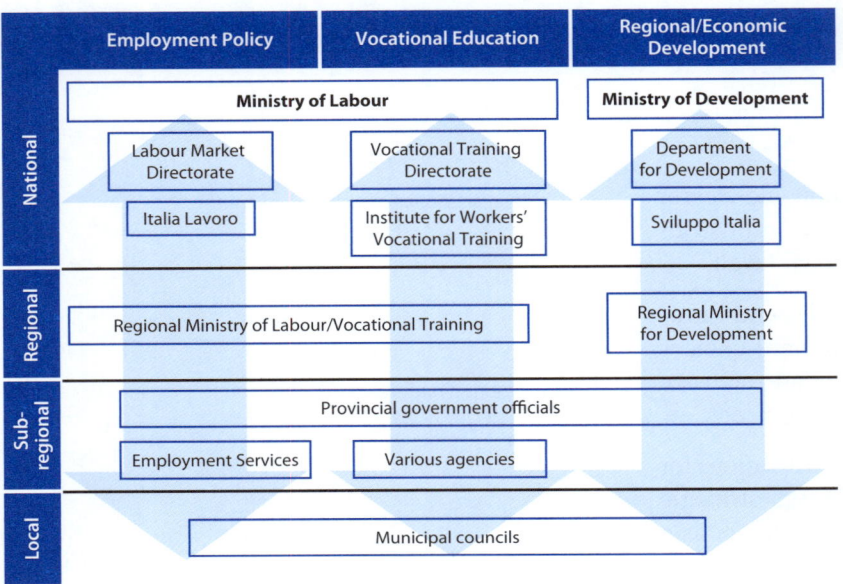

Figure 7.1. **Italy: Institutional map at national, regional, sub-regional and local levels**

Italy has a relatively decentralised governance system characterised by a high level of regional flexibility. At the national level, the Ministry of Labour takes the lead on employment and vocational training policy, supported by two national agencies: *Italia Lavoro* for labour market and employment, and ISFOL, the Institute for Workers Vocational Training for VET. The Ministry of Development is in charge of (mainly industrial) regional development policies, while the Department for Development co-ordinates and evaluates development policy.

Since 1997, however, the Italian state has transferred the majority of powers in the fields of active labour market and economic development policy to the regions. The organisational structure for delivering labour, education and vocational training policy varies from region to region. Municipal councils play a supporting role at local level through labour market analysis, partnership promotion and the creation of labour market initiatives.

Integration and co-ordination

The degree of policy integration and co-ordination at the national level in Italy was found to be relatively weak at the time of the study. Certain strategies – such as the Plan for Innovation, Growth and Employment 2005 (PICO) – combined a long list of actions relating to employment, skills and economic development policy, without consideration of the interactions or potential overlaps between them.

Other national policy strategies specified actions which converged towards the same objectives, bringing about a certain degree of integration, but no co-ordination was envisaged in terms of their implementation. The highest level of integration, when policies interact as part of a coherent and organic strategy to achieve desired priorities (Fadda, submitted), was found to be rare.

Horizontal co-ordination, information sharing and joint strategic planning was also found to be weak at the national level, particularly between labour and economic development policies. Formal co-operation was infrequent; officials responsible for employment and VET policy met once a quarter, while economic development officials met once a year. Interaction was also characterised by high levels of bureaucracy.

Vertical co-operation between the regions and the state was identified as lacking. The State and Regional Conference, made up of central government and regions, acts to fortify links and its consent is compulsory before government action with a regional impact is taken. Nevertheless, it remains a weak co-ordinating institution. Policy makers expressed a feeling of helplessness at the national level in the face of self-replicating silos from the national to the local level, and a plethora of fragmented institutions competing for resources, power and influence.

However, greater horizontal and vertical co-operation has emerged of late as a result of two main factors; emergency situations of industrial crises, and the EU programme for the National Strategic Document 2007-13 (NSD). Industrial crises threatening a large number of workers have triggered greater synergy between central administrations and social partners (see Box 7.1), while preparing the NSD led to increased communication between ministries with the aim of gathering contributions from different administrations and social partners. The Human Capital and Territorial Development project (CLUSTER) has also been noted for precipitating a higher degree of integration with regard to strategy content and partnership working.

Flexibility

Regions in Italy are marked by important inter-regional disparities (particularly between northern and southern regions) and have significant autonomy. As seen in Figure 7.2, the overall level of flexibility in the delivery of policy was rated as very high for the case study region of Puglia by both national and regional players. The perceptions of national and regional stakeholders regarding the degree of flexibility were also in close sync.

Figure 7.2. **Local flexibility**

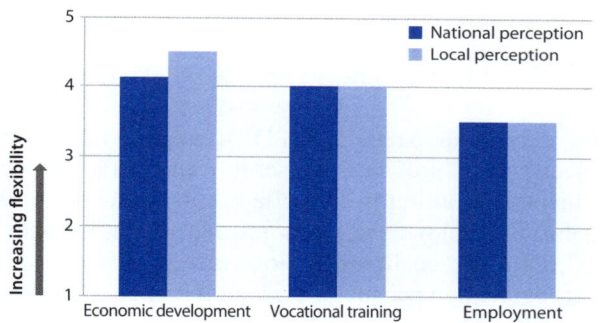

Regarding the flexibility of management tools, the ability of regional stakeholders to design programmes was perceived to be particularly high, followed closely by performance management and budgets (see Figure 7.3). The legal framework was considered to be the least flexible, attaining a "mixed" scoring.

The extent to which this flexibility is passed down to those operating at the sub-regional or provincial level (the level of local labour markets or travel to work areas) in Italy is less clear, however. The autonomy given to the regional level has led to a great deal of variation in the allocation of powers between regions, provinces and local authorities and it is not uncommon for serious conflicts to arise between the region and local government regarding such distribution of power. It is usually at the discretion of regions how much power to delegate to the provinces and municipalities and there is an ongoing debate as to whether more flexibility would be desirable at sub-regional level. It was felt by some regional officials that decentralisation to the provinces would not be effective due to low capacities to deliver services at this level.

Currently, flexibility at sub-regional and local level is restricted by the fact that funding is often controlled at the regional level. In the case study region of Puglia, provinces received funding for specific projects by bidding for projects within a tendering process (*bandi territoriali*) – essentially long lists of potential actions identified at the regional level. Regions then evaluated and selected applications in co-operation with provinces. Funds provided by the region were allocated for specific projects, with limited reference to other priorities, and could not be moved to other projects, thereby limiting flexibility. The funding of multiple individual projects also led to a lack of focus on potential synergies and the need for trade-offs between different actions. Pugliese provinces were also able to obtain finance for employment and vocational training policies from a variety of additional sources, including the European Social Fund, the Ministry of Labour, as well as from the province's own budget.

Figure 7.3. **Puglia: Flexibility of management tools**

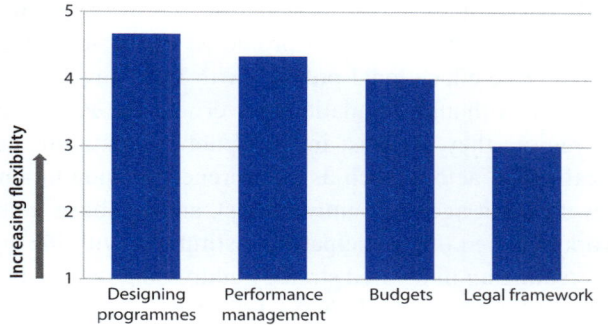

Figure 7.4. **Puglia: Integration between policy areas**

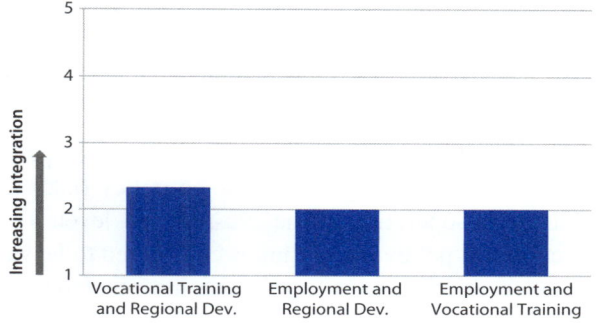

Co-operation and policy integration at the regional and local level

Regional and local policy co-operation and integration was found to be weak and ad-hoc in the Puglia region, as shown in Figure 7.4. Vocational training and regional development were considered the most integrated. Employment and regional development, and employment and vocational training received a "weak" integration scoring.

As seen in Figure 7.5, the policy sector considered to engage in local co-operation to the greatest extent was economic development, with employment and vocational training both receiving lower ratings. Significant regional variation exists in Italy in how regional administrations, directorates and agencies operate and the tools available for co-ordination, partnership arrangements and the distribution of functions; for example, some regions have a unified regional ministry for labour and vocational training, whereas others split the functions between two ministries.

Figure 7.5. **Extent of engagement in cooperation at the local level**

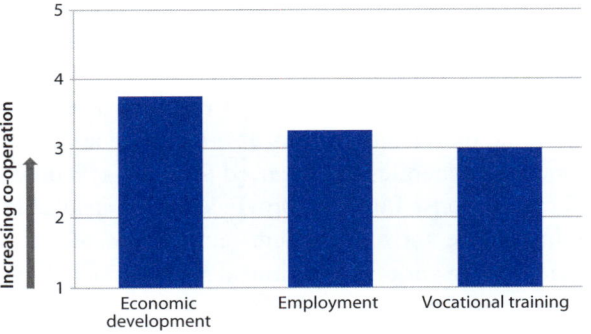

The splitting of functions and diversity of approach can result in confusion. Frequently communication is left to personal informal contacts and when institutions do collaborate, it is not uncommon for them to continue to manage their own plans without reference to collective strategies. Local agencies and partnerships are also at risk of being capitalised on to pursue personal interests, or raise political profiles.

Patti and PITs (see Box 7.1) have been developed in Italy to strengthen integration between policy fields and encourage co-operation at the sub-regional level. Their impact on real policy integration is considered to be variable, however. Within the Puglia region it was found that

such bodies "are taken up with formal procedures, and do not provide an environment for substantive co-operation" (Fadda, submitted).

> *"Stronger integration between local development planning and labour and vocational training is intended to take place through the PITs and Territorial Pacts ... However such integration is more likely to exist on paper than be actually implemented."*
>
> Italy Country Report

The national employment agency *Italia Lavoro* has launched a national SPINN project which, in part, assists with the management of PITs in integrating labour market policies with development, and encouraging better links with, and more active participation by, other public and private partners. This kind of national level technical assistance was considered to be important to ensure that co-operative working at the local level led to real local policy integration.

Box 7.1. **Patti and PITS – what are they?**

Patti (territorial pacts) and PITs (integrated territorial projects) have provided a useful framework for local partnership working in Italy. Based on the model of the territorial employment pacts introduced in Europe in 1997, Patti are coalitions of local actors (local government, public and private bodies, entrepreneurs, workers' representatives etc.) who have joined together to plan and implement an agreed set of strategies for local development. PITs are sets of intersectional actions shaped around the "*idea forza*" – the strategic idea – for the development of a specific territory, and are financed as part of Regional Operational Programmes (ROPs). They are designed to integrate different policy sectors and lead to coherent strategies for regional development.

In Puglia, as in many Italian regions, training is still "centralised" at the regional level. However Local Education Pacts have been promoted at the local level to integrate educational policies with local development policies. Although regulations governing the Pacts vary by region, they all must involve public institutions and local social actors (such as entrepreneurs, trade unions, development agencies, universities), and establish a network between the participating institutions with the aim of creating an integrated strategy addressing the needs of the territory, sector or industrial district.

Capacities

Capacities at the local level were seen to be lacking in Italy, particularly in relation to skills levels. Local actors in the Puglia region considered skills levels to be quite low: in the field of economic development, skills and resources were equally rated, but in employment and vocational training skills were rated significantly lower than resources. Resource levels in employment were perceived to be "strong" and as "average" in the vocational training sector.

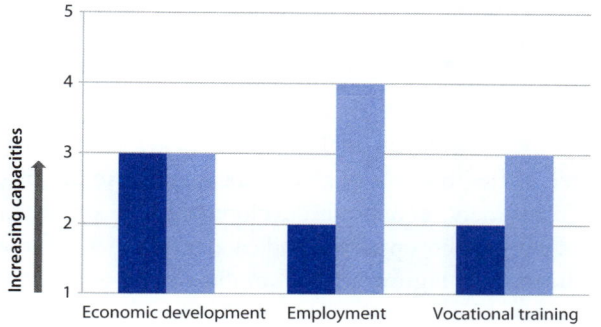

Figure 7.6. **Puglia: Average capacity of organisations**

Resources

Capacities are weakened in Italy by poor local data collection. Proximity to local labour markets does not lead to a better targeting of local policies, because "many local and regional institutions have a superficial and insufficient knowledge of labour market dynamics" (Fadda, submitted). At the time of study, organisations established to observe labour and training patterns in Puglia were not yet fully operational, adding to a lack of knowledge among decision makers on the dynamics of local markets and weak analysis. Information that was available was frequently unevenly distributed, meaning many participants lacked sufficient knowledge to make informed decisions.

Skills

The low level of skills among institutions, officials and private bodies was seen as one of the main obstacles to policy integration. There was a perceived lack of strategic capacity at the provincial level: programmes frequently consisted of "wish lists" of desired outcomes and a wide range of parallel targets, with no priorities, sequencing or mechanisms to give them strategic direction, shaped by

local conditions. While this "scatter gun" approach made it easier for stakeholders to embrace strategies, they do not become responsible partners in achieving a coherent and realistic approach. There was also a perceived absence of fixed, quantitative targets in the delivery of policies which meant that programmes were difficult to evaluate in terms of the effectiveness of their outcomes.

Box 7.2. **Case study region: Puglia**

STRENGTHS AND CHALLENGES	
STRENGTHS	CHALLENGES
• Favourable geographic location with rich natural and cultural resources; • Widespread education and vocational training system; • Large number of SMEs, R&D services and growing FDI.	• High unemployment and low labour market activity rates; • Low levels of public and private investment and innovation; • Declining standard of living; • Significant intra-regional disparities.
OPPORTUNITIES	THREATS
• ICT development potential; • Growing demand for artistic/cultural related tourism; • More powers devolved to local government ; • Strengthening urban centres and links with neighbouring countries.	• Growing competition from other regions and countries; • Deteriorating educational attainment; • Shift in labour market towards lower skills demand; • Extension of irregular economy and growth in criminal activity.

Industrial crises: triggering a more integrated approach

The Puglia region is located in Southern Italy and has a population of 4 078 100 (2008). The Puglia regional administration holds most powers concerning labour, vocational training and development policies. Despite this significant autonomy, however, silos between the three policy fields were evident at the time of study - particularly between employment and economic development.

Planning, integration and cooperation by social partners have increased as a result of industrial crises in the region. In the area of Murge a "Protocol of agreement" was set up to tackle the problem of a declining furniture manufacturing sector. Numerous representatives from national, regional and local level (e.g. the ministries of labour and of the economy, trade unions, associations working with small and medium enterprise) came together to examine ways to strengthen the sector. Actors agreed on an array of support measures which included putting in place arrangements with banks to restructure the debt of local firms, fiscal relief towards lowering labour costs, training, incentives to encourage the acquisition of new skills, and support for innovation and internationalisation by firms.

Similarly, the Nord Barese/Ofantino Pact was created in 1998 by eleven municipalities in an area particularly affected by industrial restructuring. The area has a high density of small firms clustered around the textile sector, and has experienced declining employment and income levels over the last decade.

In response, the Pact partnership created an "Agency for Employment and Development of the Area Barese/Ofantino" whose mission was to substantially restructure and modernise the sector and support the growth of tertiary employment. Intensive work was carried out to provide analysis of skills requirements, improve vocational training provision, and foster further education and training for other professionals, in collaboration with the regional branch of Italia Lavoro. A significant degree of integration between the Pact's strategies and partners was reached, partly due to the ability of the pact to access European funding which made it possible to bypass regional bureaucracy to some extent.

Despite the wide array of initiatives and policies coming from PITs and Patti, municipalities, provinces, European programmes, regional/local branches of national ministries, the study found that no institutional structure or body existed in the Puglia region capable of coordinating such a network of activities. There was an absence of effective "network governance" to coordinate the activities generated; those policies and strategies which operated within the same territory each worked with their own targets, timing, tools and interest groups. A Regional Planning Commission has been set up in Puglia to plan, monitor and evaluate labour market and vocational training policies and bring together regional institutions and social partners, but local development planning was not within their scope.

Conclusions

Figure 7.7. **Attention Areas**

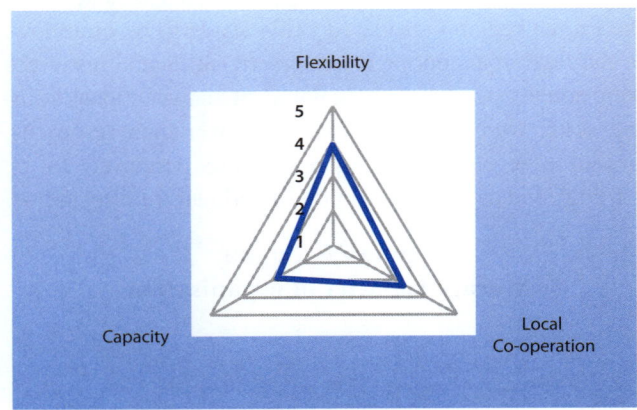

It was evident that in Italy there is a relatively high degree of flexibility available to local actors in the fields of employment, economic development and skills policies, However, co-operation and capacities are weaker. As can be seen in Figure 7.7, the combined responses at the local, state (where applicable) and national level returned 3.9 for flexibility, 3.3 for local co-operation and 2.8 for capacity from a maximum of 5.0.

The wide breadth of flexibility open to regions to design, co-ordinate and implement employment, education and skills policies coupled with the absence of policy integration indicates that while flexibility is a certainly a pre-requisite for integration, additional supports need to be in place for it to become a reality. Thus, despite the opportunities presented by Italy's decentralised regional and local government system, the lack of capacity, poor strategic planning, paucity of accurate and relevant data, and institutional failure to collaborate is reducing the ability of regional and local participants to exploit these opportunities and align policy fields more fully.

New strategic governance mechanisms are required at the local level in Italy to develop genuinely cross-sector approaches to opportunities and problems outside of crisis situations. Such frameworks will need to avoid overburdening an already overcrowded institutional structure. A cultural shift is also required to build trust between the institutions at different governance levels, with the aim of working together on achieving longer-term goals and priorities.

Recommendations

- National strategies should be based on real consultation with local and regional actors, producing a common organic programme with strong prioritisation. Local actors also need to be more involved in the design of strategies developed at the regional level.

- Measures must be taken to improve the skills levels of institutions within the public sector and among stakeholders involved in local partnerships and greater attention must be paid to skill levels when recruiting staff.

- New strategic governance mechanisms are required at the level of local labour markets to develop cross-sector and long-term approaches. Such a "connecting mechanism" should be supported by more effective information sharing, and a fair division of costs and benefits.

- A better analysis of labour market dynamics is needed, particularly at the local level. Labour market observatories should be significantly developed to meet these needs.

- Local strategy development needs to be improved. Appropriate actions must be selected and prioritised, and a planning framework is necessary to ensure all actions are integrated and joint ownership for outputs. Greater technical evaluation of strategies is required, with less reliance on the tendering process.

- Local stakeholders should take more responsibility for the results of strategies. This implies assigning targets to action plans, referring to final/ outcomes and moving away from process to impact. Care needs to be taken in defining actors' roles, selecting appropriate performance indicators and guaranteeing the technical capacity and impartiality of evaluators.

Note

1. This synopsis is based on the following country report: Fadda, S., "Integrating Employment, Skills and Economic Development in Italy", submitted 2008.

NEW ZEALAND[1]

National policy integration and co-ordination

The institutional landscape has changed quite considerably in New Zealand over recent decades. Between 1984 and 1994 the New Zealand government introduced a programme of wide-ranging reforms which transformed the economy by providing macroeconomic stability and a competitive market policy framework.

Institutional framework[2]

Figure 8.1. **New Zealand: Institutional map at national, regional and local levels**

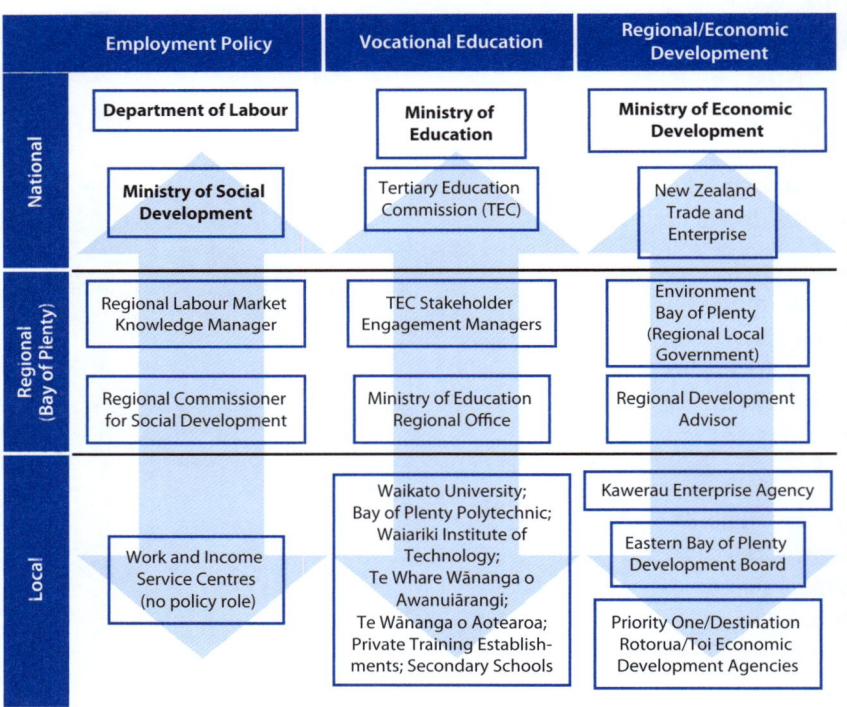

At the time little attention was paid to regional economic development as it was expected that national policies would benefit all regions and any focus by central government on one particular region would disadvantage others. This changed in 1999 following a general election, and policy focus shifted to developing partnerships between central government and regions for sustainable, locally driven, economic development. Since then this form of development has become much more centre stage in the implementation of policy.

Four ministries oversee the policy areas of economic development, vocational education and training (VET), and employment. The Ministry of Economic Development co-ordinates whole of government responses, working alongside New Zealand Trade and Enterprise. The Ministry of Education leads the overall direction of the education system, co-ordinating with the Tertiary Education Commission (TEC) – the national body responsible for tertiary education. The Ministry of Social Development provides employment and income assistance and its responsibilities have been extended in recent years. The Department of Labour is responsible for tasks such as advising government on employment policies, analysing labour market trends and evaluating the effectiveness of employment policies.

Integration and co-ordination

Co-ordination and policy integration between national ministries was found to be strong in New Zealand. The Department of Labour, Ministry of Social Development and TEC consulted weekly on policy priorities, strategies, programme design and delivery, and frequently collaborated with other stakeholders. Vertical integration between national and regional government was also well developed and was strengthened by significant national representation at the regional and local level and a multi-agency environment which drives initiatives to further integration. For example, under the heading of "sustainable cities" a three-year partnership was established in 2003 involving Auckland regional council, a number of government agencies and the region's local councils. It was recognised that the programme increased the capability of central and local government to work together in the Auckland region, with partners having built networks vital for cross-sector work. Building on this, four central agencies set up a shared policy office – Government Urban and Economic Development Office (GUEDO) – to act as a hub for information sharing and co-ordinate national-regional stakeholder involvement.

Close ministerial collaboration is in no small part a result of labour market conditions. From 2000 onwards significant skills shortages were experienced nationally and drove central government to strengthen joint working in order to come up with an integrated response (see Box 8.1). A Skills Action Plan, overseen by a committee of senior officials from nine central government agencies, was formed to speed up the matching of skills with job opportunities and keep people informed of education and training options.

Regular contact with employers was also evident; the Ministry of Social Development works closely with industry and training organisations to identify skills shortages and employers' needs and tailor training strategies accordingly. The Horticulture and Viticulture Seasonal Labour Strategy was an example of a whole-of-government response to significant labour shortages. An important industry in many regions which has long experienced severe shortages of skilled workers, a working group of ministerial representatives, industry groups and trade unions was set up alongside smaller working parties to devise an integrated response. The output document, Medium – Long-term Horticulture and Viticulture Seasonal Labour Strategy (2005), was viewed as having successfully provided a framework for developing sustainable seasonal labour.

Flexibility

The study found a high degree of flexibility available to policy makers at the local level in New Zealand. Figure 8.2 illustrates that the flexibility of economic development and employment policy in the case study region of the Bay of Plenty were rated very highly by both national and regional participants, receiving a scoring of "flexible" and greater; in both cases national participants perceived flexibility to be slightly higher than their local counterparts. Flexibility levels in the vocational training sector were perceived to be significantly lower.

Figure 8.2. **Local flexibility**

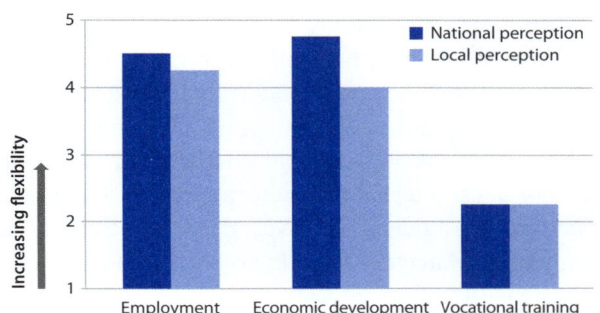

Figure 8.3 indicates mixed degrees of flexibility pertaining to management tools in the Bay of Plenty. Budgets were perceived to be the least flexible, and the scope for local stakeholders to influence programme design and performance management was "mixed". The legal framework received the maximum possible score of "very flexible", and indeed was the only country in this study to attain this. This result was borne out by the comments of interviewees; no serious legal barriers were identified by any players and, as one stakeholder noted, it was felt that it would not be too difficult for an agency's minister to amend any legislation that proved to be inhibiting.

Performance management and management by objectives were quite widely used; policy makers in each of the three policy areas generally reported back on the achievement of objectives set by the national and regional levels.

Figure 8.3. **Bay of Plenty: Flexibility of management tools**

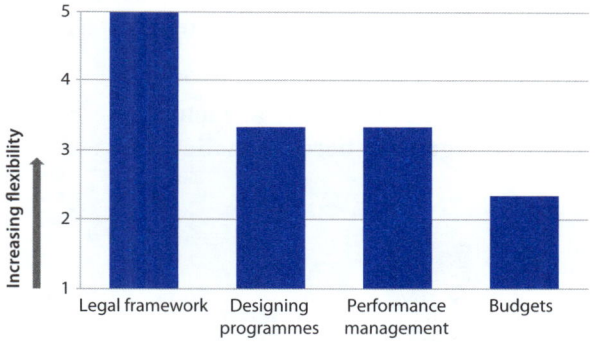

Different regional branches of central government agencies were found to enjoy different degrees of freedom. The Ministry of Social Development sets national targets as part of its Statement of Intent but allows regional commissioners considerable autonomy in determining how to work towards those targets and in allocating discretionary funds to spend on local issues. As a result of this flexibility, the regional commissioners have considerable influence and a strong leadership role at ground level.

In the area of regional development, New Zealand Trade and Enterprise were seen to have a great deal of discretion in encouraging local initiatives within national policy guidelines and refining proposals in consultation with regional economic development advisors. Although final funding decisions are made nationally as per set guidelines, in practice there was flexibility to design appropriate proposals that meet the required criteria.

In the field of education, the TEC makes its decisions at the national level meaning there is little regional flexibility. However, local tertiary education providers do have considerable autonomy in determining what courses and programmes they will offer in response to nationally determined funding.

Co-operation and policy integration at the regional and local level

New Zealand was found to have a high level of regional and local co-operation. Figure 8.4 shows the level of integration between policy areas in the Bay of Plenty. As can be seen, the lowest level of integration was found to occur between vocational training and regional development, rated between "weak" and "average". Employment and regional development were found to be slightly more integrated, while employment and vocational training were considered to be the most integrated, receiving a rating of "strong" – indeed, the highest integration score given to these two policy areas from all participating countries.

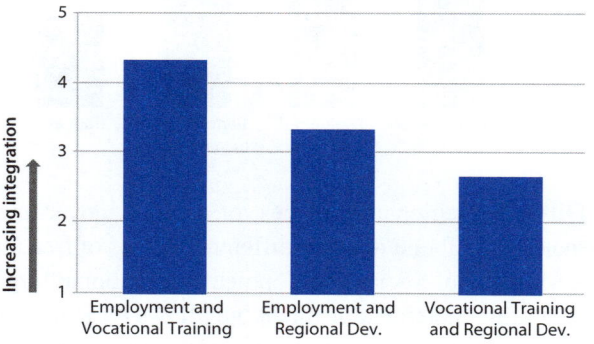

Figure 8.4. **Bay of Plenty: Integration between policy areas**

Figure 8.5 depicts the extent of engagement in co-operation at the local level – a combined factor based on the number of partners with which the organisation has ongoing active communication, the extent to which co-operation goes beyond formalities to involve substantive collaboration, participation in multi-stakeholder partnerships, and the extent of information sharing. Overall ratings were very high. Economic development and employment were considered to engage in the most local co-operation, both attaining the rating of just under "very strong". Vocational training was thought to engage in a slightly above average level of co-operation.

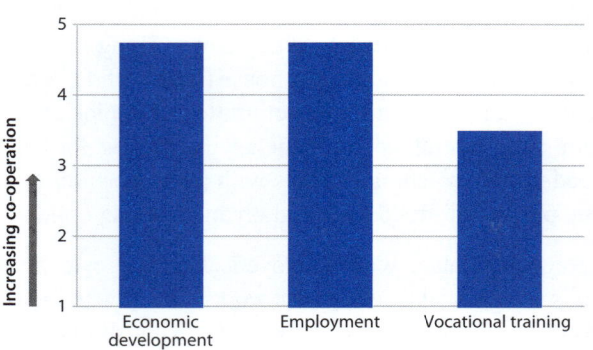

Figure 8.5. **Extent of engagement in cooperation at the local level**

A range of central and local government actors provide leadership in integrating the three policy fields at regional and local level, including economic development agencies, regional commissioners for social development and enterprising community advisors. Economic development agencies are responsible for leading the Regional Partnerships Programme (RPP), established in 2000 – drawing in part on research carried out by an OECD LEED programme – by the Ministry of Economic Development.

A three stage programme, RPPs part fund regional economic partnerships to devise regional economic development strategies, as well as drive capability building and major regional initiatives. Early progress results showed that the RPP was performing well against policy objectives and has led to improved local co-operation and trust, more collaborative approaches and a more strategic regional focus. The RPPs have since been consolidated to a smaller number of larger regions.

On the employment side, the regional commissioner for social development (under the Ministry of Social Development) is seen as playing a particularly important role in bringing local policy makers, colleges and companies together.

At the time of the study there was concern that the restructuring of the TEC and recentralisation of staff back to Wellington would undermine the local strategic approach to education and skills. While previously the TEC had a strong regional character in addressing skill shortages, internal restructuring resulted in 14 area offices being reduced to five. However, Stakeholder Engagement Managers have been put in place to communicate with tertiary education providers in the regions, and polytechnics have been given new responsibilities to take a strategic role at local level, galvanising partnerships and planning for the longer term. Such a role may be challenging as it will require that institutions think outside of their own institutional goals.

Despite the willingness to co-operate at the local level there was evidence of some duplication of processes and actions between policy makers. Each policy area was found to run a separate strategic planning process in the regions, each with its own timescales, creating confusion, "contested claims" for leadership, partnership fatigue and decreasing engagement by business representatives. Following this study, one mechanism identified to resolve this issue was the alignment of central government agencies' annual Statements of Intent.

Another concern was the difficulty in engaging with a disparate private sector – for example, a number of regional stakeholders in the Bay of Plenty commented that they did not have the capacity to deal with the large numbers of SMEs on their databases.

Capacities

Capacities were seen to be lacking in New Zealand. As illustrated in Figure 8.6, local actors considered the average resource and skills capacity of organisations in the Bay of Plenty region to be "average" in all three policy sectors, with the exception of resource capacities in employment which was more poorly rated as "weak".

Figure 8.6. **Bay of Plenty: Average capacity of organisations**

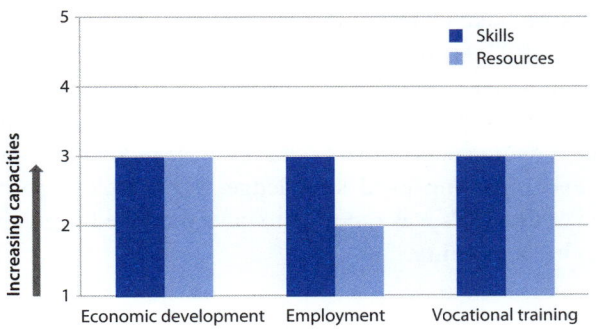

Box 8.1. **Case study region: Bay of Plenty**

STRENGTHS AND CHALLENGES

STRENGTHS	CHALLENGES
• Declining unemployment rate and no longer well above national average; • Significant ethnically diverse population; • Strong forestry and horticulture sectors; • Wide range of public and private tertiary education providers.	• Highest national unemployment rates experienced in Eastern Bay of Plenty districts; • Higher unemployment rates among some ethnic groups; • Eastern Bay of Plenty region identified as having acute needs.

OPPORTUNITIES	THREATS
• Service sector potential to deliver large gains; • Linkages between industry, public agencies and education institutions; • Distinct regional identities and visions; • Merging of 3 regions to create a more viable critical mass.	• Growing skills shortages, particularly in horticulture sector; • Significant intra-regional disparities; • Parochialism and a "silo mentality" between the three regions.

Addressing skills shortages: partnership led approaches

The Bay of Plenty is on the east coast of New Zealand's North Island and has a population of 269 800 (2008). It comprises seven city/district councils and three regions as outlined by the RPP, each with its own economic development agency (EDA): Western Bay of Plenty – Priority One EDA; Rotorua – Destination Rotorua EDA; and, Eastern Bay of Plenty – Toi EDA. Each region is very distinct and this is reflected in the unique visions put forward in their strategic economic development plans. While such diversity ensures that each region retains its unique identity, it has also encouraged parochialism and a "silo mentality". There are almost twice as many Māori in the region as the national average and their unemployment rates were about three times as high as the European population (2006).

The Bay of Plenty's regional EDAs have developed a number of initiatives addressing the endemic skills shortages experienced nationally since 2000. Priority One launched the innovative INSTEP programme which aims to strengthen business – secondary school links. It created a database of over 9 000 businesses available to participating schools and initiated projects to help raise the profile of local industry opportunities among secondary school students and teachers.

For example, each year INSTEP organises the "Principals' Big Day Out" in which school principles are partnered with businesses to showcase local industries experiencing skills shortages.

A further example of a partnership led approach to skills shortages is the Rotura Employment Skills Project. Commissioned in 2002 by the Waiariki Institute of Technology, Work and Income, the TEC and Destination Rotura to identify employment skills gaps, a reference group was convened from local education organisations and key industry sectors to guide the project. Approximately 1 400 local employers were surveyed and nine main industry sector group workshops were held, with each sector group meeting twice to develop key action points. These were merged by the steering group to create the Rotorua Employment Skills Strategy (2003), which served as the basis for joint work between national and regional decision makers to develop a range of new training opportunities designed to address immediate sector specific skills shortages.

However, it was recognised in the region that work on better aligning education and training with industrial need was mainly focused on "plugging the gap" in meeting short-term skills shortages, rather than focusing on longer-term economic development. Such firefighting also ran the risk of preventing necessary restructuring and investment in further productivity which could undermine future living standards. At the same time more complex issues, such as the labour market exclusion of the Maori, were not being adequately addressed.

Resources

The most often cited barrier to effective working was "financial constraints". As noted by one participant, the ability to commit financial resources was seen as key to effective participation in regional partnership. Regional commissioners and regional economic development advisors were in a position to provide strong leadership as they had autonomy over local funding or could access national funding sources, with considerable flexibility to adapt this to regional needs. There was some unease that certain projects might be thought to be "double-funded", meaning they are not necessarily cohesive, unified governmental responses.

In addition, inadequate labour market analysis was a common theme at the national and regional level. Four different agencies (New Zealand Trade and Enterprise, the Department of Labour, the Ministry of Social Development and the TEC) were found to produce disparate analysis for their own purposes rather than combining resources for a more sophisticated level of analysis. Analytical and strategic capacities at the local/regional level were seen as weak and most analysis was done in Wellington, as a result of which much was too aggregated to be of use to local stakeholders, and there was little regional ownership of it. It was felt that there was a need for labour market research and information which is credible and reliable, disaggregated to at least city/district council level and informed by a regional long-term economic development strategic plan. Stakeholders argued that this must be in a form all agencies could use and with an emphasis on "an authentic blend of wide-ranging local knowledge with robust statistical analysis" (Dalziel, submitted).

At the time of the study, 16 regional Labour Market Knowledge Managers were in place to help gather and distribute relevant information, but the posts had limited budgetary power and have since been discontinued. The Department of Labour has more recently developed a series of analytical tool sets customised to regional needs which may go some way towards addressing the labour market information issue.

Skills

Some concerns were raised regarding local skills to implement longer-term local strategies. It was suggested by some stakeholders at the national level that in the first round of RPPs not all strategies were of the same quality and in some cases it was apparent that strategies were produced to meet funding criteria rather than arising from genuine engagement with regional industry leaders or encompassing local knowledge. Nevertheless, round two of the RPPs was reported to have produced strategies of a higher quality.

Conclusions

Figure 8.7. **Attention Areas**

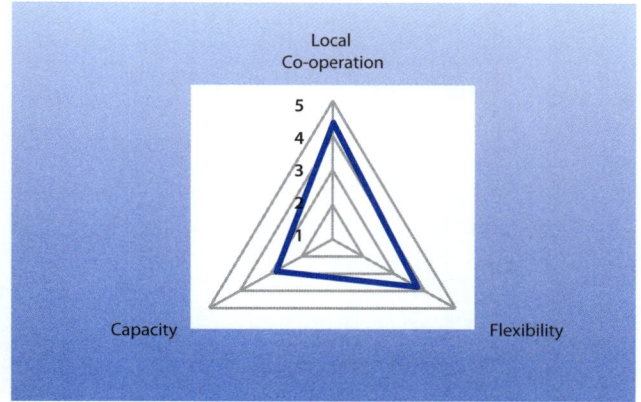

In New Zealand a high degree of local co-operation and flexibility was found to be available, allowing regional players to adapt national policy to regional and local needs. However, capacities were considered to be at a lower level. As seen in Figure 8.7, from a maximum score of 5.0 the combined responses at local, state (where applicable) and national level returned 4.3 for local co-operation, 3.7 for flexibility and 2.8 for capacity. The main concerns highlighted in relation to capacities were a lack of financial resources and inadequate data at ground level. Thus, while local officials enjoyed significant degree of flexibility and co-operation, the lack of critical resources to back this flexibility up with concrete actions was undermining the potential for further integration.

Emerging skills shortages in the last decade have boosted national and regional efforts to integrate skills and vocational training policies with labour market policies and the general view is that these have been successful. However, there are concerns that the results may not be well integrated with longer-term regional economic development strategies. There is a need to proceed cautiously when aligning vocational training and employment policy strategies and avoid the risk of short-termism. Longer-term local policies are needed that also prioritise skills upgrading in enterprises, and improvements to productivity and skills utilisation.

Recommendations

- National policy frameworks should be better aligned and policy goals in the various areas should incorporate a regional/local dimension. Further consideration needs to be given to how national and regional targets can be brought together to set these goals and use partnership processes. This would also provide the opportunity to clarify roles and responsibilities of central and local government along with other stakeholders.

- A co-ordinating mechanism is needed for identifying areas of overlap and complementarity between ministries and improving policy integration. The Statements of Intent produced by central government agencies should be aligned as one mechanism for resolving/integrating contested claims for leadership in this multi-agency environment.

- A wide range of central government and other agencies require reliable disaggregated analyses of regional labour markets to develop and deliver effective regional policies. A multi-agency senior officials working group should be created to consider how resources could be pooled to produce more sophisticated regional labour market analyses.

- Strategic capacities should be enhanced, notably through training and budget provision.

- Policymakers should note the concerns that current skills and VET policies at regional level tend to be driven by existing labour market shortages without necessarily being integrated with regional economic development strategies. Specific guidelines should be developed for TEC Stakeholder Engagement Managers to require high level statements of regional tertiary education needs, gaps and priorities to take into account relevant economic development strategies.

- Many regional initiatives are moving to three year plans which may conflict with the annual work plans typically required of central government regional officers. Consideration should be given to moving towards three-year work plans, perhaps supplemented with annual milestones.

Notes

1. This synopsis is based on the following country report: Dalziel, P., "Integrating Employment, Skills, and Economic Development in New Zealand", submitted 2007.

2. This was the institutional landscape at the time of the study. Since then Regional Labour Market Knowledge managers, Stakeholder Engagement Managers and Regional Development Advisors have been disestablished.

POLAND[1]

National policy integration and co-ordination

Institutional framework

Figure 9.1. Poland: Institutional map at national, regional, sub-regional and local levels

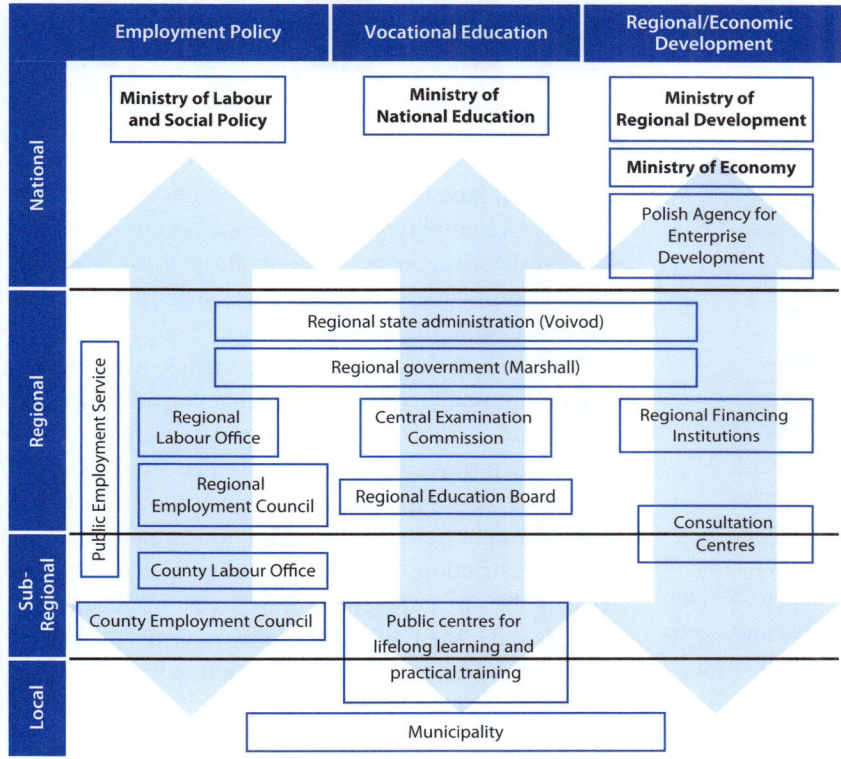

A series of reforms introduced in the 1990s decentralised responsibility for policy design and implementation in Poland and created a relatively unique institutional framework; the country was divided into 16 administrative regions, each equipped with regional government, and 380 counties. As a result national level influence was limited and regional and local autonomy was strengthened.

The Ministry of Labour and Social Policy co-ordinates labour market policy, structuring the activities of the public employment service and developing an annual National Plan of Activities in Support of Employment. Most responsibility, however, has been devolved to regional, sub-regional and local levels. Regional governments base their annual plans on the national plan and provide guidance for the public employment service at the local level, where most projects are designed and implemented according to local requirements. Similarly, vocational education and training (VET) is mainly managed at the regional and sub-regional level. The Ministry of National Education has responsibility for developing targets, programme requirements and allocating resources but its role in implementing policy is limited; budget allocation is its only real means of influence and is employed as a management tool. The Ministry of Regional Development directs regional development policy. Two strategic documents define the general priorities to which the activities of particular ministries are subordinated in this field – the National Development Strategy 2007 – 2013 and the National Programme of Reforms in Support of the Lisbon Strategy, which focuses on actions to retain economic growth and stimulate new job creation.

Integration and co-ordination

The study found a low level of horizontal integration and co-ordination at the national level, partly as a result of the devolution of powers. Ministries were not seen to sufficiently monitor how national policy was applied locally, and co-ordination between the three ministries governing employment, education and regional development appeared largely short-term and operational, with an emphasis on procedural matters rather than active policy discussion. Negotiations on European regional operational programmes (ROPs) had increased communication between the ministries and it was hoped that this would lead to further cross-ministerial collaboration. Participation, however, in the negotiations was obligatory and all the ministries did not feel that they were necessarily equal partners in the collaboration process.

Flexibility

Poland's decentralised governance system has granted a high degree of flexibility to regional and local players. As evident in Figure 9.2, national stakeholders considered vocational training to be "very flexible", followed by economic development, and employment policy was regarded as the least flexible. Regional participants rated economic development as the most flexible, followed by vocational training and employment. National stakeholders perceived flexibility to be at a higher level in each policy area than their regional counterparts.

Figure 9.2. **Local flexibility**

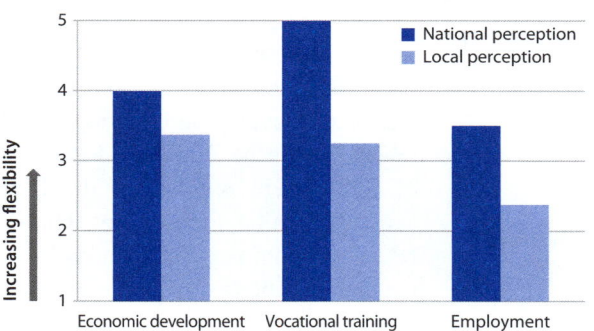

The general framework of labour market policy is set at central level, but regional and local units are able to develop their own policies according to local conditions and needs and the vast majority of instruments are implemented at the local level by county labour offices. County labour offices enjoy a large degree of flexibility and the heads of local labour offices are influential figures due to their knowledge and experience of labour markets. The heads are elected locally but they receive funding directly from national government rather than the county budget which ensures them a strong and autonomous position locally, and budgets do not have to be spent according to specific budget lines.

As shown in Figure 9.3 all management tools received an "average" rating. "Management by objectives" appears to function relatively weakly, with minimal vertical performance reporting. Local labour offices provide indicators to regional administration but this varies between regions and a standardised approach to data collection and evaluation was found to be lacking at the national level. Employment agencies were governed by local boards which were made up of employers and other stakeholders, and this had allowed a certain degree of relaxation in relation to vertical performance targets.

Figure 9.3. **Krakow: Flexibility of management tools**

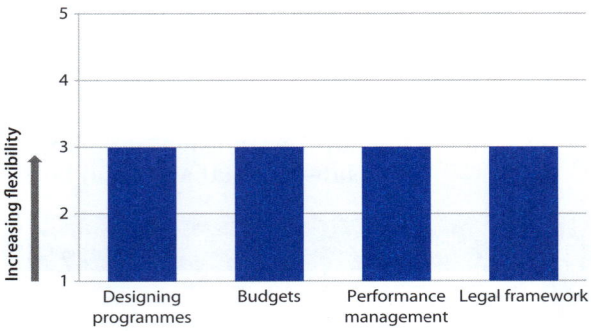

However, labour market legislation governing eligibility for active employment schemes was considered to be overly restrictive. At the time of study, those who could avail of employment schemes were strictly defined and people not belonging to the six target groups (*e.g.* elderly, disabled, youth, those in employment) were seen as almost impossible to assist.[2] Many consider that such an approach made it difficult to take preventative measures, or help those at a greater distance from the labour market. At the same time the reliance of local authorities on government transfers for funding was also felt to represent a restriction on their flexibility. Local authorities were unable to supplement resources with additional funds, leaving them little autonomy in terms of spending resources and acting as a break to policy integration.

Co-operation and policy integration at the regional and local level

At the regional and local level the institutional landscape was found to be complex and not conducive to co-ordination, particularly as different governance levels were responsible for different policy fields. This is partly as an outcome of the governance structure at the regional level in which two administrations operate; the elected regional council and its administration (the Marshall office), and central government representation (the *Voivoid*). The Marshall office is responsible for regional economic and social matters and its influence appeared to be growing; the *Voivod's* role is to ensure the delivery of national policies and is mainly limited to constitutional arrangements. Within each region there are counties (*Powiats*), with 22 counties existing in the case study region of Malopolskie (see Box 9.1 below).

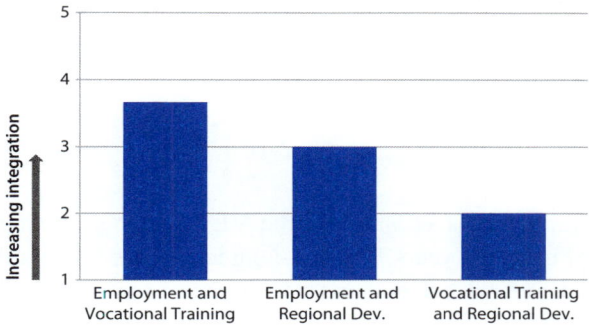

Figure 9.4. **Krakow: Integration between policy areas**

Figure 9.4 illustrates mixed levels of integration between policy areas in the case study region of Krakow. Vocational training and regional development policy areas were considered to be the least integrated by local stakeholders, followed by employment and regional development. Integration levels between employment and vocational training received the highest rating of slightly less than "strong".

Regional government defines the strategic development of a region, decides on budget and resource allocation and develops a Regional Plan of Activities in Support of Employment and labour market programmes. Most tasks related to employment promotion are performed at county level and municipalities are responsible for increasing educational levels and providing social assistance.

Economic development is mainly managed by *voivodships* and local authorities. Labour market policy is strongest at sub-regional level, managed primarily by local labour offices and county employment councils, which work closely with local businesses and schools to adjust training programmes to employer needs and subsidise job creation.

County employment councils review employment projects, suggest modifications and work towards achieving full county employment, introduced by national government to increase policy integration. The councils generally meet every three months and are made up of representatives from a variety of public and private sectors but their effectiveness varies widely depending on the county they are operating in, the quality of leadership and the political strength of the more powerful labour office. At the time of the study they were seen to function mainly as "rubber stamping" bodies for decisions taken by the local labour

offices and there was a lack of ownership and vision regarding their potential role, stemming partly from the fact that they were implemented from above rather than emerging organically "bottom up".

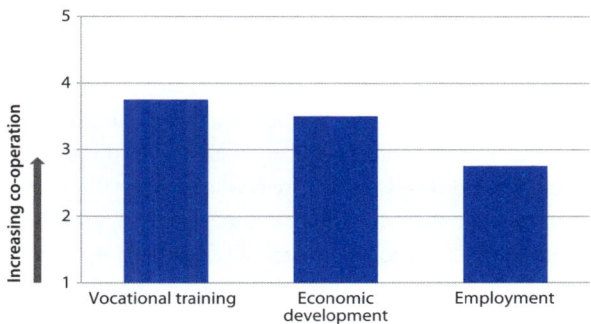

Figure 9.5. **Extent of engagement in cooperation at the local level**

Education policy is also a county level competence and in this field the regional level is restricted mainly to advisory activities and educational promotion. The Malopolskie Council of Education was set up in 2005 as forum for exchanging ideas and to develop ways to enhance the region's educational system, for example (see Box 9.1). Co-operation was found to be limited between education institutions and business interests in the case study region: the private sector was enthusiastic to work with labour offices in creating subsidised work places (and thereby lowering their own costs) but was less willing to work with schools directly and engage in apprenticeship training. There was also weak collaboration between employment and social policy and a lack of vision on how to align these policies more closely.

In addition, social policy was seen as doing little to bring people with low employability back into the labour market and break dependency on social assistance, partly because employment was managed sub-regionally while social assistance was a local level competency. Co-operation between county and municipal level administration was generally weak and there was little interaction with the NGO (non-governmental) sector.

Local collaboration in Poland is further hampered by competition between local authorities with rural counties, which were likely to have fewer resources than their urban counterparts. Nevertheless, policy integration has increased in recent years and the greatest degree of joint working is between education and employment policy which are subordinated to the same administration. It was also common for labour offices, the local employment council and school headmasters to co-ordinate directly with each other.

Capacities

Weak capacities were found to be an issue at the local level. As shown in Figure 9.6, the skills and resource levels in organisations in Krakow were considered to be "average" in each policy area. While local policy makers were felt to know their fields relatively well and had learned the "trade" of local development by trial and error, they tended to turn to national level for guidance and did not take full advantage of the freedoms available to them in what is a highly decentralised system. Building capacity therefore needed to include empowering people to take on more responsibility and an increased tolerance for risk-taking. National capacities were also felt to be lacking, in particular due to the politicised nature of the state administration.

Resources

Funding levels were felt to be low across the board. For example, the public employment service was found to be poorly funded compared to the European average and is struggling in terms of the quantity of human resources and quality: there was also little outsourcing of training and labour market services.

Figure 9.6. **Krakow:** Average capacity of organisations

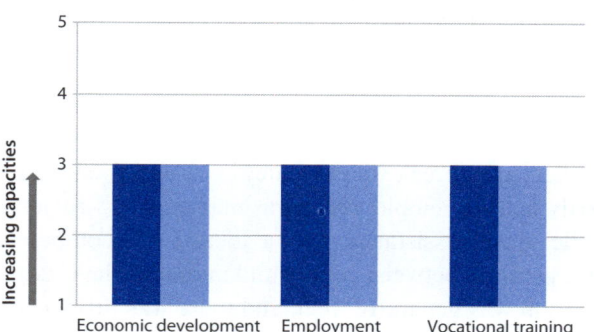

Another important issue was the absence of useful data at the local and regional level. Data originating from the national statistics agency was found to be overly aggregated and lagged and there was no standardised approach for data collection. While new projects to create more accurate data have been outlined as part of European

funded projects, as of yet there is no concerted effort to ensure that they feed into local strategies. It was also found that there was little in the way of monitoring and evaluation of the impact of policy interventions on the labour market and lessons learnt were rarely fed back into the local strategic planning system.

Skills

Capacity issues have hit the VET sector particularly hard in recent years. The life-long learning system is felt to be under-developed and slow to meet local needs, with few mechanisms to respond to the demand side of the economy. This is, in part, a result of restructuring: during the 1990s many vocational schools closed and private schools biased towards "low cost" fields of education such as finance and teaching became more widespread, resulting in an oversupply of these skills. By the late 1990s Poland's vocational sector was seen to have all but collapsed. Investment in VET has continued to decline and some local governments are reluctant to provide more support to this sector, preferring to shift support towards academic education. This has created a serious shortage of skilled workers, compounded by emigration.

Box 9.1. **Case study region: Malopolskie**

STRENGTHS AND CHALLENGES	
STRENGTHS	**CHALLENGES**
• Strong labour market and high job creation rate; • High agricultural employment; • Kraków and popularity as tourist destination; • Above average educational attainment.	• Prevalence of subsistence agriculture; • Below national average level of life-long learning; • Weak institutional structures; • High number of long-term unemployed.
OPPORTUNITIES	**THREATS**
• Leading region in terms of human capital potential; • Growing labour force; • Establishment of council of education to further collaboration; • Improved collection and sharing of data.	• Declining vocational education sector; • Prevalence of "hidden unemployment" in agriculture; • Growing inter-regional disparities.

The Malopolskie Region is located in South Poland. The region went into decline immediately following the post-socialist transformation and has a per capita regional income which is lower than the national average. However, from 1995 to 2004 the region had the third highest growth rate in Poland, mainly due to the increasing metropolitan functions of Kraków.

The region has strong employment in agriculture and relatively low unemployment rates. However, there is significant "hidden unemployment", as farmers are registered as economically active, regardless of the hours they are able to work.

In 2006 the Regional Observatory of the Labour Market and Education was established with the aim of providing reliable regional labour market information to enable regional development planning. Its goals include collecting and sharing information on regional labour markets and providing this to all institutions operating at the regional level.

The regional administration is obliged to develop an annual Regional Plan of Activities in Support of Employment (RPASE), linked to a national plan in support of employment and the regional strategic development plan.

The 2007 RPASE plan focused on the following key priorities:

- Increase in the adaptability of the labour force;

- Professional reorientation of employees in declining sectors;

- Improving skills and competencies of the unemployed;

- Equal chances and reintegration of excluded from the labour market;

- Improving regional conditions for business activity;

- New jobs creation through investment;

- Improving competitiveness and innovativeness;

- Developing institutional potential, and;

- Improving education opportunities in relation to the labour market

A number of regional institutions are engaged in delivering the plan including regional government (the departments of regional and spatial policy, the structural funds, economics and infrastructure, and education and sport), regional centres for social policy, regional development and voluntary work and the county and regional labour offices.

The regional population (3, 283, 100 in 2008) is slightly better educated than the national average; a larger share of the population hold a university degree and more people attend basic vocational schools. However, in keeping with national trends, the number of those attending vocational schools has dropped significantly in recent years and more are attending general secondary schools.

A key challenge is ensuring that the children of the long-term unemployed living in poverty in the region have equal educational chances. In order to help tackle this, the regional government has established a Programme for Promotion of Gifted Youth aimed at rewarding outstanding school achievements and providing assistance to students from disadvantaged families.

Conclusions

Figure 9.7. **Attention Areas**

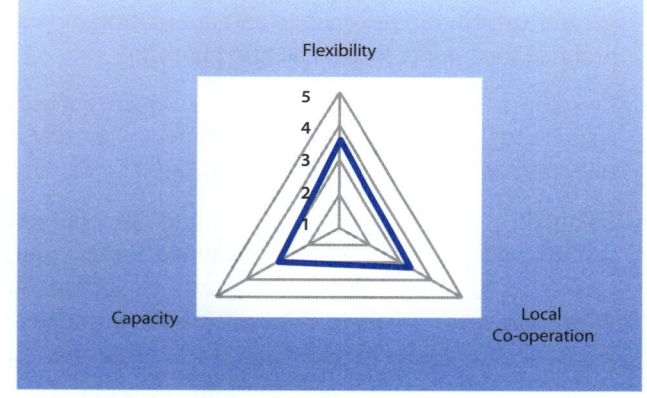

As seen in Figure 9.7, from a maximum score of 5.0 the combined responses at local, state (where applicable) and national level returned 3.3 for local co-operation, 3.6 for flexibility and 3.0 for capacity.

The level of flexibility within the employment, training and economic development systems was found to be strong in what is relatively decentralised system; however this was not matched by sufficient local capacities or local co-operation. As a result the employment services and education system are failing to deliver the human resources required by the private sector.

There is clearly a need to better exploit the flexibility available to local level actors to develop targeted and holistic local development strategies. More effective collaboration is required with the private sector in relation to skills upgrading, apprenticeships and vocational training.

Local actors could also more effectively use local information and data, and put in place more robust mechanisms for monitoring and evaluation. Local accountability structures need to be made more robust, with mutual accountability for the achievement of local strategic goals. Human resource development also needs to be further co-ordinated and tied in with local economic development strategies, requiring better co-ordination across the different governance levels.

Recommendations

- Create incentives for the local/sub-regional/regional government levels to better co-ordinate and integrate policies locally.

- Build capacity at all levels of government to generate relevant data and expertise, introduce standardised monitoring of labour market policies, and provide greater information exchange and circulation of best practice to support local strategic planning.

- Develop a local governance culture which encourages mutual accountability accompanied by a greater tolerance for innovation and risk taking.

- Establish sub-regional strategic plans for human resource development with implications for training, labour market policy and social assistance and linked with long-term economic development strategies. These should be based on locally owned information and data, with the involvement of business and trade unions.

- Create stronger links with major local employers and vocational schools.

- Provide local employment offices with more autonomy in defining target groups and conditions for providing assistance within local employment policy. In particular, policy instruments must be addressed not only to the unemployed but to high risk groups.

- Expand the remit of employment councils to allow them to take a holistic medium-term strategic approach, and/or encourage their replacement with "bottom up" sub-regional platforms where necessary.

Notes

1. This synopsis is based on the following country report: Gorzelak, G. and M. Herbst, "Integrating Employment, Skills and Economic Development in Poland", submitted 2007.

2. Following the global economic downturn, greater flexibility has been awarded to local labour offices in this area to tackle harder to reach groups.

PORTUGAL [1]

National policy integration and co-ordination

Institutional framework

Figure 10.1. **Portugal: Institutional map at national, regional and local levels**

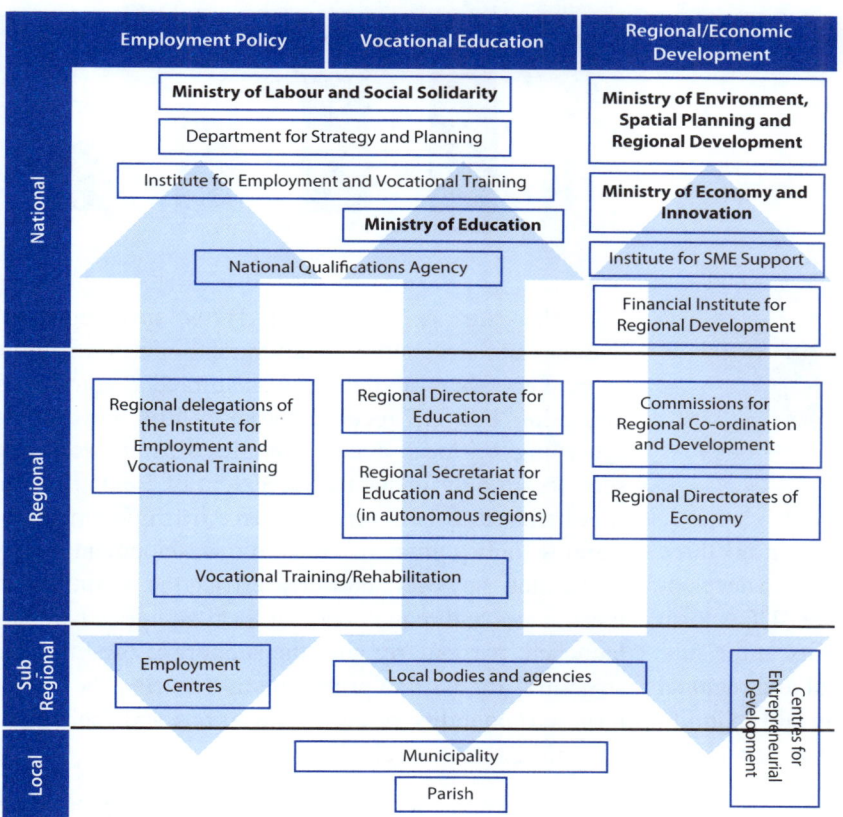

Portugal maintains a centralised governance structure. Despite the country being divided into five regions on the mainland and two autonomous island regions, the mainland regions were created for administrative processes only and do not have an elected body or local government status. The regions are used mainly for planning purposes in the context of European Structural funds and are managed by Commissions for Regional Co-operation and Development (CCDR).

There are, however, 308 municipalities in Portugal and with an average of 34,000 inhabitants they rank among the largest in Europe. The municipalities have long been the central governance unit at the sub-national level and people are more likely to identify with their local municipality or parish rather than with their wider region.

Portugal has recently being undergoing extensive institutional and economic reform, with an increasing policy focus on shifting the country towards a knowledge-based economy. At the same time there has been an effort to modernise the government, with 2006 seeing the introduction of the PRACE programme (*Programa de Reestruturação da Administração Central do Estado*) with the aim to improve efficiency and the quality of public services. PRACE envisages a redefinition of the role of state administration at the regional level and an increased proximity to citizens through decentralisation processes, balanced by a simultaneous emphasis on targets, organisational rationalisation and a search for efficiency.

Integration and co-ordination

Co-ordination between different policy areas at the national level has increased in recent years. The Portuguese National Sustainable Development Strategy (to 2015) is acting to bring together a number of different policy domains behind a single common framework. Four common issues – "qualification and skills", "competitiveness and innovation", "territorial approach to growth and innovation" and "modernising public administration" – have been identified and incorporated within diverse sectoral strategies, providing the overall strategic framework for European funding. The implementation of the Strategy requires intense cross-sectoral co-ordination among the different policy fields and its close connection with other national frameworks and plans has led to the creation of a dedicated co-ordination cabinet which reports directly to the Prime Minister. This cabinet is a high-level political entity, created with the aim of increasing coherence and avoiding duplication.

Co-ordination has also been increasing between employment and vocational training policy. The Ministry of Labour and Social Solidarity and the Ministry of Education meet frequently and have introduced joint actions such as the New Opportunities Initiative, first launched in September 2005 and which seeks to raise skills levels within the Portuguese population. A National Qualifications Agency, answerable to both the Ministry of Labour and Social Solidarity and the Ministry of Education, has also been created.

Flexibility

Figure 10.2. **Local flexibility**

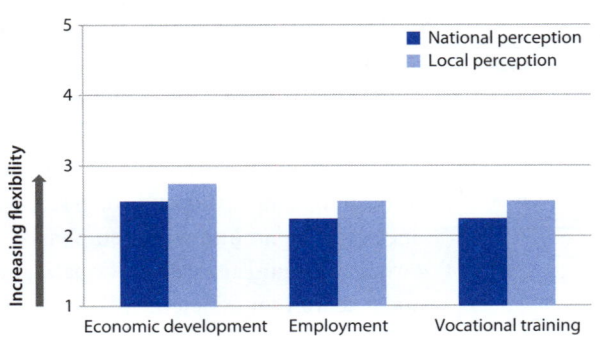

The study identified a lack of flexibility in all three policy areas of employment, skills and economic development in Portugal, with concerns that the PRACE reform did not appear to be strengthening flexibility at the sub-national level. Figure 10.2 outlines national and regional stakeholders' perception of the degree of local flexibility available. It can be seen that flexibility was considered to be low in all three policy areas by both administrative levels, with all rated slightly above "inflexible".

In all cases local agencies perceived flexibility to be higher than was thought by national policy makers. However it was widely accepted that local and regional stakeholders are given limited space to manoeuvre. Although local bodies were consulted when policies, programmes and services are developed, there was little real participation when it came to shaping policy. Regional and local players were unlikely to be able to influence the mechanisms used for performance management and accountability and they also had to respect budgetary frameworks decided centrally.

Figure 10.3 indicates how flexible management tools were considered to be in the case study region of the Algarve. The legal framework and budgets both received

an "average" rating, designing budgets was scored slightly above "inflexible", and performance management received the lowest rating of "inflexible".

Figure 10.3. **Algarve: Flexibility of management tools**

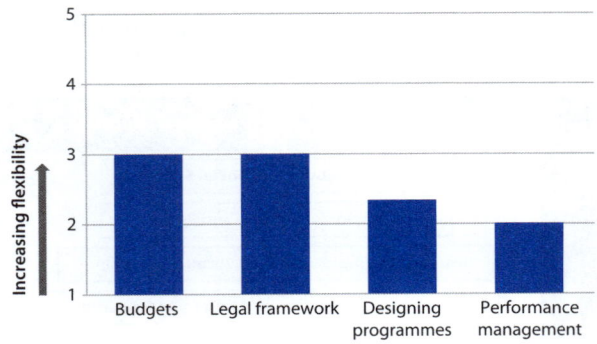

In the Algarve (see Box 10.1) the involvement of regional and local actors in designing policies was found to be very weak and there was limited possibility of allocating budgets received from central government according to local needs. The legal framework was seen to strongly influence the extent of flexibility, and was believed to be more restrictive in employment and training policy than in economic development policy. It did not, however, entirely restrict the initiatives of local actors and many concrete local activities had been launched, particularly with the support of the European structural funds. The problem was ensuring the longer-term sustainability of such innovations and their main-streaming into normal policy.

Municipalities were perceived to have a higher degree of influence and flexibility, being the only body to have decentralised competences at the regional and local level. Designing and implementing a regional development strategy was found to depend hugely on the pro-active-ness and support of municipal policymakers in Portugal, who were key catalysts in generating co-operation, policy integration and synergy among policy areas. The mayor and elected members were found to play a central role in decision making and could go beyond conventional areas such as infrastructure investment to promote broader domains such as economic development, entrepreneurship.

Overall the timescales of delivery, priorities and targets of programmes are strictly formulated by the central bodies and there are few opportunities to alter them to closer align with local needs. While the heads of local labour offices were appointed locally, this seemed to have had a limited effect on encouraging local autonomy or flexibility. Stakeholders have highlighted the need for greater involvement in defining targets, particularly for employment and vocational training policy, which would lead to more relevant and co-ordinated policies. Local actors also stated that greater flexibility in management tools would lead to more creative partnership working with other institutions. There are signs, however, that local agencies are being given more freedom to use more initiative and negotiate their own outcomes; targets for employment policy, for example, are now negotiated with local employment offices.

Co-operation and policy integration at the regional and local level

Policy integration at the local level in Portugal appears to be highly influenced by the degree of integration at the national level. While employment and vocational training policies were considered strongly integrated in the Algarve, the integration between employment and regional development, and vocational training and regional development was identified to be weak.

Figure 10.4. **Algarve: Integration between policy areas**

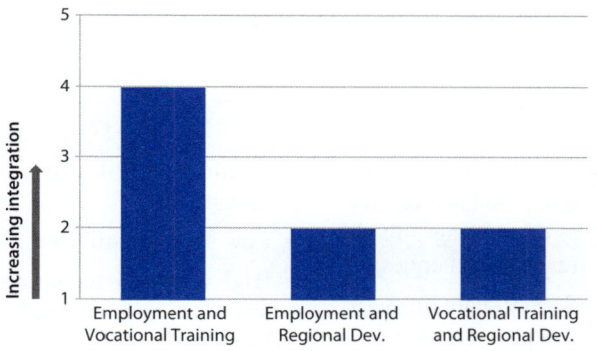

However, economic development actors were found to be the most active collaborators at the local level. They were more likely to participate in multi-stakeholder partnerships and substantive collaboration and to share information in the Algarve (see Figure 10.5). Employment and vocational training actors were found to engage considerably less.

Figure 10.5. **Extent of engagement in cooperation at the local level**

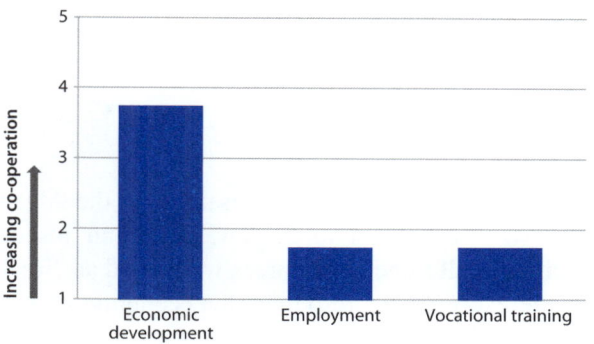

The study found that a strong sub-regional platform to encourage multi-stakeholder partnership did not appear to exist in Portugal. Regional horizontal co-ordination was facilitated by cross-sectoral co-ordination councils which brought together different ministry branches, as organised by the CCDRs, but this could nevertheless be a difficult process to co-ordinate. The various ministries did not have equivalent competences and decision making autonomy varied at the regional level. This made it difficult to develop strong action plans or a consistent vision.

Geographical and administrative boundaries were also found to pose a strong challenge to co-operation locally. However, municipalities had recently been allowed within the law to create municipal associations at different governance levels and for different purposes, thereby increasing their flexibility.

The search for an appropriate scale to harmonise the deconcentrated bodies of the central government was a key feature focus of the PRACE reform. However, it remained unclear whether the changes orchestrated through PRACE would improve local or sub-regional policy co-ordination. Interviewees expressed the opinion that the ongoing reform risked reinforcing sectoral priorities. They also pointed to a re-centralisation of the decision making process for European programming in Portugal, which was not seen as conducive to encouraging greater collaboration at the local level.

In the absence of more formal mechanisms for vertical and horizontal co-operation, there was a strong reliance on personal relationships and lobbying to develop local initiatives. While this was useful in getting individual projects funded it was more difficult to ensure that such innovations led to institutional learning. European programmes, such as LEADER, for example, had encouraged many local development initiatives (including 17 development partnerships in the Algarve alone) but there had been little opportunity to mainstream the learning of these programmes.

Capacities

The average capacity of organisations in the Algarve region was considered to be low. Skill and resource capacities in all three policy areas were rated as "weak", with the exception of resources for economic development which achieved an "average" scoring.

Figure 10.6. **Algarve:**
Average capacity of organisations

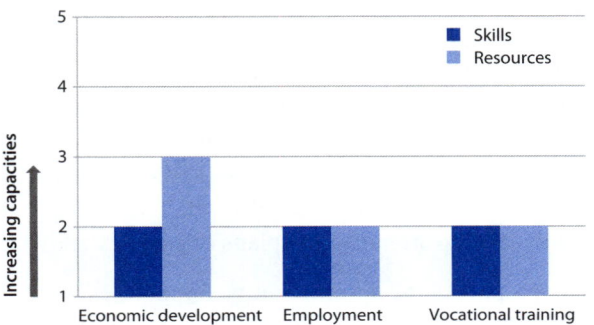

Resources

Local development agencies were one example of a potentially "integrative" local institution that had been undermined by resourcing issues. Local development agencies exist across Portugal, strongly stimulated by European experimental programmes such as LEADER which set up "local action groups" in the early 1990s. Where local development agencies and municipalities worked together in the Algarve, the impact could be strong. However local development agencies were generally low level and, despite their cross-cutting focus, had limited capacities to deliver initiatives outside of local municipal boundaries. Because of their limited funds they often performed an operational role rather than a strategic one and ended up focusing on keeping their own organisation afloat through access to European grants and programmes.

Skills

Despite the obstacles to co-operative working, local regional and sub-regional actors did appear to have the skills necessary to develop effective strategies. In the Algarve local organisations mentioned the lack of a formal global regional strategy with which they could identify, but put a strong value on the quality of planning documents prepared by the CCDR Algarve. These offered a coherent framework within which to situate regional challenges and provide clear criteria for priorities to be managed as part of the European Algarve Operational Programme. Despite this, the education and training system was not seen as fully effective in providing the specific and generic skills required for partnership working and designing local development strategies, such as visioning and team working.

Box 10.1. **Case study region: Algarve**

STRENGTHS AND CHALLENGES	
STRENGTHS	CHALLENGES
• The fastest growing region in Portugal; • Unemployment rate below national average; • Transformation from under-developed region to one of the most developed; • Portugal's main tourist region.	• Poor quality urban environment; • Environmental protection problems; • Seasonal labour demand and short-term employment contracts; • Prevalence of small-scale firms which are less open to innovation.
OPPORTUNITIES	THREATS
• Growing product specialisation in areas such as tourism, agro-food & renewable energies; • Supply chain linkages from current industries to potential growth sectors.	• Declining traditional industries; • Low skills equilibrium; • High unemployment rate among immigrants and low employment rate amongst women.

The Algarve region, a tourist destination in the South West of Portugal, is made up of 16 municipalities and has 428 200 inhabitants (2008). The economic activity of the region is reliant on three key sectors; tourism, the building industry and commercial activities. Despite recent economic growth, this has created a labour market based primarily around low skilled employment. Workers commonly experience seasonal unemployment and short-term contracts.

In recent years the region has sought to tackle this issue and reinforce its competitiveness by specialising in potential growth sectors such as niche tourism, environmental protection and renewable energies. The CCDR Algarve has played a central role in developing regional strategies such as the Regional Development Strategy 2007-13 and the Regional Spatial Plan, to create a coherent vision for the region aligned with European and national strategies.

A strong focus of these strategies is the need to boost innovation and upskill local people to compete within the knowledge economy. Stakeholders agreed that these interventions are based on a shared and comprehensive understanding of the key problems facing the Algarve, thereby increasing their value. However, they were seen to offer little guidance on management and implementation. This, and the limited flexibility available to local actors, undermined putting them into practice.

At the same time there was a concern that innovative and valuable local initiatives (such as those funded by European programmes) had a short life span and did not lead to policy learning within local or national institutions.

The +Algarve Programme, for example, was cited as an example of successful concrete partnership working which had not proved sustainable. Created "top down" in 1999 by the ministries for economy and employment, it sought to tackle a specific local issue – namely, the large number of people engaged in seasonal employment.

Under the programme seasonal workers were offered stable contracts in the winter season and given the opportunity to enrol in training courses to develop tourism related skills. The programme was viewed as successful by local actors and led to a more efficient use of public resources by turning costly unemployment subsidies into investment in human capital. Nevertheless it was ended by the national government in 2004 without a formal evaluation, and local stakeholders felt disillusioned regarding their lack of involvement in the decision making process.

Another example of concrete local collaboration was the establishment of the Local Observatory of Loulé in 2007 to increase information and knowledge sharing within the municipality. The observatory set up a local internet platform in the field of "employment and training" with links to the websites of several local partners (municipality, employment centre, training centre, schools, employers associations, etc.) and information on their activities. The Observatory has also implemented a survey to identify the employment and training needs of new firms being created in the locality.

Conclusions

Figure 10.7. **Attention Areas**

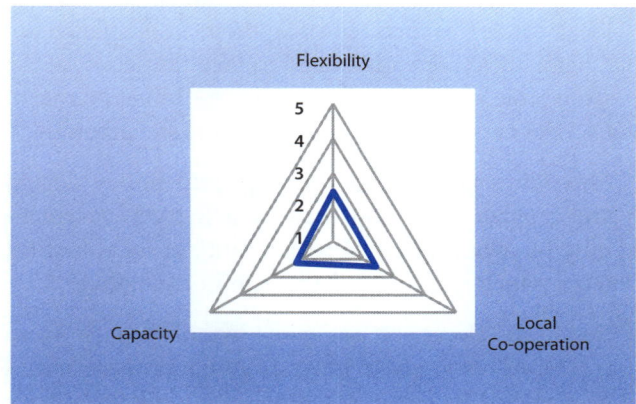

Sub-regional and regional policy makers were found to suffer from a lack of capacity, limited flexibility and insufficient meaningful co-operation in the context of a strongly centralised government in Portugal. Based on combined responses at national, local and state (where appropriate) level, Portugal received a low overall rating; 2.2 for capacity, 2.4 for local co-operation and 2.5 for flexibility from a maximum score of 5.0. Despite significant investment from the European Union in the last decades, with its associated emphasis on capacity building and the development of the partnership principle, the public sector is only just opening up to change.

Well co-ordinated actions between the three policy areas of employment, economic development and skills would be promoted by building on the existing strength of municipalities and local development agencies in order to develop sub-regional strategic platforms at the level of local labour markets or travel to work areas.

For such sub-regional platforms to produce lasting change, local policy makers in the employment and vocational training fields need to have more autonomy to adapt their programmes and commit to long-term common objectives.

Recommendations

- A local interface is required (at a sub-regional level) which would facilitate the development of targeted local strategies and enforce their implementation. Such a structure would need to take into account the strong role of municipalities. The co-ordination role of CCDRs at regional level also requires stengthening.

- Flexibility needs to be injected into policy design and management. This can be achieved incrementally by awarding greater flexibility to local institutions which have proved their ability to deliver.

- Local development agencies would benefit from increased resources to move from operational bodies to strategic ones, developing long-term strategies which cover a number of different municipal areas.

- Central government must provide incentives for civil servants to take local strategies into account when implementing programmes. There should be better mechanisms for translating national goals into local goals and vice versa, and greater negotiating of targets with local actors.

- There should be greater involvement by people involved on the ground in setting goals for local employment and vocational training policy, contributing towards greater relevance of local policies.

- Greater data availability and an investment in analytical skills would reinforce strategic planning locally. Skills for leadership and partnership working may also need a boost.

- National policy makers can learn from local initiatives which are already in place at the local level. An evaluation of policies and strategies already out there would provide a sound basis for developing systematic institutional change.

Note

1. This synopsis is based on the following country report: Henriques, J.M., "Integrating Employment, Skills and Economic Development in Portugal", submitted 2008.

ROMANIA [1]

National policy integration and co-ordination

The main actors in the field of employment policy in Romania are the Ministry of Labour, which defines policies and strategies for passive and active employment measures, the National Employment Agency (ANOFM), the main implementing body for policies and programmes, and the County Employment Agencies (AJOFM), who are in charge of implementing employment measures. Local authorities do not have formal responsibilities in this area.

Institutional framework [2]

Figure 11.1. **Romania: Institutional map at national, regional, sub-regional and local levels**

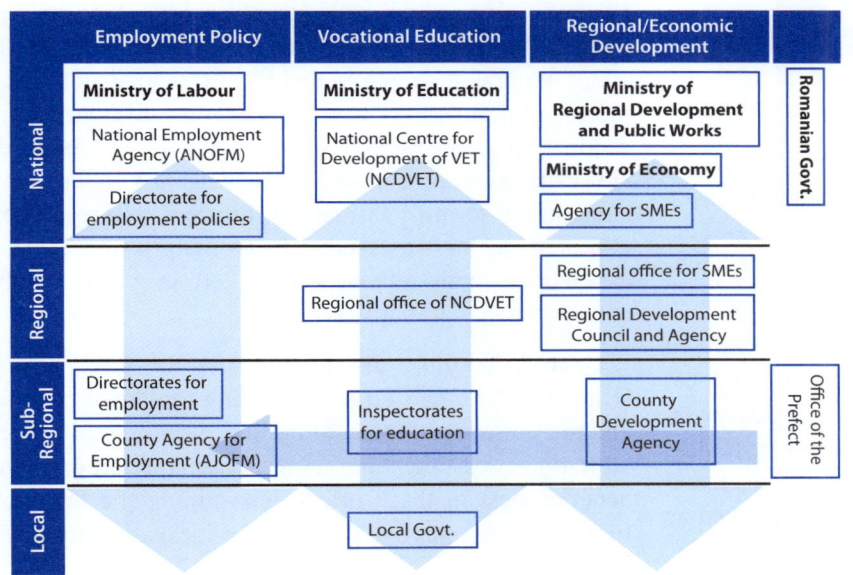

The Ministry of Education oversees national education policy in conjunction with the National Centre for Development of Vocational Education and Training (NCDVET) which supports the VET system. The Ministry of Economy and Energy (MEE) leads regional and economic development, and industrial policy. The Ministry of Regional Development and Public Works (MRDPW) oversees the development, co-ordination and implementation of regional policy. State policy for regional development is set out in the Regional Development Act and includes, inter alia, priorities such as decentralisation of management and the enhancement of partnerships with local authorities.

Integration and co-ordination

Romania has maintained a centralised governance structure and the division of work between the ministries favours a predominantly sectoral approach. Ad-hoc vertical governance structures operate and each ministry is focused on establishing and maintaining its own chain of command through its local offices.

Operational plans are generally centrally controlled and sectorally implemented, with the exception of European regional operational programmes (ROPs). At the time of study there was little input into ROPs at the regional or local level and their strategic compatibility was mainly assured at the central level, if at all.

Horizontal co-ordination and communication between national and sub-national levels was found to be thin on the ground. The greatest degree of co-operation could be seen between education and employment institutions and was based mainly on cross-sectoral relations between the regional offices, with communication between them intermediated by the Office of the Prefect.

Flexibility

Little flexibility was found to be available to policy makers in the three sectoral fields of employment, economic development and vocational training. Regional and local level authorities, in general, were seen to lack the power to influence the system at a high enough level to ensure "critical mass" in policy delivery, and had little say on policy content, activities and programmes. According to one local stakeholder "those who know the problem best have relatively little power (and money) to act on them, and those with power and resources do not have direct responsibilities and a direct interest to take part in such efforts." Resource constraints were flagged as a contributory factor but the lack of autonomy available to local officials was held as the principle reason for a failure to increase local policy integration.

As shown in Figure 11.2, stakeholders at both national and regional level (from the case study region of Timiş) rated overall regional flexibility as quite low. The economic development sector was given the highest rating by both hierarchical scales; vocational training was also rated highly by national stakeholders but given the lowest rating by policy makers. Employment was given the lowest rating by national policy makers and a medium rating by local policy makers. It is interesting to note that in two policy sectors local flexibility was more highly rated by national policy makers than by their local counterparts.

Figure 11.2. **Local flexibility**

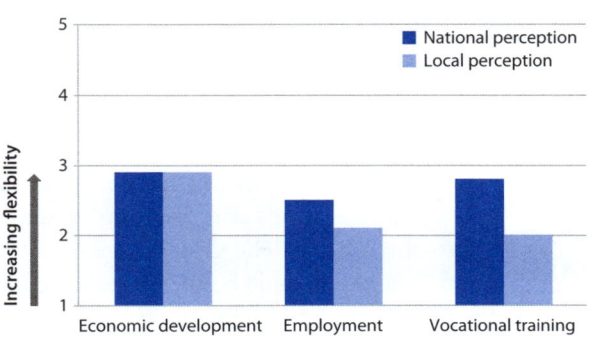

Employment policy was found to be particularly centralised in Romania. Regional and local players were seen to lack the power to intervene and shape policy to meet local needs by influencing programme design, the delivery of budgets and deciding on which people to target.

Figure 11.3 indicates that, overall, the flexibility of management tools was considered be very low by local stakeholders. The autonomy to design programme content was given the lowest rating, closely followed by performance management. Budgets were awarded the second highest level and the legal framework was perceived as the most flexible, but still falling within the "inflexible" to "mixed" category.

Figure 11.3. **Timiş: Flexibility of management tools**

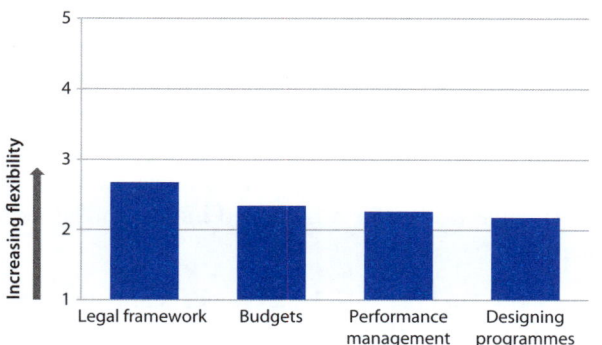

Local governments were also seen to have little say in how national programmes were managed and delivered. While in principle they can choose to top-up nationally launched schemes with their own funds or launch similar programmes, few were able to do this at the time of study due to a lack of financial resources.

In principle, investment promotion powers lay within the tiers of local government and the Regional Development Agency (ADR) but the instruments at their disposal for this purpose were found to be limited; sub-national governments may offer property tax exemptions or enter into economic agreements with private operators, but generally the number of viable initiatives was limited, the preparatory work difficult and public scrutiny high due to political sensitivities.

It was considered that the budgetary process reduced flexibility levels and limited incentives for policy integration. On paper local governments have the authority to adopt integrated strategies and local financial autonomy increased significantly from 1998-99 onwards when non-conditional grants for local governments were introduced. However, a large part of their budgetary allocations came in the form of earmarked transfers, and resources allocated in this way tended to go mainly into current expenditure with relatively little left over for locally owned strategic initiatives.

Overall, funding allocation across the three policy fields was seen to a large extent as a top down process and the same broad menu of options were offered across all regions, with the "market response" (*i.e.* programme beneficiaries) to these offers determining the focus of future programmes and the extent of local adaptability.

Co-operation and policy integration at the regional and local level

Historically, cross-departmental co-operation and policy integration at the sub-national level has not been strong and local authorities have little involvement in designing and implementing policy, particularly in the labour market and education sectors. The deconcentrated offices of central government departments possess the most influence sub-nationally, and their functions are primarily limited to implementing national mandates. For example, as decentralised branches of the central agency, county level employment offices are not able to encourage local job creation. Consequently, local authorities often have little interest in working more closely with these offices. Local politicians also tend to place more emphasis on improving hard infrastructure, an area which is easier to conceptualise and control, rather than tackling more abstract labour market issues.

Figure 11.4. Timiş: Integration between policy areas

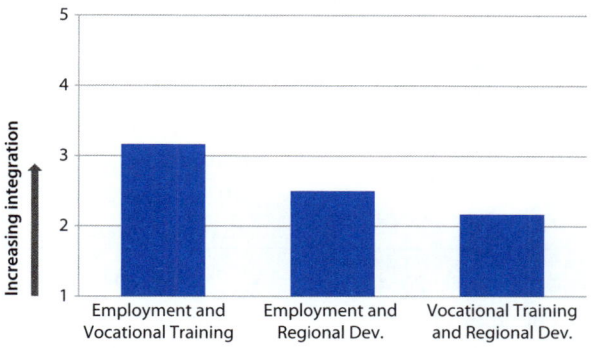

As can be seen from Figure 11.4, integration between policy areas was perceived to range from "weak" to "average". Employment and vocational training displayed the greatest degree of sectoral integration, followed by employment and regional development. Vocational training and regional development were classed as the least integrated.

Figure 11.5. Extent of engagement in cooperation at the local level

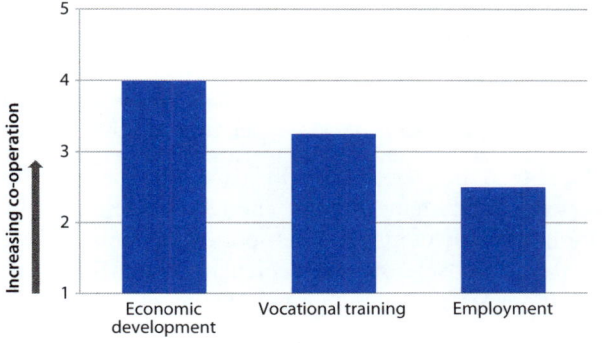

Figure 11.5 shows the estimated extent of engagement in co-operation in the case study region of Timiş. According to the views of regional players, there was a strong level of co-operation in the economic development sector, a slightly above average level in vocational training, and employment policy had the weakest level of co-operation.

Contributing to poor levels of co-ordination were the lack of incentives in place to encourage stakeholders

and heads of county agencies to engage in high-effort, high-risk policy activities where the potential for long-term benefits may have been higher (such as designing special measures to increase employment among Roma communities). When incentives were in place there was more likelihood of a greater level of integration, but municipalities still had to contend with a limited budget or a restricted remit to act as cross-sector co-ordinators.

The study identified integrative institutions at the local level, however, such as ADRs and regional development councils. ADRs in particular act as "interfaces" which support integrated approaches and co-operative working with other local actors and their cross-sectoral mandate enables a broad focus within local development policy.

European funding programmes had also provided the framework for greater co-operation. The pre-accession EU funded PHARE programme in particular stimulated some excellent co-operation on anticipating future skills needs in Timiş through an initiative known as TVET. The programme was successful partly because it had strong local and regional ownership, and in part because the programme insisted that investment in physical infrastructure should be limited to one third of total spend, ensuring that other "softer" issues such as human resources and training were also addressed. However, ultimately the strategic planning achieved through the TVET process failed to have a significant impact due to the inability of stakeholders to have any significant "traction" to influence skills provision regionally (see Box 11.1 below).

Co-operation between the public and private sector also remained limited, with previously strong links between VET schools and the private sector weakening in the face of industrial restructuring and privatisation. Even though attempts were being made to strengthen co-operation, it seemed to be educators rather than entrepreneurs who were playing the principal role in initiating collaboration.

Capacities

As can be seen in Figure 11.6, skills and resources were felt to be highest in the economic development sector in the case study region of Timiş. Employment and vocational training organisations were seen as having "weak" skills levels, with higher levels of resources. In all three policy areas, resources were felt to be the same as or greater than skills levels. This was borne out by the comments of local actors who felt that the resources available to them were higher than their skills levels – due mainly to the influx of European regional funds.

Figure 11. 6. **Timiş:** Average capacity of organisations

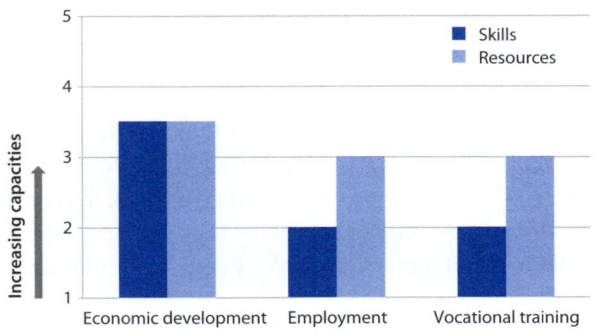

Resources

In recent years EU programmes have injected a large amount of finance into the Romanian system and have become the main platform for policy making and co-ordination at all governance levels. They have provided an important degree of "learning in practice" in new public management and also improved information and data collection practices.

However, some stakeholders commented that notwithstanding the obvious benefits of regional financial assistance, such was the scale of financial assistance that the main priority of local authorities had been to absorb as much of the funds as possible. Consequently, planning and utilising the funds has taken up the strategic and administrative capacity of the public sector, and regional and local development plans were heavily reliant on the relatively complex agendas set out in funding programmes. This was less a problem within the PHARE programmes which preceded accession to the European Union, and which, on the contrary, provoked relatively strong local co-operation using fewer resources.

Despite the influx of European funds, certain regions continue to lack resources within mainstream policy delivery and services, preventing them from taking advantage of flexibility provisions in the institutional framework.

Box 11.1. **Case study region: Timiş**

Responding to skills shortages and an outdated VET model

STRENGTHS AND CHALLENGES	
STRENGTHS	CHALLENGES
• Declining unemployment • Unemployment rate below national average; • Fertile land and strong agricultural tradition; • Booming real estate market.	• Restructuring of labour market; • Educational system struggling to meet demands of regional labour market; • Skills supply and demand mismatch.
OPPORTUNITIES	THREATS
• Continuing low unemployment; • Continuing salary growth.	• Tight labour market as a result of migration and increased demand for workforce; • Skills shortages.

Timiş County is located in the West of Romania and is a region, with a population of 674 800 (2008), known for its fertile land and strong agricultural traditions.

In the years leading up to the economic downturn, the region was increasingly facing skill shortages. There was increased demand for skilled people in agro-related jobs and services, with forecasts predicting falling demand for routine and manufacturing jobs. Unfulfilled labour market demand added to inadequate supply created a mismatch of approximately 25 per cent in 2004.

Educational institutions in the case study region were not seen to be changing fast enough to keep pace with regional labour demand. The pool of students for vocational training schools was decreasing, pointing towards falling popularity among potential students. Over half of the companies responding to a local survey in the region reported at least one vacancy for which no VET school could provide graduates with matching skills, and many local companies found VET graduates deficient in both specific job related skills and interpersonal skills.

Despite suffering the consequences of skills shortages, local firms were themselves reluctant to invest in employee training in the fear that newly up skilled workers would either be poached by competitors or move abroad.

The Timiş Education Inspectorate responded by helping

training institutions to diversify their services and used marketing tools to boost enrolment, but in the face of adverse demographic trends, declining educational quality, staff demotivation and lack of interest from potential employers, these initiatives were seen as no more than short-term stop gaps. Active public employment programmes attempted to fill the gap, but it was noted that directly run public schemes tended to be of lower quality than privately provided training and rarely functioned as designed.

Successful joint working to help address these issues was established under the pre-accession European Commission PHARE programme. Regional consortia (including representatives of development agencies, county councils, county employment agencies, school inspectorates etc.) identified priorities for VET education and developed a VET regional action plan (PRAI) and a VET local action plan (PLAI), based on analyses of current labour market trends and strategic forecasts.

However, while the strategies developed as part of the regional plans were generally far sighted and targeted, the PRAI and PLAI lacked political influence and were only able to influence training curricula at the individual school level. This limited their ultimate impact.

As local authorities are required to co-finance European funding programmes this means that capacity to promote regional development through wider actions was found to be limited. However, there was evidence that capacity shortages could trigger innovative policy responses to raise funds, and could serve as an impetus to strengthen co-ordination between local governments when it was in their interest to co-operate. For example, the AJOFM and vocational schools exchanged personnel for training programmes, creating avenues for communication and curriculum adaptation.

Skills

> "... the general impression is that the strategies are written without a great deal of regard for the competencies and tools of intervention that sub-national authorities actually have, especially as far as economic development is concerned."
>
> Romania Country Report

While material resources were generally not lacking, the skills to conceptualise and produce integrated strategy could be. Strategies and action plans often contained a wealth of data and a strong level of analysis, but the general impression is that the strategies are written without a great deal of regard for the competencies and tools of intervention that are actually available to sub-national authorities, especially as far as economic development is concerned. Objectives were often not clearly set out by local decision makers, potential trade-offs were not effectively highlighted, and integrative attempts often ended up as long wish lists.

Skills capacity issues could also affect the delivery of sectoral operation programmes (SOPs), particularly comparatively large SOPs. Capacity shortages were also evident within intermediary bodies implementing the structural funds; a survey of intermediary bodies at the local level found that staffing levels were below 40 per cent, few staff members had the necessary professional skills or experience of working with EU programmes, and poor focus, lack of co-ordination and "strategy fatigue" were noted by many working within the system of EU assistance.

Conclusions

Figure 11.7. **Attention Areas**

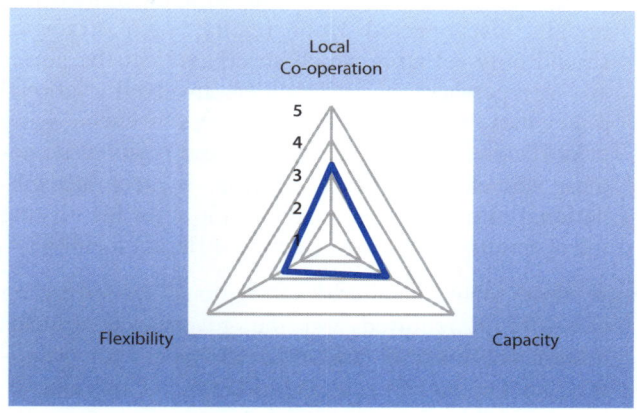

It is clear that capacities, co-operation and flexibility are all areas needing considerable attention in Romania in the coming years if policy integration is to be improved. The combined responses at national, local and state (where appropriate) level for the relevant indices awarded were 2.8 for capacity, 2.5 for flexibility and 3.3 for local co-operation from a maximum of 5.0, as highlighted in Figure 11.7.

As these scores indicate, the area requiring the most significant attention is policy flexibility. Whatever variability exists in the implementation of national programmes, it is almost entirely created by the variable rate of absorption of different components of the national programmes; an uptake often characterised by a passive response at the local level, limited by the rigidity of public sector institutions.

If key decisions and budget allocations continue to follow the vertical logic, the administrative tradition of poor horizontal co-operation and policy integration will continue to be reinforced, with negative effects on competitiveness and social cohesion.

Recommendations

- Functions and responsibilities must be clearly assigned to the different tiers of government in a transparent and stable process in order to align administrative competences with political accountability.

- Further flexibility needs to be available to local level offices within both the employment and VET sectors, alongside training and capacity building. Greater decentralisation of resources and increased power to make decisions at the local level will increase the likelihood of policy integration at sub-national level.

- Rather than developing advanced and complex policy documents at the local level with strategic aims which remain disconnected from reality, such strategies should only set aims which strictly reflect the power and competences of stakeholders involved. National policy makers can assist in this process by encouraging prioritisation and realism in local and regional strategies, and ensuring the availability of accurate sub-national information and data as a tool for identifying the overriding problems affecting different localities.

- A more robust local and sub-regional co-ordinating structure is required and the governance vehicles designed at this level need to have broader responsibilities than the implementation of EU funds. Such amendments would harmonise local concerns as expressed by local authorities with national policy and EU goals.

- The inter-ministerial committees set up to co-ordinate important strategic areas relating to EU accession should play a more important role. It is necessary to link policies at the central level to increase the likelihood of sub-national integration.

Notes

1. This synopsis is based on the following country report: Ionita, S. (2006), "Integrating Employment, Skills and Economic Development in Romania", submitted 2006.

2. A Ministry of European Integration existed at the time of this study, but it responsibilities were absorbed by the Ministry of Regional Development and Public Works when the country joined the EU at the beginning of 2007.

UNITED STATES[1]

National policy integration and co-ordination

Institutional framework

Figure 12.1. USA: Institutional map at national, regional, sub-regional and local levels

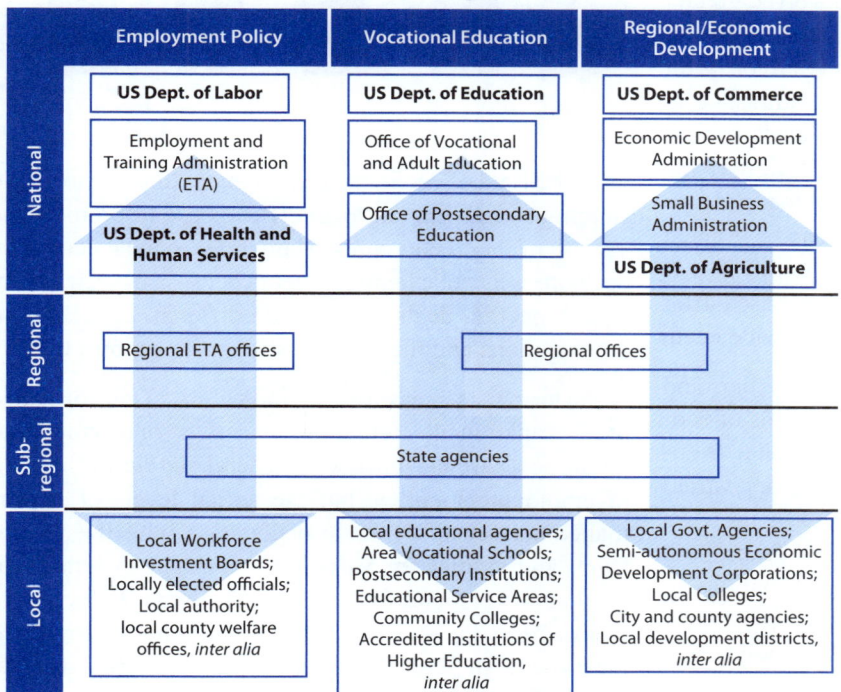

Integration and co-ordination

Governance structures in the United States are relatively decentralised, particularly in relation to vocational education and training (VET) and economic development.

In employment and VET policy the Federal Departments of Labor and Education play a leadership role, often guiding and funding employment and VET initiatives, but considerable latitude is left to states and localities to determine the details of programme delivery.

No single federal statute or programme governs economic development at the sub-national level, with activities instead carried out by numerous agencies. At the time of the study, economic development policy was split between ten different federal agencies, with 27 sub-agency units and 73 programmes.

The sheer number of agencies involved in economic development sometimes made it difficult for this policy area to be co-ordinated effectively with employment and VET policies at the national level. Increased co-ordination between these policy areas at the national level has been a sought after goal across multiple administrations in recent years. Historically, there has been a modest level of co-operation between employment and vocational training programs as both were driven by a "supply side" focus in years past.

However, beginning with enactment of the Workforce Investment Act of 1998 in the Clinton Administration, employment and training efforts have focused increasingly on the demand-side as well, aligning employment policy more closely with economic development through a "demand-led" approach.

These efforts to increase alignment across policy silos and focus employment and training on the needs of both workers and employers were major goals of the Bush administration and continue to be major goals under the Obama administration. In fact, in a renewed effort to increase the number of Americans who attain postsecondary credentials and employment in high-demand occupations – a major goal of President Obama – the Obama Administration is working with Congress on ways to establish career pathways, sector-based and other innovative initiatives that align the continuum of education (from adult basic to postsecondary education), training and economic development programmes to help individuals persist and succeed, and to attain high demand employment and progress.

Flexibility

In recent years, efforts have been made to transfer greater responsibility down to state and local actors in the employment and VET fields. In the employment sector the 1998 Workforce Investment Act (WIA) established local workforce investment areas and business-led workforce investment boards (WIBs), responsible, with locally elected officials, for the design and oversight of local workforce systems.

The WIA was intended to fundamentally change the way workforce development systems were provided across the US and provided extensive authority to states and local areas, allowing them to design their own employment programmes and provide varying levels of service to individuals in industries according to their importance to the local economy.

In the field of VET policy, the 2006 Perkins Career and Technical Education Act (CTE) also devolved greater authority to sub-federal authorities; no national standards or curriculum were set, and maximum authority for programme design and implementation was allocated to states and local school systems. Local officials have substantial influence over training programme design. In the case of Texas, for example, if a new programme is identified as necessary by local actors, approval can be granted rapidly by the state (usually within one month) if it is classified as a "local needs course", to be assessed after three years to ascertain whether there is a statewide need.

Overall the study found that flexibility at state and local levels was high in the three policy domains of economic development, employment and vocational training, yet the flexibility available to local actors varied significantly between states and localities. In the case study region of the Lower Rio Grande Valley, Texas, both national and regional stakeholders perceived flexibility to be high; with economic development rated the most flexible by both tiers (see Figure 12.2). In all three policy sectors local players perceived their flexibility to be higher than their national counterparts.

Figure 12.2. Local flexibility

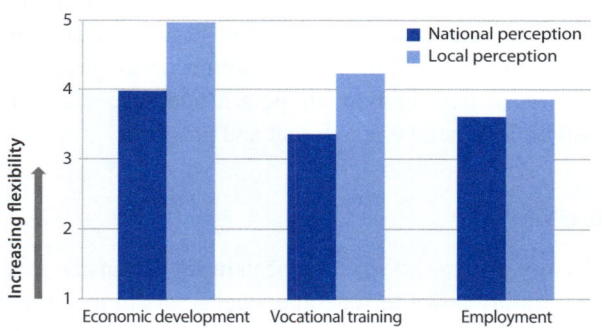

The four management tools of programme design, budgets, performance management and legal framework were perceived to be very flexible in the case study area of McAllen, Texas, across all policy areas.

Figure 12.3. McAllen, Texas: Flexibility of management tools

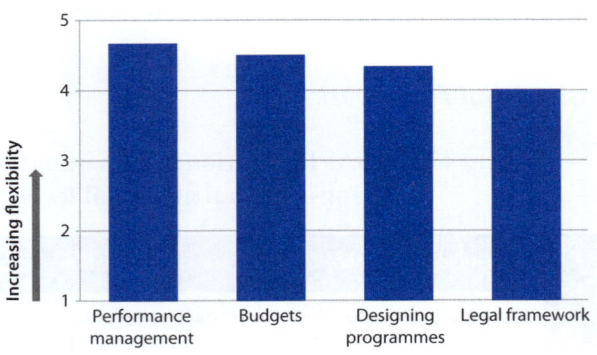

In the field of economic development there is no single funding source that all local officials use to promote the growth of their economies. Many refer to local economic developers as policy entrepreneurs because of their ability to put together deals that include different agencies and organisations and the funding streams to support them.

Performance measures, or indicators of performance (*e.g.* employment, retention, earnings and credential attainment) are established in federal statute in the field of employment policy, but the actual levels of performance are set by states in negotiation with the federal level, and significant variation is evident in how local level actors respond to these targets. Some WIBs regard them as just the starting point, while others struggle to meet them. In Texas, local actors are encouraged to set additional targets to those set at "baseline" by the state, based on local strategic priorities through a two-tier system of "formal" and "less formal" measures. Formal measures are consistent across workforce programmes and include mainly output targets, while less formal measures are often outcome based and consistent with local strategic plans. Local workforce boards report to the state on both sets of measures.

For vocational training, while core indicators of performance are defined in federal law, levels of performance are determined by the states and localities. In the economic development field targets vary considerably by programme, but there has been an increased emphasis on accountability in recent years.

The legal system was identified as providing a mechanism for the Department of Labor to influence the actions of states and localities beyond the rather limited operation of federally funded programmes. However, in recognition of the potentially restrictive influence this could have, a "waiver" system has been established to allow states to apply for additional flexibility in implementing workforce strategies and initiatives. Many states have taken advantage of the system, with 331 being approved by 2006. Texas, for example, obtained waivers to expand the target group of people eligible for training and to relax the required 50 per cent employer match for customised training. The Workforce Investment Board in the Lower Rio Grande Valley took advantage of the former waiver to create a "local activity account" using USD 1 million of its local WIA allocation to broaden eligibility to training locally.

When local level players in Texas came up against an obstacle in this state they felt free to telephone state authorities to seek changes in policy, although the capacity to do this varied depending on personal relationships and lobbying power. There was some contradiction in the way in which federal policy makers and auditors interpreted the management framework for employment policy in the United States, however. While federal and state leadership wanted in many cases to promote a more creative, flexible set of programmes, programme auditors often interpreted legislation more narrowly. This had left many local WIBs "timid" and reluctant to implement innovative strategies in the delivery of workforce services.

Co-operation and policy integration at the regional and local level

Maryland Workforce Development Board's promotional slogan of "workforce development is economic development" highlights the increasing overlap between the aims and objectives of policies to promote employment, economic development and skills at sub-federal level. Figure 12.4 shows that integration between policy areas in McAllen, Texas, was considered to be very high, achieving the highest overall rating of all participating regions in the study. The extent of engagement in co-operation in each of the three policy fields at the local level was also scored very highly both here (see Figure 12.5) and in Maine.

However, the extent of co-operation varies considerably in the United States, with some localities reporting strong inertia in the management of political and institutional systems and identifying that policy areas continued

to operate in silos. Community leaders were not always aware of other ways to do business or they concluded that the difficulties associated with trying to achieve real integration were too great – like most change – and not worth the political or emotional effort required to transform them into realities.

> *"… there are many more areas that operate in relatively traditional silos with little creativity across programs or funding streams."*
>
> United States Country Report

Figure 12.4. **McAllen, Texas: Integration between policy areas**

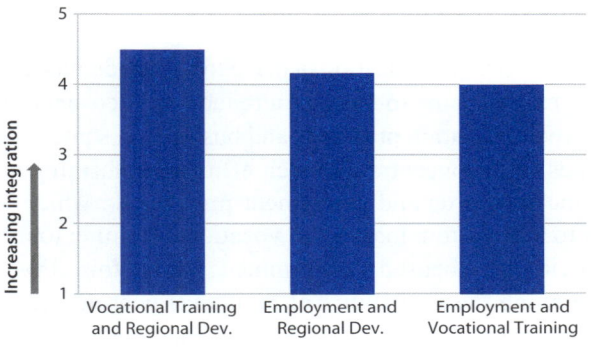

Figure 12.5. **Extent of engagement in cooperation at the local level**

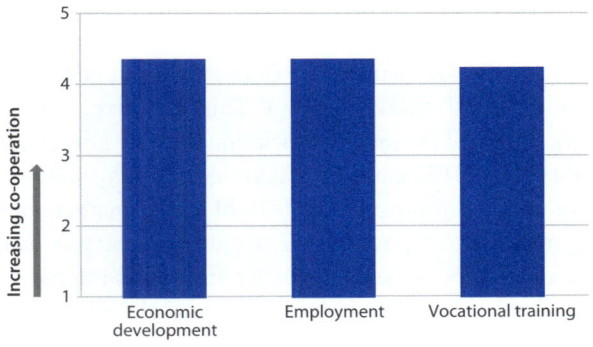

In the field of employment policy, integration has been encouraged across the United States through a WIA requirement that local areas establish at least one comprehensive "one-stop center" through which job seekers and employers could access all WIA services. The local WIBs have also played a strong role in strengthening integration with employment policy and are strongly business led. Elected at the local level, they have served as intermediaries in bringing businesses, community college, and other community organisations together around labour market and economic growth issues. However, the extent to which they deliver local co-operation varies considerably across the country, and in some cases WIBs are seen as purely formal bodies bypassed by other efforts to create co-operative approaches.

Further collaboration was encouraged under the Bush administration through the Workforce Innovations for Regional Economic Development (WIRED) scheme which encouraged workforce development actors to take a leadership role in building collaborative approaches regionally. USD 250 million was invested in the scheme which was intended to catalyse the creation of high-skill, high-wage opportunities for workers and a stronger human resource base for business.

In the field of education, a drive to lift academic standards has led some to identify a reduction of co-operation between education providers and business in some states. States have concentrated much effort on reforming academic standards and assessment procedures, which has led to a shift from market led vocational training to more individually focused programmes. While this drive is improving the availability of high level generic skills to local employers, concerns have been expressed that this is at the cost of vocational learning, meaning that education and local employers' needs are less integrated.

A federal initiative which has had some success in galvanising better linkages between educators and industrial sectors is the Department of Education's Career Cluster initiative (see Box 12.1 below). This initiative, which is overseen by the National Association of State Directors of CTE (NASDCTEc), has been adopted by many states and regions and customised to their local labour market needs. Job profiles are mapped across an entire industry so learners and workers can see how different careers interact and rely on one another. Within each career cluster there are anywhere between two to seven career pathways from secondary school to college, graduate schools, and the workplace. The network of clusters is delivered through a partnership approach involving state, schools, educators, employers, industry groups, and other stakeholders who have worked together to create curriculum guidelines, academic and technical standards, assessments, and cluster professional development materials.

Figure 12.6. **Career Cluster Model**

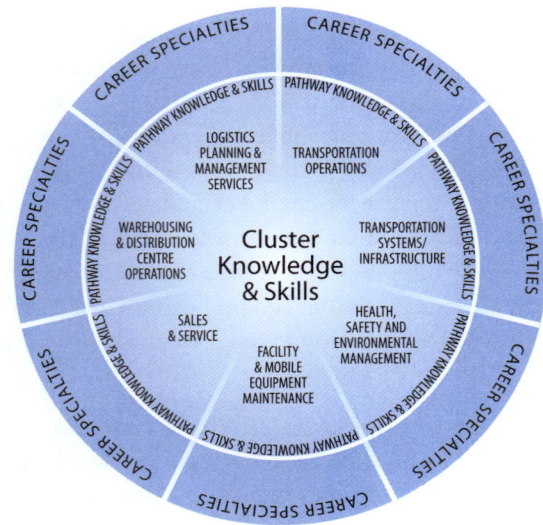

Source: National Career Technical Education Foundation (NCTEF) and National Association of State Directors Career Technical Education consortium (NASDCTEc), *http://www.careerclusters. org/resources/ClusterDocuments/tdldocuments/brochure.pdf.*

Mapping local activities

Attempts to both map and consolidate the number of programmes operating on the ground in all policy fields has been found to aid policy integration in the United States. Texas, for example, merged ten agencies into one new agency in 1995 to create the Texas Workforce Commission. Similarly when the state of Maine received funding under the WIRED programme (see above) they started work by mapping all employment, training and vocational education organisations' funding sources, services and target populations. Such efforts reduce ambiguity and complexity and make it easier for agencies to collaborate.

While in some states policy integration is rather ad-hoc and led by individuals, in other states co-operation it is much more formalised. In Maine collaboration was led from the top by the state governor but attempts to institutionalise collaboration at a more local level were more challenging. Texas, in contrast, has introduced systemic requirements for collaboration through a series of "Memoranda of Understanding" and through co-locating and merging agencies, which may mean that policy integration is more durable in practice. At the same time, flexibility in policy delivery meant that there was space for creativity and informal relationships on the ground.

Capacities

Of all the case study regions involved in the study, McAllen, Texas was the only one in which local stakeholders considered skills and resource levels to be high in each policy sector; organisations' skills capacity were rated "very strong", while resource capacities were rated as "strong" (see Figure 12.7).

Resources

Resources were identified as a more important factor in explaining variation in policy integration than skills levels. In particular, a common complaint by WIBs was that the Workforce Investment Act had granted them broader responsibilities to address demand side issues during an extended period of budget cuts. In some states, such as Maine, resource shortfalls were exacerbated by political pressures to disperse investments widely across the territory. As a result, there was a lack of critical mass at the local level to generate projects which could have a real impact.

Figure 12.7. **McAllen, Texas: Average capacity of organisations**

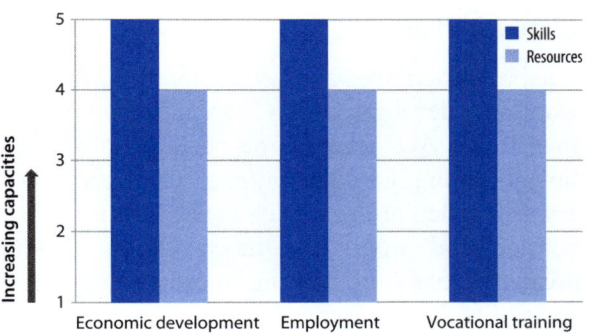

Information and data availability was raised as a further important local resource issue. In many cases local actors were forced to commission their own research to supplement disaggregated data available from the state and federal levels. Yet this had the benefit of creating strong local ownership of data which could act as a catalyst to better align local policies to tackle glaring common problems.

Skills

Local leadership is a key factor in producing integrated working in the United States, with leadership skills such

as being able to "prod" other stakeholders to act, earn trust and have an alternative vision for the future being crucial to local development. The emergence of new economic development "areas of opportunity" within the context of the knowledge economy has required a broader range of expertise and skills to be fostered within economic development, VET and employment policy.

Box 12.1. **Case study region: the Lower Rio Grande Valley, Texas**

STRENGTHS AND CHALLENGES	
STRENGTHS	CHALLENGES
• Shared vision for region's future economic development; • Strong collaboration between stakeholders; • Advantageous location and Foreign Trade Zone; • Declining unemployment.	• Performance of elementary and secondary schools disappointing; • Funding shortages limiting educational programme expansion; • Pockets of economic distress remain.
OPPORTUNITIES	THREATS
• Growing and young population base; • Development potential as "rapid response manufacturing center"; • Strong linkages between curriculum and needs of clusters; • Redesigned WorkFORCE Solutions service delivery model.	• Infrastructure and intellectual capital primarily benefitting the main cities to the detriment of regions • Declining enrolment in higher education; • Employer educational attainment criteria not being met.

Twenty years ago McAllen, Texas (population 1 202 189 in 2008) suffered from 20 per cent unemployment in an economy primarily dependent on agricultural and retail sectors. There was uncertainty about the growing number of "maquiladoras" (manufacturing plants) operating in nearby Mexico and of the implications for the region's economy. At the same time the region had a very poorly educated workforce, with a significant percentage of local people dropping out of high school.

This did not stop local leaders from developing an ambitious vision for the future. Recognising that local policy makers had in the past been working separately in a mainly reactive manner, they sought to turn economic development "from a response to a journey". Noticing the demands of manufacturers and their clients for increasingly short product life cycles, the region positioned itself as a "rapid response manufacturing centre" that could use existing companies and suppliers to move from product design to market in ever shorter time frames. The strategy sought to take advantage of the region's geographic location, relatively close to Mexico's ports on the Pacific Ocean, and equidistant between the US east and west coasts and the region is also a designated Foreign Trade Zone.

As the region progressed with its strategy, it became increasingly apparent that skills and education constituted an important part of the solution and local leaders collaborated to open South Texas College in 1993, a comprehensive community college that has grown from 1 000 to more than 17 000 students. In addition, the College and other educational institutions worked with the local WIB to document skills gaps and better use customised training funds. Regional officials have also worked with elementary and secondary schools to improve standards and develop linkages between school curriculum and local economic clusters.

Local actors took advantage of flexibility within the Texas workforce system to achieve their strategy and supported their work by commissioning a major local data survey which they reviewed together with all partners every two years. Overall, the regional strategy has been responsible for helping to attract more than 500 employers and nearly 100 000 jobs to the wider region. Although there certainly are pockets of economic distress, there has been tremendous progress since the early 1990s, with unemployment declining in Hidalgo County from 24.1 per cent to 7.7 per cent, and in Starr County from 40.3 per cent to 10.7 per cent.

Conclusions

As Figure 12.8 shows, the United States achieved high overall ratings within the study for flexibility, capacities and local co-operation based on interviews and roundtables at national, local and state level, and indeed these were the highest scores returned of all participating countries; 4.1 for capacity, 4.4 for local co-operation and 3.9 for flexibility from a maximum of 5.0.

Capacities, in particular, were thought to be important in achieving overall policy integration – and where local leaders had the capacity to take advantage of the flexibility

available to them, the results were impressive. However, local actors equally were unlikely to be penalised for failing to take co-ordinated action and the largely "carrot-based" approach to policy delivery has resulted in a situation where policy integration varies significantly state-by-state and region-by-region. The ever-present tension remains to find the appropriate balance between local flexibility and control while maintaining accountability and demonstrating a return on public investment by federal and state authorities.

Figure 12.8. **Attention Areas**

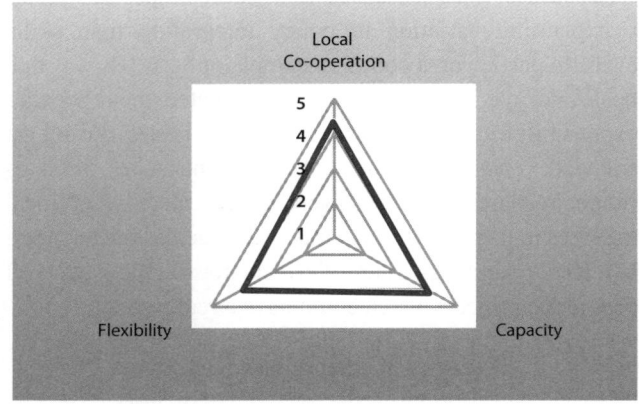

Recommendations

- The broadened roles and responsibilities allocated to workforce development bodies under the Workforce Investment Act needs to be accompanied by sufficient funding for collaboration and effective delivery. In particular there must be sufficient financial, political and programme incentives to encourage greater partnership working in order to balance the costs of collaboration.

- Trends to increase incentives for collaboration across agencies, organisations and levels of government must continue and be accompanied by increasing emphasis on systems of horizontal accountability.

- Continued strong state guidance and leadership are important in helping to create a vision, used in parallel with incentives to local areas to encourage them to use the flexibility they have to move beyond the status quo.

- Policy makers and programme auditors need to share information more effectively regarding the intended interpretation of programmes rules and regulations, particularly contained within the WIA.

This would avoid local actors being penalised for innovative actions which the federal government might actually want to encourage.

• Policy makers need to overcome the centrifugal political tendencies which encourage the approach to allow enough critical mass to create real change in localities in crisis.

Note

1. This synopsis is based on the following country report: Troppe, M., M. Clagett, R. Holm, and T. Barnicle, "Integrating Employment, Skills, and Economic Development in the United States", submitted 2007.

About the authors

Francesca Froy is a senior policy analyst at the Organisation for Economic Cooperation and Development (OECD), working within the Local Economic and Employment Development (LEED) Programme in Paris. She coordinates the work of the programme on employment, skills and local governance and has developed a stream of work on immigration and ethnic minority youth. She is the co-editor of the OECD publications *From Immigration to Integration: Local Solutions to a Global Challenge*, *Designing Local Skills Strategies* and *Flexible Policy for More and Better Jobs*. Prior to joining LEED, she was involved in evaluating European projects and helped to manage the DG Employment and Social Affairs initiative IDELE (identification and dissemination of local employment development). A British national, she has worked for the Public Employment Service and for a local municipality in the United Kingdom, where she led a multi-sector partnership to create employment and skills opportunities within social housing. She has a BSc in Anthropology from University College London and an MA in cultural theory from the University of Reading.

Sylvain Giguère is Head of the Local Economic and Employment Development (LEED) Division at the OECD. He manages a team of 25 economists, analysts and research assistants based at both the OECD Headquarters in Paris and the OECD LEED Centre for Local Development in Trento, Italy. A Canadian national, Mr. Giguère joined the OECD in 1995, first to work in the Directorate for Employment, Labour and Social Affairs (DELSA). In 2002 he was appointed Deputy Head of the LEED Programme, where he developed a policy research agenda to provide guidance on how public policies can be better co-ordinated and adapted to local conditions to improve economic and social outcomes. This work has produced a broad range of policy lessons, from labour market policy to economic development. Sylvain's work has been published widely, not only by the OECD but also by Palgrave Macmillan and Nikkei, among others. He studied economics at University of Quebec in Montreal, Queen's University (Kingston, Ont.) and University of Paris I (Sorbonne), where he obtained a PhD in economics.

ORGANISATION FOR ECONOMIC CO-OPERATION AND DEVELOPMENT

The OECD is a unique forum where governments work together to address the economic, social and environmental challenges of globalisation. The OECD is also at the forefront of efforts to understand and to help governments respond to new developments and concerns, such as corporate governance, the information economy and the challenges of an ageing population. The Organisation provides a setting where governments can compare policy experiences, seek answers to common problems, identify good practice and work to co-ordinate domestic and international policies.

The OECD member countries are: Australia, Austria, Belgium, Canada, Chile, the Czech Republic, Denmark, Finland, France, Germany, Greece, Hungary, Iceland, Ireland, Israel, Italy, Japan, Korea, Luxembourg, Mexico, the Netherlands, New Zealand, Norway, Poland, Portugal, the Slovak Republic, Slovenia, Spain, Sweden, Switzerland, Turkey, the United Kingdom and the United States. The European Commission takes part in the work of the OECD.

OECD Publishing disseminates widely the results of the Organisation's statistics gathering and research on economic, social and environmental issues, as well as the conventions, guidelines and standards agreed by its members.

OECD PUBLISHING, 2, rue André-Pascal, 75775 PARIS CEDEX 16
(84 2010 03 1 P) ISBN 978-92-64-05680-0 – No. 57717 2010